Harriet Martineau

Theoretical and Methodological Perspectives

VOLUME 5

Mary Jo Deegan, Series Editor

Women and Sociological Theory

Mary Jo Deegan, *Series Editor*

Caroline Bartlett Crane and Progressive Reform: Social Housekeeping as Sociology
Linda J. Rynbrandt

Intimacy and Alienation
Arthur G. Neal and Sara F. Collas

Harriet Martineau

Theoretical and Methodological Perspectives

Edited by
Michael R. Hill *and*
Susan Hoecker-Drysdale
With an Introduction by
Helena Znaniecka Lopata

Routledge
New York & London

First published in paperback in 2003 by
Routledge
29 West 35th Street
New York, NY 10001
www.routledge.com

Published in Great Britain by
Routledge
11 New Fetter Lane
London EC4P 4EE
www.routledge.co.uk

Routledge is an imprint of the Taylor & Francis Group.

Printed in the United States of America on acid-free paper.

10 9 8 7 6 5 4 3 2 1

Library of Congress Cataloging-in-Publication Data
Harriet Martineau : theoretical and methodological perspectives / edited by Michael R. Hill and Susan Hoecker-Drysdale ; with an introduction by Helena Znaniecka Lopata.
p. cm. — (Women and sociological theory (Routledge (Firm)))
Includes bibliographical references and index.
ISBN 0-8153-3451-6(hbk.) — ISBN 0-415-94528-3(pbk.)
1. Martineau, Harriet, 1802–1876. 2. Sociology—Great Britain—History—19th century. I. Hill, Michael R. II. Hoecker-Drysdale, Susan. III. Series.
HM477.G7 H37 2001
301—dc21 2001019121

This book
is dedicated by
Michael R. Hill
to

Donald David Hill,
actor, union administrator, and
remarkable brother

and by
Susan Hoecker-Drysdale
to

John Philip Drysdale,
scholar, tutor, loving companion

Contents

Series Editor's Preface

THIS BOOK ANNOUNCES THE COMING OF AGE OF HARRIET MARTINEAU studies in sociology. Since Seymour Martin Lipset introduced and edited her *Society in America* in 1962, Martineau slowly has gained acceptance as a founding figure in the discipline. The work of the scholars included here, however, is responsible for making this substantial recovery of a great sociologist possible. It has been a collaborative effort in this final stage, and the sociologists who wrote these chapters have contributed through scholarship and collegial friendship, a kind of Martineauian "Invisible College," to sustain and augment the effort.

One book cannot assure a field of study will be established and sustained. It can point to how and why such study is warranted. This is an exciting beginning for such an ambitious and significant goal.

Mary Jo Deegan

Foreword

THE ARRANGEMENT OF THE CHAPTERS—SUGGESTED BY MY ASTUTE AND hard-working co-editor, Susan Hoecker-Drysdale—reflects in broad terms a chronology suggesting something of Martineau's development, changing interests, evolving views, and life experiences. We begin, following Professor Lopata's introduction, with an overview in Chapter One of the current relevance of Martineau's writings and ideas in our classrooms and the discipline generally. Chapters Two through Nine provide detailed discussions of various facets of Martineau's life, development, and intellectual contributions. The book closes with a brief epilogue outlining the traits of Martineauian sociology and advocates its adoption as a professional alternative for sociological practice in the remainder of the twenty-first century.

As in most intellectual endeavors, we do not all see eye-to-eye on every matter—indeed, that is a great joy and strength of scholarly life. Thus, it behooves me to note that the views expressed in each chapter remain the responsibility of each contributor, whereas accountability for myriad editorial intrusions, failing to catch typographical mistakes, and the like, rests primarily with the first editor. In deference to my colleagues from Canada, the reader will find numerous spellings like "centre" and "labour." A noticeable degree of unavoidable bibliographic repetition is necessary to the arguments in the several related chapters, and thus I collapsed all of the chapter bibliographies into a single master reference list. The difficulty in doing this is that Martineau's many works exist in myriad editions with various paginations, dates, and publishers (Rivlin 1947). I have tried, as far as possible, to standardize the citations and references with the aim of reducing confusion for the reader, but may have achieved, inadvertently, the opposite result in a few instances.

I gratefully acknowledge the day-to-day interpersonal encouragement received during this project from: Sherry and Brad Berles, Thomas Calhoun, Miguel Carranza, Joleen Deats, Mary Jo Deegan, Connie Frey, Tim Gongaware, Kathleen Johnson, Jennifer Lehmann, Allan McCutcheon, Julia McQuillan, Terry Miller, Helen Moore, Carolette Norwood, Keith Parker, Lori Ratzlaff, Greg Rosenboom, Barb and Tim Sandusky, Bennie Shobe, F.M. Tuttle, Ana-Maria Wahl, Pat and Scott Wendt, Jeff Willett, and Yuanting Zhang. Your smiles and collegiality are invaluable.

Numerous mutual friends and colleagues in the Harriet Martineau Sociological Society, the Research Committee on the History of Sociology in the International Sociological Association, and the Section on the History of Sociology in the American Sociological Association have been wonderfully supportive of this project—a fact for which both editors are grateful, and we hope their interest augers well for the future of Martineauian studies in sociology. We are especially indebted to Helena Znaniecka Lopata for contributing the introduction to this volume. This book would not have been possible without the international support and inspiration of Mary Jo Deegan and John Drysdale.

Susan Hoecker-Drysdale gratefully acknowledges and expresses her appreciation for funding from the Social Science Research Council of Canada in support of the research reported in Chapters Six, Seven, and Nine.

This project has given me privileged insights into the professional work and personal sacrifices made by my co-editor, the co-contributors to this volume, and those who love them. The spirit of Harriet Martineau lives in them all.

Michael R. Hill
Lincoln, Nebraska

Introduction

Helena Znaniecka Lopata

THIS BOOK HAS AN INTERESTING HISTORY—RATHER APPROPRIATE BECAUSE it covers an important segment of the history of sociology. I first became acquainted with what were some of its middle beginnings in October, 1996. Reading in an ad hoc newsletter about a proposed working seminar of the Harriet Martineau Sociological Society (HMSS) on Mackinac Island, Michigan, I contacted Michael R. Hill, the newsletter editor, expressing my desire to participate. The "cosmopolitan community of scholars" is one of my focal interests, and I was pleased to find sociologists actually working with Martineau's biography and writings to the extent of coming together for a working seminar. This sounded like a time and place for meeting scholars studying a major contributor to such a community. I knew of Martineau from having taught history of sociology at Loyola University, Chicago, where most of my colleagues and students had not heard of her and were surprised at the excellence of her *Society in America.* Most colleagues were instead familiar with—or at least had heard more about—Alexis de Tocqueville's *Democracy in America.*

The 1997 HMSS seminar location, contributors, and content were fantastic or, in my grandchildren's language, "awesome." Mackinac Island is situated in Lake Michigan in the straits between upper and lower Michigan, and is reached only by boat or plane. Mission Point Resort, on the island, is a charming place to meet in the late spring. Mackinac was chosen by the organizers because it was one of the places that Harriet Martineau actually visited while on her carefully planned and extensive trip through the United States. In fact, she vividly described her early July, 1836 visit in the unabridged version of her *Society in America:*

> The island looked enchanting as we approached, as I think it always must, though we had the advantage of seeing it first steeped in the most golden sunshine that ever hallowed lake or shore. . . .
>
> The next morning all was bright. At five o'clock we descended the ship's side, and from the boat could see the commandant and his dog hastening down from the garrison to the landing-place. We returned with him up the hill, through the barrack-yard; and were joined by three members of his family on the velvet green slope behind the garrison. No words can give an idea of the charms of this morning walk. We wound about in a vast shrubbery, with ripe strawberries under foot, wild flowers all around, and scattered knolls and opening vistas tempting curiously in every direction. "Now run up," said the commandant, as we arrived at the foot of one of the knolls. I did so, and was almost struck backwards by what I saw. Below me was the Natural Bridge of Mackinaw, of which I had heard frequent mention. It is a limestone arch, about one hundred and fifty feet high in the centre, with a span of fifty feet; one pillar resting on a rocky projection in the lake, the other on the hill. We viewed it from above, so that the horizon line of the lake fell behind the bridge, and the blue expanse of waters filled the entire arch. Birch and ash grew around the bases of the pillars, and shrubbery tufted the sides, and dangled from the bridge. The soft rich hews in which the whole was dressed seemed borrowed from the autumn sky.
>
> But even this scene was nothing to one we saw from the fort, on the crown of the island; old Fort Holmes, called Fort George when in the possession of the British. I can compare it to nothing but to what Noah might have seen, the first bright morning after the deluge. Such a cluster of little paradises rising out of such a congregation of waters, I can hardly fancy to have been seen elsewhere. The capacity of the human eye seems here suddenly enlarged, as if it could see to the verge of watery creation. Blue, level waters appear to expand for thousands of miles in every direction; wholly unlike any aspect of the sea. . . .

And so Martineau continues. Mackinac, suffice it to say, is a beautiful and historic place, one that clearly made a favorable impression on Martineau in 1836 and on those who attended the HMSS seminar in 1997.

Martineau was not, however, the only important woman to visit the island in its early days. For example, Dr. Alice Hamilton, a Hull-House resident, spent her summers on Mackinac, and helping to orient the HMSS seminar participants to this particular bit of history, Mary Jo Deegan presented an illustrated slide lecture on "The Distinguished Cottagers from Mackinac Island—the Hamilton Sisters." Rounding out the historical briefing of the seminar members, a representative of the Mackinac Island State Park Commission provided a concise history and description of the island.

I realized the first day of the seminar that the presenters were no amateurs, but sociologists having extensive familiarity with Martineau and the people connected to her. The speakers expressed sorrow that Martineau has been seriously neglected in comparison to Alexis de Tocqueville (the latter had actually been less prepared and less well organized to observe American society). Formal presentations on Martineau's Unitarian background and involvement, her collaboration with Florence Nightingale, her writings on work and occupations in the nineteenth century, the meaning of her concept of "Things" in connection with Émile Durkheim's work, her systematic exploration of the "morals and manners" of people she observed and analyzed—in spite of her own deepening hearing loss, combined to indicate a complicated picture of this early feminist thinker and sociologist. Adding counterpoint and useful contrast, a paper on Victoria Woodhull, another early woman social theorist, was also presented.

Each contributor to the seminar and thus to this book has other publications on closely related subjects. Michael R. Hill, co-editor of this volume, has written *Archival Strategies and Techniques* (1993) and edited Harriet Martineau's *How to Observe Morals and Manners* (1989). Hill and Mary Jo Deegan co-edited *Women and Symbolic Interaction* (1987) and Charlotte Perkins Gilman's *With Her in Ourland: Sequel to Herland* (1997). Hill is originator and editor of *Sociological Origins*, a new journal devoted to the history of sociology. He also has an extensive bibliography of Harriet's publications in a variety of sources. Susan Hoecker-Drysdale, also a co-editor of this volume, has studied and written extensively from the numerous Martineau publications on work and occupations, treating work as subject and as agency, and is the author of *Harriet Martineau: First Woman Sociologist* (1992). She equates Martineau's theories with those of Karl Marx, Max Weber, Émile Durkheim, Thorstein Veblen and Charlotte Perkins Gilman. Mary Jo Deegan has frequently written about early women sociologists, including *Jane Addams and the Men of the Chicago School, 1892–1918* (1988), *Women in Sociology: A Bio-Bibliographical Sourcebook* (1991), and several analyses of other women and men sociologists, especially George Herbert Mead, Alfred Schutz, and W.I. Thomas. Pat Duffy Hutcheon is author of *Leaving the Cave: Evolutionary Naturalism in Social-Scientific Thought* (1996). Lynn McDonald authored *Early Origins of the Social Sciences* (1993), *The Women Founders of the Social Sciences* (1994), and *Women Theorists on Society and Politics* (1998). Patricia Madoo Lengermann with Jill Niebrugge-Brantley published *The Women Founders: Sociology and Social Theory 1830–1930* (1998), which summarizes and adds to their prior work in several sources.

Martineau's recent ascendancy in at least a few sociological circles lags somewhat behind Martineau's earlier popularity and fame among the literate public in England and America. Indeed, as I peruse my personal library, I see that the earliest discussion of Harriet Martineau in my possession is contained in Elbert Hubbard's *Three Great Women: Being Little Journeys*, "done into a book by the Roycrofters at their Shop which is in East Aurora, Erie County, New York, in the Month of April, Year Nineteen Hundred Eight." Hubbard's handsome example of arts and crafts printing also includes little journeys on Elizabeth Barrett Browning and Madame Guyon. It is high time, of course, that Martineau's contributions are remembered and discussed by today's sociologists.

The memorable 1997 seminar on Mackinac Island was followed in successive years by presentations at professional meetings and social events in members' homes, including in Toronto during the meetings of the American Sociological Association (ASA), in Montréal during the World Congress of the International Sociological Association, and, most recently, in a hotel suite in Washington, DC, again during the annual meeting of the ASA. Divers members of HMSS helped form a new ASA section on the History of Sociology, and several were voted its officers in 2000 during the section's first elections.

Volunteering to participate in any organizational activity often results in an invitation to work, and I ended up being asked to write the preface for this volume on Harriet Martineau, composed at core of revised versions of the earlier Mackinac papers. To help set the historical context of this endeavor, I contacted Michael R. Hill for information on the origins of HMSS and received an extensive response, of which the following is both a verbatim and an abridged version:

> In early 1996, Michael R. Hill, with the support of his colleague and life-partner, Mary Jo Deegan, wrote to scholars interested in Harriet Martineau and proposed forming an organizational structure to be called the Harriet Martineau Sociological Society. The envisioned organization would specifically encourage research and scholarly exchange on the sociological work of Martineau and other early women sociologists. Hill suggested that all interested persons meet at the upcoming 1996 mid-term meeting of the International Sociological Association (ISA) Research Committee on the History of Sociology (RCHS) in the Netherlands.

In Amsterdam, the RCHS session organized by Lynn McDonald included three especially relevant papers. Susan Hoecker-Drysdale presented "Analyzing Harriet Martineau's Letters on Science," Patricia Lengermann and Jill Niebrugge spoke on "Engendering Social Theory: Early Women Sociologists Theorize Domestic Service," and Michael R. Hill read a paper on "A Methodological Comparison of the American Studies of Harriet Martineau and Alexis de Tocqueville." These presenters, together with Lynn McDonald, Mary Jo Deegan, John Drysdale, Pat Duffy Hutcheon, Linda Rynbrandt, and Rosalind Sydie, comprised the first HMSS caucus. In due course, after Amsterdam followed Mackinac, Toronto, Montréal, and Washington, DC. Thus, our HMSS history continues, presumably for many years to come.

This book is a very important contribution to the history of sociology, both because it provides us with extensive analyses of an almost forgotten sociological pioneer and because it includes a comparative tie-in to the theories of other sociological pioneers and to American and British history and scholarship.

Harriet Martineau

CHAPTER ONE

Taking Harriet Martineau Seriously in the Classroom and Beyond

Michael R. Hill
Susan Hoecker-Drysdale

THE CONTRIBUTORS TO THIS BOOK, SOCIOLOGISTS ALL, TAKE HARRIET Martineau seriously as a major and consequential intellect within their chosen discipline and their classrooms. It has not always been so, at least in recent times, but Martineau has now been rediscovered by sociologists who are writing about Martineau in a growing series of books, essays, and scholarly editions. We do not all see Martineau through the same "author spectacles," as the following contributions make evident, but we do *see* her—she is no longer "invisible" to those of our students and colleagues who possess a modicum of bibliographic savvy. At several points in this book, readers are presented with contextual background and biographical details about Martineau, information that is useful and necessary for readers who are still new to Martineau's work, but it warrants notice that the time for penning generic introductory synopses of Martineau and her accomplishments is drawing to a close—several sociological introductions are readily available and are cited among the references at the end of this book. Along this line, although uncited in the present bibliography, a growing number of introductory sociology textbooks now make at least passing reference to Martineau (Hill 1998). Harriet Martineau has arrived on the doorstep of the twenty-first century sociological scene, and it is high time that the discipline's scholars, thinkers, and theoreticians take her seriously.

Giving Martineau her due is no minor matter and no small challenge. The eventual consequences for a discipline long socialized to honor only white western males as its revered founders are, of course, unpredictable. Chagrin? Embarrassment? Disbelief? Willful ignorance? These certainly are possibilities, but we hope here for understanding, enlightenment, and reflexivity—our sociological colleagues are, after all, scholars and intellectuals who profess tolerance and openness to new perspectives. The shape of sociological thought changes and grows in novel and unexpected ways when women's previously unheralded contributions to the discipline are acknowledged in literature reviews, incorporated in texts, included in lectures, and added to graduate reading lists (see for example the perspective adopted in Joe R. Feagin's (forthcoming) 2000 presidential address to the American Sociological Association). This is especially vital in Martineau's case. Two hundred years after her birth, Martineau's work remains intellectually vibrant, astutely critical, and deeply concerned with myriad substantive issues that still engage many of today's sociologists around the world.

Taking Martineau seriously demands more than honorific mention in introductory textbooks—no matter how salutatory it is to add such a remarkable "heroine" to the discipline's traditionally male-dominated founding pantheon. Martineau's work demands far more than a genteel tip of the hat. The contributors to this volume wrestle with the implications of Martineau's ideas for sociology today in the same way that disciplinary arbiters have for decades supported and argued for the continuing relevance of Émile Durkhem, Max Weber, Karl Marx, and other male theorists. Given the sheer magnitude of Martineau's published corpus, this is a daunting task and is only just now underway. Despite years of reading, writing, and thinking about Martineau's ideas, none of the contributors to this book claim a comprehensive grasp of Martineau's work as a whole, but each finds sociological gold—and the prospect of further rich discoveries—among the literally thousands of Martineau's writings. The conceptual potential is astonishing: new vocabularies, new precedents, new systems of relevance, new models of engaged sociological practice—all flow in torrents from Martineau's pen. This book offers a preview, a first effort toward what, of necessity, must be the long-term project of taking Martineau seriously. We invite your participation, your critiques, and encourage your own explorations and extensions of Martineau's work and ideas—and we are confident that Martineau herself would likewise welcome you to this exciting and progressive enterprise, not because she sought the limelight, but because she believed so deeply in the positive social results of cooperative rational industry.

Because we contend pointedly—as have others—that it is high time to take Harriet Martineau seriously within the discipline of sociology, the present volume provides several worked examples illustrating how to begin the project of giving Martineau her due: pedagogically, contextually, theoretically, and methodologically. In this chapter, we examine the opportunities and challenges of utilizing Martineau pedagogically in the sociology classroom, in introductory courses and across the broad spectrum of substantive interests that comprises sociology today. In the chapters that follow, Pat Duffy Hutcheon shows how to locate Martineau historically and intellectually within the social and religious movement called Unitarianism, providing a model for future explications of Martineau's location within other influential nineteenth-century movements of thought. Lynn McDonald approaches Martineau through the eyes of another major nineteenth-century figure, Florence Nightingale, and reminds us that our assessments of Martineau's centrality depend, in part, on the disciplinary spectacles one wears and values. Hoecker-Drysdale discusses Martineau's links with Auguste Comte, long acknowledged as one of the discipline's early male founders. Lengermann and Niebrugge favorably compare Martineau to Émile Durkheim, and Hill draws sharp methodological contrasts between Alexis de Tocqueville and Martineau. Beyond these contextual, theoretical, and methodological assessments, Martineau's continuing substantive relevance for special sociological work is also extraordinarily wide. In relation to the sociology of work and occupations, for example, Hoecker-Drysdale's two-part essay, "Words on Work," explores the complexity and sophistication of Martineau's analyses of human labor. Mary Jo Deegan, taking a very different tack, demonstrates Martineau's critical relevance for the sociology of physical disability. In sum, and in varied ways, all of the contributors to this volume provide sociological exemplars of how to take Martineau seriously.

In the remainder of this chapter, we draft the pedagogical dimensions of Martineau's biography, accomplishments, and ideas in sociology classrooms. Readers unfamiliar with Martineau's work will find the following material useful as a resource for introducing Martineau to students and also as an orientation for the substantive chapters below. From this perspective, the substantive chapters easily perform a double duty. Not only do they stand as independent scholarly explorations in their own right, but, when utilized selectively, they make excellent reading assignments in college courses, for example, in the sociology of religion, the sociology of work and occupations, sociological theory, health and disability studies, sociological methodology, social movements, and the sociology of women, to emphasize the most obvious pedagogical applications. We fully expect that—when more scholars in additional specialties begin taking Martineau seriously—the list from which to choose relevant course readings will become ever more expansive.

BIOGRAPHY AND CRITIQUE

Biographical Sketch

To the extent that any complex institutional phenomenon such as sociology can have identifiable founders, Alice Rossi (1973: 118–24) justly celebrated Harriet Martineau as "the first woman sociologist." Martineau's life is a remarkable example of sociological invention, growth and insight. Harriet, born in 1802, was the sixth of eight children in a middle-class English family. Her younger brother, James, became a well-known cleric (Jackson 1901). Her father's occupation as a manufacturer placed Harriet in comfortable surroundings, but her childhood was marred by strong feelings of fearfulness and self-doubt. She was, nonetheless, intellectually industrious and applied herself to both secular and religious studies. With the exception of two years in private, coeducational classes and a year in a boarding school for girls, she was educated largely at home by siblings and by hired tutors. Through self-study, Martineau rigorously augmented her early exposure to subjects routinely taught only to males. Education was important in the Martineau family and Harriet was both immersed and self-immersed in the classics, languages (Greek, Latin, Italian, French—she later taught herself German), literature, history, composition, mathematics, religious studies, and later as an adolescent expanded her studies in music, modern literature, philosophy, poetry and languages. Women were barred from university study, but Martineau maintained a regimen of intense, self-directed investigation throughout her life. Troubled by increasing deafness as a youth, Martineau required an ear trumpet during adulthood.

The Martineau family suffered severe economic losses in the 1820s, as well as the death of Harriet's father—and Harriet was left to her own resources. While Harriet faced the exigencies of earning her living in a patriarchal society, she wrote, "I began to feel the blessing of a wholly new freedom" (Martineau 1877b, I: 108). Martineau escaped the confines of middle-class Victorian marriage when her fiancé unexpectedly died. She was happily single and independent for the remainder of her life. She successfully supported herself as an author in a variety of genres, including: essays, tracts, reviews, novels, travelogues, biographies, how-to manuals, journal articles, newspaper columns, histories, children's stories, and sociologically-informed nonfiction.

Martineau's intellectual life is a chronicle of scholarly maturation and deepening sociological insight. Raised as a devout Unitarian, Martineau's first literary efforts were fervently religious (see Pat Duffy Hutcheon's chapter, this volume). Adoption of "Necessarianism" provided her with an intellectual bridge to a social scientific perspective, and the theoretical framework in her twenty-five volume *Illustrations of Political Economy* (1832–4) signaled her eventual departure from ecclesiastical dogma (see especially volume twenty-five, *The Moral of Many Fables*). In the *Illustrations*, she employed fiction to explicate the principles of the new science of political economy, and the results met with popular success. The *Illustrations* marked her entry into English literary society and set her on the road to financial independence.

In 1834, Martineau began a two-year study tour of the United States (see Hill's chapter on Martineau and Tocqueville, this volume; Bullock 1992). She reported her observations in *Society in America* (1837) and *Retrospect of Western Travel* (1838a). These empirical studies emerged hand-in-hand with her foundational treatise on sociological data collection. *How to Observe Morals and Manners* (1838b) insightfully articulated the principles and methods of empirical social research (see Patricia Lengermann and Jill Niebrugge's chapter, this volume; Hill 1989). This period marked Martineau's achievement of a mature and incisive sociological imagination.

In subsequent years, Martineau refined her metatheoretical orientation, and moved even farther from her Unitarian upbringing. Following a trip to the Middle East, reported in *Eastern Life, Present and Past* (1848), she openly embraced atheism in *Letters on the Laws of Man's Nature and Development* (Atkinson and Martineau 1851). In 1851, she began an English translation/condensation of Auguste Comte's *Cours de philosophie positive*. The introduction of positivist sociological ideas into the United States was greatly facilitated by Martineau's momentous rendition of Comte's (1853) most influential sociological work (see Hoecker-Drysdale's chapter on Comte, this volume).

By choice, Martineau's later years unfolded not in London, but in the Lake District where she built a house at Ambleside. She redeemed her mortgage with royalties from the controversial book with Atkinson. The beauty and peacefulness of the Lake District stand in strong contrast to the years of personal trial, illness, exhaustion, deafness, and social and literary controversy that confronted Martineau throughout much of her life. At various points, her intellectual circle included: Charles Babbage, Thomas Carlyle, George Eliot, Florence Nightingale (see Lynn McDonald's chapter, this volume), Charles Dickens, Thomas Malthus, William Wordsworth, Charlotte Brontë, Charles Lyell, and Charles Darwin, among many others.

For Martineau (1877, I: 143), her profession was a Weberian calling:

> Authorship has never been for me a matter of choice. I have not done it for amusement, or for money, or for fame, or for any reason but because I could not help it. Things were pressing to be said; and there was more or less evidence that I was the person to say them.

Martineau, like all significant sociological theorists, gave life and direction to vital intellectual questions with insight, originality, and a deep sense of personal and social mission. Harriet Martineau died at seventy-four years of age, in 1876.

Sociological Critique

It is no easy task to provide a sociological critique of Martineau's published writings. Most readers new to her work are stunned to learn of the sheer mass and scope of her writings. Joseph Rivlin's (1947) comprehensive bibliography lists dozens of separately published books. The 3,479 pages of the *Illustrations of Political Economy* alone were originally published in twenty-five separate installments, of which the last, *The Moral of Many Fables*, was a systematically arranged compendium of theoretical principles. Martineau was equally prolific as a contributor to periodical journals and newspapers. There is yet no thoroughly comprehensive bibliography of Martineau's reviews and journal articles. Several early articles were reprinted in her *Miscellanies* (1836c) and a selection of later articles appeared in her *Health, Husbandry and Handicraft* (1861). Additional articles are discovered whenever scholars scour Victorian-era periodicals. As a sociologically-astute journalist, Martineau wrote more than 1,500 newspaper columns, of which only a few have been reprinted (Webb 1959; Arbuckle 1994; Martineau 1994). In sum, Martineau's written corpus is a massive reservoir of astute sociological insight awaiting modern sociological critique and extension.

Martineau undertook pioneering studies—substantive, theoretical, and methodological investigations—in what is now called sociology. She was an ardent Unitarian, abolitionist, critic, feminist, social scientist, and avowed atheist . Her writing included such topics as: social theory, biography, disability, education, history, husbandry, legislation, manufacturing, mesmerism, work and occupations, occupational health, philosophy, political economy, religion, research techniques, slavery, sociology, travel, and women's rights.

Of Martineau's numerous works, her three-volume *Society in America* (1837) is the most widely known to sociologists in the United States. Her methodological strategy confronted the problem of ethnocentrism. Rather than compare the United States to England, she identified the moral principles to which Americans claimed allegiance, and compared them to observable social patterns—a methodologically insightful distinction between rhetoric and reality. Martineau documented a wide chasm between extant institutional patterns and the values of democracy, justice, equality, and freedom that Americans claimed to cherish. Beyond *Society in America* (typically read only in the abridged version), however, Martineau's other economic, political, and historical studies remain largely uncited by sociologists. Her substantive, systematic observations of society are directly relevant to historical and comparative sociologists who explicate the complexities of Victorian England and nineteenth-century life. Her theoretical and methodological insights remain as bright, lively, and cogent as any penned by her more widely acknowledged male co-founders of sociology.

In *How to Observe Morals and Manners* (1838b), Martineau provided the first-known systematic methodological treatise in sociology. It is a theoretically sophisticated, yet practical, guide to sociological observation. Metatheoretically, she offered the classic positivist solution to the correspondence problem between intersubjectively verifiable observables and unobservable theoretical entities. Confronting the problem of studying a society as a whole, she creatively attacked problems of bias, generalization, samples, reactivity, interviews, corroboration, and data recording techniques. She outlined studies of the major social institutions, including: religion, education, family, fine arts and popular culture, markets and economy, prisons, government, and philanthropy. *How To Observe* is also a precedent-setting work of theory. Before Karl Marx, and decades before Émile Durkheim and Max Weber, Martineau sociologically examined social class, forms of religion, types of suicide, national character, domestic relations and the status of women, delinquency and criminology, and the intricate interrelationships between repressive social institutions and the individual (Hill 1989).

Thematic study of Martineau's extensive corpus provides a wealth of untapped opportunities for modern sociologists. The metasociology of Martineau's translation of Comte's (1853) major sociological treatise is a crucial field for intellectual exploration. Her contributions to feminist thought (Martineau 1985) deserve spirited sociological review. Martineau's (1859a) mutual project with Florence Nightingale, *England and Her Soldiers*, is a *tour de force* on occupational health. Martineau provides detailed portraits of nineteenth-century industrial, agricultural, and domestic work in *Health, Husbandry, and Handicraft* (1861) and elsewhere. Her *Illustrations of Political Economy* and other didactic tales are untapped models of literature as sociology. Thematically, Martineau's sociological imagination was unbounded—it reached from micro to macro, from theory to observation, from objective description to informed critique and social action.

The majority of the major, book-length critical interpretations of Martineau have been authored primarily by scholars in disciplines other than sociology—recent examples from English literature include Valerie Pichanick (1980), Thomas Gillian (1985), Linda Peterson (1986), Valerie Sanders (1986), Deirdre David (1987), Shelagh Hunter (1995), and Claudia Oražem (1999). A substantial number of journal articles and chapters in books have also appeared. Those outside the discipline of sociology, however, often fail to appreciate Martineau's specifically sociological acumen. Pichanick (1980: 75), for example, vastly underrated Martineau's scientific discernment when she credited Martineau with having outlined nothing more than a "primitive" sociological methodology. Recent volumes by literature and language scholars typically shed little illumination on Martineau's distinctly sociological accomplishments. (To these recent offerings may be added a string of earlier works by non-sociologists, including Theodora Bosanquet (1927), Narola Elizabeth Rivenburg (1932), John Cranston Neville (1943), Vera Wheatley (1947), and R.K. Webb (1960)). These often interesting and inherently valuable—but characteristically asociological—works all pose a challenge to modern sociologists. Whatever the value of Martineau's work to literature, history, journalism, women's studies, and other disciplines, the evaluation of her original contributions to sociology requires sustained, intelligent critique by sociologically-sensitive scholars.

This sociological critique has been slowly building. One of the earliest of sociologists, Auguste Comte, was extremely pleased with Martineau's translation/abridgment of his foundational *Cours de philosophie positive*. He wrote to her:

> And looking at it from the point of view of future generations, I feel sure that your name will be linked with mine, for you have executed the only one of those works that will survive amongst all those which my fundamental treatise has called forth. (Comte, quoted in Harrison 1895: xvii–xviii)

In the hands of subsequent male sociologists, however, Comte's prophesy of Martineau's fame went unfulfilled.

Edith Abbott (1906: 615), a Chicago sociologist, attributed "the most convenient and definite statement regarding the early employment of women" in the United States to Martineau (1837, II: 131–51). Abbott (1906: 616) however, faulted Martineau's computational accounting of the occupations open to women, and argued that Martineau's underreporting of occupational possibilities for women lent unintended support to "comforting generalizations regarding the multiplication of industrial openings for women" in the decades subsequent to Martineau's report. Nonetheless, Abbott (1906: 626) appreciatively noted Martineau's perceptive and critical conclusion that "it is difficult . . . for women to earn their bread." If Martineau's specific statistics were misleading, her overall conceptual analysis was accurate and enduring. Abbott wrote that "one could not go far wrong in saying that the lot of the poor woman is still sad. Opportunity of employment is scarce now as it was then." Little more was then heard about Martineau in sociological circles—with perhaps the sole exception of Mary van Kleek's (1913: 18) citation of Martineau's data on women bookbinders in van Kleek's landmark study of the bookbinding industry.

Following a nearly half-century hiatus of significant commentary by sociologists on Martineau, Seymour Martin Lipset (1962: 39), who otherwise admired Martineau's sociological skills and went to the considerable effort of abridging Martineau's *Society in America*, suggested:

> To those who wonder why such a sophisticated analyst has been allowed to linger for so long in the obscurity of nineteenth-century editions, the answer must be that the blame rests with Harriet Martineau herself.

Lipset implied that Martineau was overlooked only because she wrote lengthy works that are "tedious to some readers." Importantly, however, he pointed out that, "In emphasizing the value system as a causal agent, Martineau was an early precursor of one of the major sociological orientations, an approach that attempts to analyze the effect of values on structure and change" (Lipset 1962: 10), and concluded that *How to Observe Morals and Manners* "testifies to the considerable sophistication" that Martineau brought to methodological issues (Lipset 1962: 37). Upon the publication of Lipset's abridged edition of Martineau's *Society in America*, John Cawelti (1963: 208) characterized Martineau as a Victorian combination of Margaret Mead and Hannah Arendt. Comparing her work to Tocqueville's well-known studies of the same era, Cawelti credited Martineau with providing a viable, alternative analysis of "the pressure toward conformity" in American society. Not only did he prefer Martineau's full-length treatment over Lipset's abridgment, he concluded, that Martineau suggested further "avenues of approach to the problem that are surely worthy of investigation by historians and sociologists" (Cawelti 1963: 213).

In subsequent counterpoint, and in concert with new wave feminist awakenings in American sociology in the 1970s, Alice Rossi (1973) designated Harriet Martineau as "the first woman sociologist," and Dale Spender (1982) critically faulted the male academic establishment for the patriarchal exclusion of Martineau's work from sociology. Paul Riedesel's (1981) apologetic exemplifies the patriarchal bias. He severely discounted Martineau even while calling attention to her work. Claiming that Martineau "left no corpus of theory," Riedesel (1981: 77) failed to cite Martineau's sophisticated methodological classic, *How to Observe Morals and Manners* or any of her equally resilient and intellectually vibrant works. At best, such essays damn with faint praise.

In an important pedagogical article, James Terry (1983: 253) argued in *Teaching Sociology* that Martineau and Charlotte Perkins Gilman are "two women who have been excluded from the sociological canon whom I consider on a par with the traditional masters." He concluded, Martineau's "writings in political economy and scientific methods, her comparative study of American and European societies, and her insights into the subordination of women in American society in the 1830s deserve recognition and study in their own right" (Terry 1983: 253–4). Robert Nisbet (1988: 173–4) followed suit, asserting that—compared to Alexis de Tocqueville's (1835–40) *Democracy in America*—Martineau's (1837) *Society in America* "is a better study of American life." Michael R. Hill (1989) outlined Martineau's scientific logic and traced her epistemological development in his long introduction to the sesquicentennial edition of Martineau's *How to Observe Morals and Manners*. Hill (1989: li) argued that any *one* of Martineau's recognized major accomplishments, specifically, (1) writing the first book on sociological methodology, (2) completing an insightful and methodologically sophisticated analysis of American society, and (3) translating and condensing Comte's foundational work, warrants her unconditional election to the rank of major sociologist. And, in the same year, Shulamit Reinharz (1989: 92) reminded us that Martineau's methodological treatise, *How to Observe Morals and Manners* not only predates Durkheim's *Rules of Sociological Method* by sixty years but is also "nearly analogous." In her survey of the "continuities among women as subjects and objects of intellectual work," Reinharz (1989: 92) noted:

> There were the continuities of not being remembered—e.g. the fame of de Tocqueville vis a vis Harriet Martineau, although both wrote at the same time about the same topic; and the fame of Durkheim's treatise on method as compared to Martineau's although hers predates his by sixty years and is nearly analogous.

Two years later, Mary Jo Deegan (1991: 13–14), in her introduction to *Women in Sociology: A Bio-Bibliographical Sourcebook*, assessed Martineau's sociological preeminence as

> equal to, if not greater than, that of any man in her era, including the relatively overpraised Comte and de Tocqueville. Martineau's lucid translation of Comte's work contributed significantly to his recognition as a founding sociologist. She condensed his voluminous Cours de philosophie positive and made it more accessible to those who later established sociology in the English-speaking world. In addition, her travels in the United States were more insightful, comprehensive, and methodologically creative than those of de Tocqueville. Martineau is a giant in sociology, and her undisputed leadership is recognized here.

The longest sociological analysis to date, Susan Hoecker-Drysdale's book-length sociological assessment, *Harriet Martineau: First Woman Sociologist*, appeared in 1992. Hoecker-Drysdale's compact biography examines the life and thought of this Victorian radical and specifically outlines Martineau's multifaceted work in political economy, history, journalism, and sociology—work based on Martineau's premise that scientific knowledge is essential to social progress. In sum, by the last decade of the twentieth century, the paradigmatically revolutionary case for Martineau was amply made.

Now, in the Kuhnian tradition of normal science, a number of paper presentations at professional sociological meetings, articles, and book chapters—several by the contributors to this book—are starting to appear with greater regularity. The chapters in this book are offered as points of departure for ever more exhaustive and comprehensive explications of Martineau's metasociological framework, sociological theories, methodologies, and empirical findings, analyses, and social critiques. The astonishing breadth of this prospect points not only to an exciting future of new scholarly work *per se*, but also to vital pedagogical opportunities in academic classrooms.

PEDAGOGICAL ISSUES

James Terry (1983) recommended including Martineau's work in the basic sociology curriculum, and with good reason. For the authors of this chapter—as well as for many sociologists of our acquaintance—Martineau's insights inform every sociology course we teach, and we cannot imagine teaching sociology without including her sage observations and sociological perspective. We have taught Martineau in a wide range of courses. For example, Hill utilizes Martineau in: Sociological Research Methods, Regional Geography, Introduction to Sociology, Sociology of Marriage and Family, Social Problems, and Sociological Theory. Hoecker-Drysdale has taught Martineau in courses on Feminist Sociological Theories, Sociology of Sex Roles, Women and Work through Literature and Sociology, Victorian Sociology, The Feminist Tradition in Sociology, Feminist Perspectives in Social Science, and Classical Social Theory. Experientially, we conclude that Martineau's works merit mature study and intelligent analysis throughout the sociological curriculum. Academics who teach university courses have much to gain in taking Martineau seriously in the classroom.

Martineau was a nineteenth-century writer, however, and her prose is challenging for today's students, in the same way that the works of Charles Dickens, Jane Austen, and other Victorian writers speak often to universal issues but in the language and diction of an earlier era. We recognize that students unfamiliar with nineteenth-century prose may sometimes find her word choices exotic to the modern eye and ear. This is, of course, a pedagogical opportunity, first, in terms of the wider mission of liberal arts education—that we do not jettison the wisdom of our predecessors just because their words now ring with a peculiar timbre, and second, as a pointed sociological illustration of linguistic, cultural, and institutional change. Our experience has been that students quickly develop the comprehension skills for (get the knack of) reading Harriet Martineau, in part because they are drawn by the lively empirical descriptions which are interspersed in her analyses and because Martineau speaks to so many contemporary social issues.

We suspect, however, that any strangeness or difficulty perceived by would-be instructors and/or their students in reference to Martineau's language is largely a straw figure. Linguistic difficulty is given no salience by those who seriously teach and read the works of Adam Smith, Max Weber, Émile Durkheim, Karl Marx, Georg Simmel, Alexis de Tocqueville, and the like—all authors who are indeed challenging to the average college student. Reading sociological theory in the original or in translation almost always requires discipline and a sympathetic willingness to understand—so too for Martineau. That Martineau has not been widely taught in sociological theory courses is a problem that lies not primarily in Martineau's prose style, but in the traditions of patriarchal pedagogy. When Martineau is presented with the same energy, veneration, erudition, integrity, and authority with which astute Marxists discuss *Capital* or discerning Durkheimians dissect *The Elementary Forms of Religious Life*, for example, we contend that her work too becomes as "richly textured," "complex," "thoughtful," "brilliant," "significant," "foundational," and "masterful" as any authored by members of the traditional male pantheon.

In Martineau's case, there is a further complication on the linguistic and conceptual front—she wrote frequently and explicitly for the literate public of her era, and rarely for academicians. Much of her sociological writing is directly accessible to neophyte readers, especially her didactic fiction and many of her newspaper "leaders" and articles in popular British monthlies. Here, the pedagogical difficulty is that students may miss entirely the sophisticated logic and structure of her theoretical views and focus instead on story line or substantive, topical content (although, clearly, substantive content gives life to theory). Indeed, some readers at the time noted that they read her didactic tales more for the story than the moral. This is a general problem faced by instructors who teach about such writers as Martineau, Jane Addams, Charlotte Perkins Gilman, and W.E.B. Du Bois, writers for whom it was axiomatic that their sociological ideas ought to be presented at least part of the time in prose accessible to non-specialists. Thus, such writings tend to forgo the esoteric footnotes, arduous definitions, and abstracted languages in which so much sociological theory is shrouded and encapsulated. Pedagogically, the task is to make the implicit theory more explicit, in much the same way that we must often show students how everyday speech is theory-laden and replete with metascientific presuppositions. With reference to formal theories, this is nothing more than the obligation to excavate and/or reconstruct "missing" elements in metascientific worldviews, and to demonstrate how such elements are logically interconnected (Hill 1984: 66). Interestingly, Martineau provides worked examples of just this process in her *Illustrations of Political*

Economy, wherein each fictional narrative is supplemented by a tightly worded précis outlining the theoretical principles that underlie each didactic novel in the series.

Martineau's *Moral of Many Fables*, the last volume of her *Illustrations*, is a logically integrated compilation of the brief theoretical summaries from each novel. Here, for example, is the précis from Martineau's *The Hill and the Valley* (1832–4, no. 2: 216):

> CAPITAL is something produced with a view to employment in further production.
> Labour is the origin, and
> Saving is the support, of capital.
> Capital consists of:
> 1. Implements of labour,
> 2. Material, simple or compound, on which labour is employed, [and]
> 3. Subsistence of labourers.
> Of these three parts, the first constitutes fixed capital; the second and third reproducible capital.
> Since capital is derived from labour, whatever economizes labour assists the growth of capital.
> Machinery economizes labour, and therefore assists the growth of capital.
> The growth of capital increases the demand for labour.
> Machinery, by assisting the growth of capital, therefore increases the demand for labour.
> In other words, productive industry is proportioned to capital, whether that capital be fixed or reproducible.
> The interests of the two classes of producers, labourers and capitalists, are therefore the same; the prosperity of both depending on the accumulation of CAPITAL.

Explicating and interconnecting the logical arguments in summary form for Martineau's myriad other works is an instructive exercise for professor and student alike, and one that is required if the theoretical import of Martineau's writings and the theoretical shifts in her work over time are to be fully appreciated in courses wherein selections from her writings are made assigned readings.

Researching Martineau's Intellectual Biography

Professors preparing new lectures on Martineau's intellectual biography as a sociological pioneer have many available sources on which to draw. Her birth at the dawn of the nineteenth century and subsequent career in England, however, make it relatively more difficult for North American instructors to locate primary information to use in reconstructing Martineau's professional life. Mary Jo Deegan (1988) shows how to use various library aids to build biographical portraits of neglected women sociologists, but the library tools she recommends are best suited to American women who became active professionally in the late nineteenth century and thereafter. Somewhat different strategies are required to construct an intellectual biography of Martineau as a sociologist, but the mine of readily available material is happily large.

In addition to the several literary biographies, noted above, and Hoecker-Drysdale's (1992) sociologically-framed account, most students begin with the major data source on Martineau's life, her *Autobiography* (1877b), written in 1855, but published posthumously in 1877 together with Maria Chapman's biographically important *Memorials of Harriet Martineau* (1877). The most available edition is the Virago 1983 publication of the *Autobiography*, but, unfortunately, it contains neither the *Memorials* nor an index. Martineau (1877a), ever sensible and efficient, also wrote her own obituary notice and self-estimate! Readers should be warned, however, that Martineau's reflections on herself are often self-deprecating and thus do not adequately convey an objective estimation of her intellectual accomplishments.

Numerous personal experiences are reflected in Martineau's *Household Education* (1849), *Life in the Sick-Room* (1844b), and *Berkeley the Banker* (a didactic novel in her *Illustrations of Political Economy*, 1832–4). Her adult conversion to atheism, from a spiritual life of devout Unitarianism, is chronicled in *Eastern Life, Present and Past* (1848). Glimpses of personal life are found readily in Elisabeth Arbuckle's edited collection of Martineau's correspondence with Fanny Wedgwood (Martineau 1983) and in Martineau's *Selected Letters* (1990) edited by Valerie Sanders. A selection of Martineau's letters regarding America written between 1835 and 1867 was edited by R.A. Burchell (Martineau 1995). Regarding material in archives, a large collection of Martineau manuscripts and letters in the Birmingham University Library, Birmingham, England, are now available on microfilm—a collection for which there is a published guide: *Women, Emancipation and Literature: The Papers of Harriet Martineau, 1802–1876* (Adam Matthew Publications 1991). Second in size and importance only to the Birmingham papers is the Reinhard S. Speck Collection of Harriet Martineau papers now deposited at The Bancroft Library, University of California, Berkeley. An inventory of the collection is available via the internet and from the Library.

Social context and perspective on the times as well as the intellectual debates of Victorian England can be gained by more general reading in the journals in which Martineau published, such as the *Atheneum*, *Edinburgh Review*, *Household Words*, *Once A Week*, *Westminster Review*, *Cornhill Magazine*, *Chambers Magazine*, and others. The *Wellesley Index to Victorian Periodicals, 1824–1900* is a helpful tool in this regard. As was common practice in Victorian periodicals, many of Martineau's articles and reviews were unsigned or published under pseudonyms. Modern scholarship is slowly providing a corrective, however. For example, Lohrli (1973) provides a complete list of the articles Martineau wrote for Charles Dickens during his editorship of *Household Words*. Francis E. Mineka (1944) lists the articles Martineau wrote for the *Monthly Repository*, and Arbuckle (1994) has updated R.K. Webb's (1959) invaluable handlist of the hundreds of unsigned leaders that Martineau wrote for the London *Daily News*. *Poole's Index to Periodical Literature*, under "Martineau, Harriet," furnishes references to a representative selection of nineteenth-century reviews of her publications, and to use *Poole's Index* to find representative articles written *by* Martineau, consult the useful but not wholly reliable *Cumulated Author Index for Poole's Index to Periodical Literature, 1802–1906*. There is at this writing, however, no comprehensive bibliographic guide to either Martineau's magazine articles or to contemporary critiques of her writing.

Martineau's biography intersected with many of England and America's most notable personalities. To recreate this exciting intellectual world, energetic students may be put on the hunt for references to Martineau in autobiographies and "life and letters" volumes written by her friends and contemporaries. For examples of these genres, see Charles Knight (1864), Jane Carlyle (1883), James Payn (1844), Gordon Haight's (1954–5) edition of the letters of George Eliot, and John Stuart Mill (1967). The index to Martineau's (1877) *Autobiography* (unfortunately not provided in the 1983 Virago edition) furnishes a long list of names to begin investigating for this type of biographical scavenger hunt. The importance of names as starting points for biographical and archival searches cannot be overemphasized. For examples and discussion of this approach to sociobiographical research, see Hill (1993: 27–36). By cross-indexing who wrote about whom in their letters and memoirs, a dense sociogram of Martineau's intellectual world can be constructed as a class project.

Teaching Martineau across the Sociology Curriculum

Martineau wrote so many varied books, articles, and newspaper "leaders," that her materials are relevant to virtually every sociology course. The institutional sweep of *Society in America* and *Retrospect of Western Travel*, for example, is complete: family, religion, law, education, economy, polity, art, literature, language, etc. A host of graduate theses using the general formula, "Harriet Martineau's Theory of (fill in a social institution of your choice)" are waiting to be researched and written. Instructors will find the following primary works especially cogent and pertinent to the courses noted:

- **Introduction to Sociology:** Martineau is now mentioned in more than a dozen introductory sociology textbooks (Hill 1998) and we suggest supplementing such texts by carefully selecting an article or chapter by Martineau that fits the topics emphasized—and the teaching strategy adopted—by individual instructors. The excerpts reprinted in Lengermann and Niebrugge-Brantley (1998) are excellent models of the types of substantive materials that can be selected and assembled for use in introductory undergraduate settings.
- **Sex and Gender; Sociology of Women:** Yates's edited collection, *Harriet Martineau on Women* (Martineau 1985), is an outstanding exemplar of drawing from Martineau's works for a thematic purpose. Feminist sociological interpretations of Martineau are particularly appropriate (and challenging—given her sometimes conservative views) in sex and gender and women's courses. Lengermann and Niebrugge-Brantley's (1998) recent text/reader relates Martineau and her work to other important early women sociologists and social scientists whose work was at once foundational and feminist.
- **Theory and Methods:** *How to Observe Morals and Manners* (1838b) is the first systematic and substantive treatise on the methodology of sociological research. It explores the thorny problems inherent in drawing theoretical conclusions from direct observation and interview data. With guidance, the work is accessible to undergraduate majors. It also teaches important theoretical points. Consideration of Martineau as a theorist of reform, including valuable excerpts of her writings from a variety of sources, are found in McDonald (1998: 138–65). In addition, Martineau has been examined by McDonald (1994) as a nineteenth-century woman methodologist. Martineau, before Marx and well before Durkheim and Weber, examined social class, religion, types of suicide, national character, delinquency, penology, and the intricate interrelationships between social institutions on the one hand and the individual on the other.

  Advanced students will find an engaging epistemological discussion in *Letters on the Laws of Man's Nature and Development* (Atkinson and Martineau 1851; Hoecker-Drysdale 1995). Martineau's translation of *The Positive Philosophy of Auguste Comte* (see Chapter Nine, this volume) is not only a classic in its own right, but is also a paradigm example of translation as sociological labor as later practiced by C. Wright Mills, Talcott Parsons, and others who produced translations of Marx, Durkheim, Weber, etc. An introduction to Martineau's theory of political economy is found in the nonfiction treatise on *The Moral of Many Fables*, the last installment of her twenty-five–part *Illustrations of Political Economy* (1832–4). Advanced students interested in the theoretical development of free-trade economics should be offered *The Factory Controversy* (1855) and *Corporate Tradition and National Rights* (1857b).

- **Historical and Comparative Sociology:** Martineau comes brightly to the fore when she turns her methodological and analytical skills to complex empirical topics—and she does this best in *Society in America* (1837). Her attempt in *Retrospect of Western Travel* (1838c) to write pure, uninterpreted description is a useful companion work. *How to Observe Morals and Manners* (1838b) articulates the research design for these large studies and should be read in conjunction.
- **Health and Occupations:** Martineau was a keen observer of occupations and the relation of work to health problems. Though presently scarce, her *England and Its Soldiers* (1859a) is a *tour de force* of occupational health studies. There, she compared the hazards of military life with a wide range of civilian occupations. Modern students in social change courses can be challenged to document and compare the health risks of these several occupations in the past and in the present.

  Martineau's (1861) collected articles in *Health, Husbandry and Handicraft* show her acumen in carefully observing manufacturing processes, including the production of straight pins—a topic close to the heart of classical economists such as Adam Smith's dissertation on the manufacture of pins in *The Wealth of Nations* (see also Chapters Six and Seven, this volume). Concerning the sociology of health *per se*, Martineau's *Life in the Sick-Room* (1844b) chronicles her own bout with a serious illness and is instructive as an exemplar of reflexive participant observation. Her controversial cure by hypnosis is detailed in *Letters on Mesmerism* (1845) and relates directly to modern discussions of alternative treatments and the social construction of illness.
- **Sociology of Literature:** No course in the sociology of literature is complete without a substantive bow to Martineau. Her work includes deceptively uncomplicated examples of writing novels as sociology. She viewed fiction as an experimental mode in which the theoretical principles of the social sciences can be worked out. Martineau's method is the empirically-grounded thought experiment (Hill 1987). This method is best seen in the first twenty-four numbers of the *Illustrations of Political Economy* (1832–4), in the tales pub-

lished as *Poor Laws and Paupers* (1833), and in *Forest and Game Law Tales* (1845–6). She explored her abstract ideas in these works and was sufficiently audacious to make the practical import of her sociological theories intelligible to a mass, popular readership.

Turning to another genre, Martineau's (1877b) *Autobiography* is receiving critical attention in literary studies (e.g., Peterson 1986) and should be included in courses on sociobiography—an emergent field in sociology (Long 1987; Denzin 1989). Examples of Martineau's own excursions in biography are collected in *Biographical Sketches* (1869).

As genres of popular literature, Webb (1959) and Arbuckle (1994) lead readers to reams of Martineau's newspaper columns. The *Miscellanies* (1836c) and *Health, Husbandry, and Handicraft* (1861) provide a wealth of sociologically-informed essays and journal articles. *Deerbrook* (1839a) is her major experiment in writing a pure novel and is readily comparable to the works of Jane Austen and similar novelists of that era. Both George Eliot and Charlotte Brontë praised *Deerbrook* and claimed to be inspired by the novel. *The Hour and the Man* (1841) is a full-length excursion in historical fiction focused on slavery in Haiti.

- **Social Problems, Social Change, and Race Relations:** Martineau was an outspoken critic of slavery, injustice, and oppression. She advocated reform measures on the basis of consistently argued sociological principles. Her insight into northern resistance to the abolition movement in America is surprisingly modern. Her analysis of slavery as a debilitating social institution is particularly cogent in *Society in America* (1837) and this aspect is well-preserved in Lipset's abridgment of that work (Martineau 1962). Her observations are continued in *Retrospect of Western Travel* (1838c). *The Martyr Age of the United States* (1839b) lays out the dynamics of the American abolitionist movement. Martineau's *Demerara* in the *Illustrations of Political Economy* (1932–4, no. 4) depicts the ill-fated economics of slave systems. *The Hour and the Man* (1841) explores, through historical fiction, the dynamics of the slave revolt in Haiti.
- **Criminology:** Martineau conceptually and empirically analyzed prison systems in *Society in America* (1837, III: 179–90) and, in *Retrospect of Western Travel* (1838c, I: 199–227), vividly illustrates her pluck as a penal investigator. Whereas Tocqueville interviewed only prison officials during his American tour, Martineau visited several prisons, interviewed their wardens, and arranged to talk, unchaperoned, with several male inmates. Thus, her conclusions on prison systems—and her denunciation of the Auburn scheme—have superior empirical grounding and are candidates for inclusion in all introductory crimi-

nology courses. From her writings as a whole, one can assemble insightful, interrelated readings on morality, religion, law, education, economics, criminality, and penal reform.

Availability of Martineau's Works

Students and instructors alike could not benefit from Martineau's pioneering sociological work if text and reference copies were not readily available for assignment and study. Although first published during the nineteenth century, several of Martineau's core works are still in print. Others can be purchased as microforms or as Books-on-Demand (to check current availability, consult *Books In Print*—preferably the online version for the most up-to-date information). Book prices range from relatively inexpensive paperbound editions to high-priced library bindings. The wave of the future is signaled, perhaps, by the recent offering of *The Hour and the Man* in an electronic version, or e-book, at lower cost than any of the traditional paper editions.

Most volumes not available in smaller libraries can be easily located online via OCLC's *WorldCat* and obtained through interlibrary loan. The first volume of the Osgood edition of Martineau's *Autobiography* is now available online, without charge, via the Victorian Women Writers Project, courtesy of Indiana University. It seems reasonable to expect that additional Martineau works will become available in this way in future years. The bibliographical details of Martineau's separately published works in their various paper editions are sufficient to fill a monograph in its own right (Rivlin 1947) and are not reproduced here. Although rapidly rising in price over the last two decades, many first and early editions of Martineau's works are also available on the rare book market, and the occasional "bargain" can still be had by academics who want to build personal Martineau collections.

Martineau's works are ripe for compilation and class assignment as professor-generated photocopy packets. Photocopy packets of selected readings—and even entire books—can be readily compiled and/or reproduced inexpensively for course adoption. It is especially important to note that all copyrights to Martineau's works are long expired, thus reducing costs to students and eliminating considerable red-tape—no "permissions" to make multiple copies are required. A further advantage is that all of Martineau's works appear in English—her entire corpus, unlike that of many European theorists, is immediately accessible to English-speaking students in Canada, England, the United States, and around the globe.

We offer one cautionary admonishment when recommending Martineau to students. Where renewed interest in Martineau's sociology is likely to spark increased student use of rare or fragile early editions, local librarians should be alerted and encouraged to remove these volumes from open stacks, prohibit their circulation, and curtail their unsupervised use. Photocopies, microfilms, or modern reprints should be made available in their stead.

A CONCLUDING COMMENT ON SERIOUSNESS

We have emphasized in this chapter the importance of taking Harriet Martineau seriously, in the classroom and beyond, but it would be a mistake, if, in so doing, we failed to underscore the personal enchantment and intellectual delight that we, our colleagues, and our students, have experienced when reading, studying, and writing about the life, times, work, and ideas of Harriet Martineau. Martineau's works open exciting windows on the earliest origins of sociology as a modern discipline; the study of her life and work results in a clearer understanding of the roots of our own intellectual commitments. In short, she helps us connect with a discipline that is otherwise too often abstracted and abstruse. Her criticism often sparkles, her insights are frequently provocative, and her empirical descriptions almost always impart that immediate sense of presence that makes our collective social past more palpable to us in the present. We are serious in our studies of Martineau because she inspires us, makes us smile in admiration of her industry, and engages our sociological imaginations.

CHAPTER TWO

Harriet Martineau and the Unitarian Connection

Pat Duffy Hutcheon

THOROUGH KNOWLEDGE OF A SUBJECT'S SUBCULTURAL MILIEU IS A CRUCIAL launching pad for the sociologist—no less than for the biographer—in any attempt to understand what made that person what she was and enabled her to do what she did. More than most, we are aware of the impact of socialization. It would therefore seem that one of the most important things sociologists need to know about Harriet Martineau is the fact that her family was a leading light in a community of Unitarians in one of the manufacturing centres in northern England. Both the location and the religious affiliation have a significance not immediately apparent to many of today's Martineau admirers—and this significance warrants detailed exploration.

A DISSENTING TRADITION

Unitarians were the most notorious of the Dissenters—as the non-Anglican Protestants had come to be known in eighteenth-century England, and have, subsequently, played an important role in the history of sociology. Deegan and Rynbrandt (2000), for example, document significant links between thc Unitarian female ministers' tradition and Chicago Sociology, from 1892–1918. My focus here, however, concerns the very earliest ties between sociology and Unitarianism, as reflected in the life and works of Harriet Martineau. An understanding of the origins of Unitarianism helps us better comprehend the religious issues that Martineau confronted and eventually transcended.

In spite of the relatively small number of Unitarian adherents, this particular Dissenting denomination had a unique history and performed similarly singular cultural roles in both England and America throughout the entire nineteenth century. Although the original philosophical or theological roots of Unitarianism can be traced to the fourth-century heretic, Arius (the founder of Arianism), the movement was revitalized in the fifteenth century by Lorenzo Valla, an Italian Renaissance man who was the secretary to Pope Nicholas V. Valla's famous *Annotations on the New Testament* employed historical criticism to challenge the authenticity of both the "Donation of Constantine" (a document justifying papal supremacy in Western Europe) and the Nicene Trinitarian creed which had been issued by the Council of Nicaea in 325 AD in order to demolish the claims of Arianism. Somewhat later, Erasmus—influenced by Valla—further nourished the roots of the new anti-Trinitarian perspective with his discovery that the verse in the Vulgate version of the *New Testament* justifying the Trinity was nowhere to be found in the original Greek.

This was revolutionary in the extreme, and few there were in the Europe of that day who dared consider it. Christianity, by its very nature, was an intolerant world view, based on the belief in only one revelation, one Saviour, and one single path to salvation. In fact, Luther launched the Reformation in 1517 with the publication of his 95 Theses which did little more than criticise the reigning priestly orthodoxy, particularly their selling of indulgences. Heavily influenced by the German mystics and fundamentally opposed to the humanism of the times, Luther soon proceeded to move much further, however. He insisted on the arbitrariness of God's Will in the bestowal of the grace of salvation upon impotent, sinful humankind, and on the ineffectiveness of good works and sacraments. By 1537, when Calvin assumed leadership of the new Protestantism, Luther's reforms had become an established Christian orthodoxy, and its doctrines were being imposed with a passion and intolerance surpassing even that of the priests of Rome.

THE WELLSPRINGS OF UNITARIANISM

In the interim, Lutheranism had remained more or less confined to Germany and the Scandinavian countries—except for the Anabaptists (a term employed to lump together the more extreme currents within the new movement). These dissenting groups were soon drifting far afield to escape persecution by Luther for their insistence on equality for the downtrodden within the new religion, and on that freedom of individual choice in forms of worship which they thought had been promised by the reforms. From such radical roots there eventually sprang a host of independent Christian movements such as the Mennonites, Baptists—and *Unitarians*. During this same period, Calvinism was evolving into the Huguenots of France, the Puritans of England, the Presbyterians of Scotland, and the Reformed Church of Holland.

Although Erasmus had died in 1536, his ideas lived on to inspire Sebastian Castellio of Basel (1516–1563), to write *Concerning Heretics*. Published in 1554, the book was a defence of skeptics such as Michael Servetus (1511–1553). Servetus, the author of *On the Errors of the Trinity*, had escaped the terrors of the Spanish Inquisition only to be captured and burned at the stake by Calvin. Castellio's courageous book on this and similar events stands almost alone as a call for tolerance during the latter part of the sixteenth century. No doubt this publication was at least partly responsible for the fact that the fire which reduced the body of Servetus to ashes failed to destroy the spirit of skeptical inquiry in that dangerous era. It may well have helped to spread throughout Europe the sparks igniting a radically new movement for religious reform: one far removed from both Luther's original mystical Protestantism and the subsequent, more rigid dogmas of John Calvin.

One of Castellio's disciples was a scholar at the University of Leyden in Holland called Jacobus Arminius. He attempted to forge a less "hard-line" form of non-Catholic Christianity than that of either Luther or Calvin. His was a version which left room for some degree of human free will and the possibility that salvation was open to everyone, not only to those whose souls had undergone a sudden and tumultuous union with the Holy Spirit. Each man participates in Divinity, Arminius said, and does not require immutable doctrines and creeds interpreted by previously designated authorities. In the early seventeenth century his teachings—known as Arminianism—came to influence the more reform-minded among those Puritans who escaped the tyranny of Charles I by emigrating. Many had spent time in Holland before setting sail for the Colonies where they established settlements in Salem, Massachusetts and on Old Providence Island. There, on the shores of what came to be known as New England, we will leave that particular thread of our story for the moment.

SOCINIANISM

According to Martineau, Comte once claimed that the "total demolition of Christianity was provided by three reformers of the Reformation era—Luther having overthrown the discipline, Calvin the hierarchy, and Socinus the dogma" (Martineau 1877b, II: 46). To learn about the latter, we return momentarily to the mid-sixteenth century and the height of the Reformation to join, in our imagination, yet another group of reformers. These were Italian Humanists who, in seeking freedom from the excesses of the new Protestants as well as the persecution of the Catholics, carried the anti-Trinitarian ideas of Servetus to Switzerland and finally to Poland. Here, in an intellectual soil made fertile some five decades earlier by Copernicus' deathbed publication of *On the Revolutions of the Heavenly*

Spheres, this scientifically oriented religious reform movement evolved even further. Eventually, under the leadership of Faustus Socinus (1539–1604), it became known as Socinianism.

The new religion, based on reason and respect for evidence, spread rapidly into bordering countries as well. By 1618, in Poland alone, more than 300 Socinian congregations are thought to have existed (Mendelsohn 1985). However, a fierce Jesuit-led struggle was mounted against them early in the century, with orders to root out the Socinian "heresy" once and for all. A vigorous policy of persecution and systematic extermination was pursued, with Socinus himself falling victim to brutal attacks. He was killed on the streets of Krakow in 1604, and in the space of a few ensuing decades, virtually all the Socinian church records in Poland were destroyed.

A small contingent of members managed to escape into Transylvania where they joined the fragments of a declining denomination there who shared many aspects of the liberal approach of Socinianism. These people, known as Unitarians, possessed a remarkable recent history. Their religious reform movement was one of the surviving remnants of those radical and spiritualistic sects grouped under the general label of Anabaptism. Their forebears had made their way into the Transylvanian mountain area of what is now Romania in the years of persecution by Luther following the Peasants' Revolt of 1525 in Germany. A man named Francis David (1510–1579), the most outstanding religious leader of the country, had been the chief inspiration of the Transylvanian Unitarians. In 1568, at the height of his influence, he had persuaded the only Unitarian king in history, John Sigismund of Transylvania, to issue the Western world's first edict of religious freedom and toleration. Unfortunately, this unique example of pre-Enlightenment tolerance lasted only until the death of King John three years later. In 1579, John's successor ordered David thrown into prison, where he died of exposure, hunger, and disease. His followers were tortured, imprisoned, and executed. However, a few scattered congregations had managed to survive to welcome the Socinians from Poland when they fled to Transylvania some four decades later; and eventually, with the newcomers' help, to carry the flickering candle of Unitarianism into the future.

UNITARIANISM IN ENGLAND

Unitarianism, as a belief system, was subsequently pioneered in England in the early eighteenth century by leading deists such as Isaac Newton and John Locke. However, the form in which it eventually developed there owed more to the Socinianism of Poland than to the Transylvanian version whose name it adopted. Whereas the Transylvanian Unitarianism reflected many of the more spiritualistic and mystical aspects of Anabaptism, that which evolved in England out of the Socinian experience was, from the beginning, marked by a focus on reason and empiricism.

It was not until 1774, however, that the first Unitarian church in the country was founded by Theophilus Lindsey, a former minister of the Church of England. Among the large congregation in attendance at the first meeting in a London auction room were Benjamin Franklin and Joseph Priestley. Fortunately for the new movement, Priestley (1733–1804) almost immediately joined Lindsey as the co-founder of English Unitarianism. An innovative minister, scientist, and philosopher, he had long been influenced by the ideas of the Scottish moral philosophers, Thomas Reid and David Hartley. Priestley accommodated their theory of common-sense reasoning to the earlier Enlightenment concepts of necessary cause and argument from design. The result of all this was a philosophical perspective, known as "necessarianism," which placed great value on the search for cause and effect in organic as well as inorganic nature, while holding to a belief in individual agency, a commonly experienced external world, and an ultimately designing God. Although the latter belief may strike the modern observer as being in conflict with the findings of science, in the era preceding Darwin's breakthrough, it accorded quite satisfactorily with available knowledge. Within this framework, inductive reason or empiricism was thought to be a necessary tool not only in the natural sciences but for the testing of religious beliefs as well (Hutcheon 1998: 24).

Because of the influence of Joseph Priestley, "necessarianism" became one of the defining currents within the world view of early nineteenth-century Unitarianism. This was especially the case in Birmingham where, in 1780, Priestley succeeded in establishing a close-knit, politically and theologically radical, and financially and politically powerful, congregation. Birmingham was an obvious choice for there was a ready nucleus of rationalists in that city who happened to be well-known industrialists and scientists. Although some of these remained with those other radical Dissenters, the Quakers, many became supporters of the new Unitarian chapel.

The Birmingham Lunar Society—of which Erasmus Darwin (the grandfather of Charles) was a prominent member—had already been playing a leading role in the intellectual community of the area (Davidoff and Hall 1987: 235). For well over a decade they had been attempting to insert an emphasis on science into the school curriculum, and had even been encouraging fathers to educate their daughters—albeit only in their homes. It may well be that the Unitarian influence played a role in the decision made subsequently by Erasmus Darwin to publish his 1797 treatise, *A Plan for the Conduct of Female Education in Boarding Schools*. This, in its turn, no doubt helped to create a milieu within the Unitarian community which made it possible for the parents of Harriet Martineau to consider the education of girls in a more favourable light than was then the norm in England.

UNITARIANISM IN NORTH AMERICA

We cannot leave Priestley's story, however, without tracing the course of his influence, and that of Unitarianism, into North America. His Birmingham ministry had ended precipitously on Bastille Day in 1791 when he and his family, all set to celebrate the revolution, were attacked by a mob and their home destroyed by fire. It was not only Priestley's political allegiances that had infuriated the populace; his scientific approach to religion was inflammatory as well. In his sermons, Priestley often attacked the notions of Father, Son, and Holy Ghost as superstitions, and expressed sympathy for the political revolutionaries of the time. He also worked actively for the separation of church and state. All this made him a ready victim for established interests within both groups, who encouraged the populace to consider him a traitor. This is how it happened that a leading British scientist—the discoverer of oxygen and a prestigious member of the Royal Society—was virtually run out of his country. He fled with his family first to London where he found himself an outcast, shunned even by fellow members of the Royal Society. His sons, forced to emigrate to the United States to find work, settled in Northumberland, Pennsylvania. Priestley's friend, Thomas Jefferson, invited him to Philadelphia, then the intellectual centre of the country and the capital of the nation. Soon after Priestley arrived in 1794, Jefferson introduced him to President George Washington as well as to John Adams (the second president of the United States) and Benjamin Rush (a member of the Constitutional Committee). By 1796, Priestley had succeeded in establishing the First Unitarian Church in Philadelphia and in gaining a number of the leaders of the community as supporters.

This event did not mark the actual beginning of Priestley's influence in America, however, for his radical religious perspective had previously been popularized in New England by an itinerant preacher called William Hazlett (C. Wright 1954: 213). As a result of Hazlett's activities, a congregation based on Priestley's ideas was established in Maine in 1792. This, in turn, had been followed in 1794 by the first church in North America actually called Unitarian—in Northumberland, Pennsylvania (Scott 1964: 40). In fact, the Priestleys soon moved from Philadelphia to join their sons in Northumberland, where Joseph almost immediately became minister of the Unitarian church now called The Priestley Memorial. It was here that Harriet Martineau was to visit during her trip to America some four decades later.

SUBCULTURAL SOURCES OF SOCIALIZATION

This historical background is required to understand that the middle-class Unitarian subculture into which Harriet Martineau was born in 1802 was a particularly defining and determining one. Like most of the Unitarians of the time, Harriet's father had become attracted to the denomination because of his family history. He was of Huguenot descent, his ancestors having emigrated to England from France following the revocation of the Edict of Nantes in 1685. Harriet's mother was descended from a Dissenting vicar who had been ejected from his living after the passing of the second Act of Uniformity in England in 1662, which excluded all non-Anglican Protestants or "Nonconformers" from public office. This situation held until the passage of the Toleration Act of 1689 giving the right to vote and freedom of worship to all but Roman Catholics and Unitarians (Burns 1955: 547). From 1695 on, however, there was no serious attempt to silence the Unitarians although, even in Harriet Martineau's time, the denomination had to depend on Anglican theological schools to train their ministers. The Catholics, on the other hand, were still being considered "seditious" by the British government until after 1829.

It is not surprising that the Martineau parents came together as members of these most heretical of all the Protestant Dissenters: the Unitarians. There is little doubt that the experience of being raised within the Unitarian community founded by a scientific rationalist and radical political thinker contributed in large measure to the fact that Harriet grew up to ". . . rattle the bars of her gender-defined cage and rage against its strictures" (Hutcheon 1996: 72).

There were, of course, other sources of socialization in the Martineau family setting. Harriet's birth order as the sixth of eight children was important, as well as the fact that the failure of her father's manufacturing business in the depression of the 1820s was followed by his death—leaving the widow and her three youngest offspring in straitened circumstances. (A number of years later this led to the perception, shared by the entire family, that Harriet would assume responsibility for the mother and dependent siblings.) Other early socializing influences were the obstacles to normal childhood social interaction caused by Harriet's developing deafness from the age of eleven and her congenital lack of the senses of taste and smell. Ironically, however, it was those very handicaps, plus two major decisive factors in her immediate sub-cultural environment, that ultimately provided her with an advantage not generally available to females. These were (1) a childhood home where the entrepreneurial spirit was a fact of life, along with an early experience of suddenly straitened circumstances, if not real poverty; and (2) the Unitarian connection.

It has been said that the Unitarians (along with other Dissenting factions of the time) made the best capitalists in these early stages of Britain's industrial revolution (Stromberg 1963: 464). The fact that entrepreneurial capitalism, in its beginnings, was a *radical* response to economic challenges—and that it was looked down upon by the aristocratic establishment—is seldom appreciated today. In later life, Harriet recognized that the intimate knowledge about manufacturing and commerce provided by her family environment, along with the early propulsion into a situation of severe financial hardship, had given her an experience of "the real world" rare in the life of an intellectual, most of whom were of the established gentry. She was grateful, she once said, for this "loss of gentility" which, in fact, allowed for some loosening of the bars of the gender-cage.

It is possible, however, that she was not as aware of the advantages of the Unitarian connection which, for many years, opened intellectual windows and political and social doors. How could it have been otherwise? No more than a fish is conscious of the distinctive features of the water in which it swims could Harriet have fully appreciated the advantages of the rich sub-cultural milieu that had been hers from birth. Indeed, the unique intellectual culture resulting from the theological "openness" of Unitarianism was to provide a fruitful seed bed for radical thought during the entire century, and Harriet (knowingly or otherwise) benefited greatly from this. The fact that the denomination could claim a preponderance of members who belonged to the intellectual elite both in England and the United States was in itself remarkable and was to have significant consequences for Harriet's career.

Another defining feature of membership in a Dissenting denomination was the experience of being an outsider. In the popular culture and the general society of the time, the religion of Harriet's family was viewed at best with considerable suspicion and puzzlement, and at worst with loathing and resentment because of its denial of the divinity of Jesus and many other central doctrines of Christianity. All this was bound to have had far-reaching consequences for a young person maturing within sight and sound of the challenging teachings and the many admirable role models of Unitarianism.

What this particular girl-child gained from the physical and cultural contingencies of her growing-up was a marginality that provided her with an abiding curiosity about how people operate, along with the observer status and detached, objective stance that were to serve her all her life (on the sociological concept of marginality, see Simmel 1950; Park 1928; Deegan 1994, forthcoming). Martineau was *necessarily* different, both physically and culturally, so she felt less fettered by the cage of sex- and work-role expectations than did her fellow females. The marginal attitude of the social critic is often furthered, as well, by the experience of injustice.

In spite of the liberalism of her parents, as a child Martineau had been the recipient of unjust and occasional harsh treatment from her family. She had been cut off from much of the normal family interaction by her advancing deafness, and sometimes been made to feel unwanted and very much alone. As a female, she was expected to fill her days with needlework and other housekeeping pursuits and to accept without question her exclusion from formal schooling until the age of eleven. However, she did receive tutoring at home in the form of instruction from her older siblings.

In fact, precisely *because* of the family's Unitarian connections, Harriet was presented with an opportunity that few girls of her generation were to experience. By a fortuitous combination of circumstances she was, for a couple of periods, provided with formal schooling. In 1813, her sister and she attended a school run by a minister, Isaac Perry, who had converted to Unitarianism and thereby lost most of his male pupils. Then, at the age of sixteen, she spent fifteen months at the Bristol School for Girls, operated by her aunt and uncle. Of her Aunt Kentish, she later wrote, "I was to find, for the first time, a human being of whom I was not afraid" (Martineau 1877b, I: 69).

Nonetheless, even for a female in a Unitarian family, and for one as motivated as Harriet, obtaining an advanced education had its difficulties in those days. "When I was young," she once wrote, "it was not thought proper for young ladies to study very conspicuously . . . thus my first studies in philosophy were carried on with care and reserve" (*Ibid.*: 77–78). An important focus of these studies was the life and work of Joseph Priestley, which led to her discovery of his "doctrine of necessity." This, in turn, brought the prescient sociological insight that "All human action proceeds on the supposition that the workings of the universe are governed by laws that cannot be broken by human will . . . the constitution and action of the human faculty of will are determined by influences beyond the control of the possessor of that faculty" (*Ibid.*: 85). "How awful and how irremediable," she concluded much later, "are the evils which arise from that monstrous old superstition—the supposition of a self-determining power, independent of laws, in the human will. . . ." (*Ibid.*: 85).

With such a background it is no wonder that, throughout her life, Harriet Martineau fought for equality of opportunity for women. That the struggle began early is evidenced by her first two publications which, like so much in her early life, resulted from her religious connection. Her first publication, "Female Writers on Practical Divinity," appeared in two parts in the Unitarian *Monthly Repository* (Martineau 1822c, d). The second, published in the same journal during the following year, was titled "Female Education" (Martineau 1823b). Both were published anonymously under the pseudonym, "Discipulus." The latter article addressed the lack of educational opportunity for females. There, Martineau (1823b: 77) noted:

> The boy goes on to continuously increase his stock of information . . . while the girl is probably confined to low pursuits . . . and thus before she is sensible of her powers, they are checked in their growth, chained down to mean objects, to rise no more; and when the natural consequences of this mode of treatment arise, all mankind agrees that the abilities of women are far inferior to those of men.

CAREER ADVANTAGES OF THE UNITARIAN SUBCULTURE

However, gender bias was clearly not an issue for the Unitarian periodical which continued to accept Martineau's contributions on a regular basis, providing her with the writing practice and self-confidence that every would-be writer will recognize as invaluable. For this was no ordinary denominational newsletter. A number of its editors and contributors went on to join the nation's literary elite. Their standards were high, and Harriet was quick to benefit from suggestions and advice regarding her frequent submissions of poems, stories and essays. This supportive "leg up" into journalism no doubt had much to do with the subsequent clarity of style and keen ability to organize and integrate ideas that marked Martineau's professional writing for the rest of her life.

Almost as important as the early start in writing for publication was the network of powerful intellectual contemporaries provided by the Unitarian connection. Although Charles Darwin was seven years her junior, she came to know him well through her close friendship with his older brother Erasmus. She mentioned her respect for Charles' ". . . simple, childlike, painstaking . . . qualities as a scientist and human being" (1877b, I: 268); and he is said to have admired her mental capacities (Webb 1960: 175). Through the Darwins, Martineau met another Unitarian, Charles Lyell, the famous geographer. It is likely that the exposure to these powerful scientific minds had a great deal to do with her subsequent evolutionary and naturalistic approach to social theory. She also became familiar with a conflicting philosophical perspective when the young transcendentalist Unitarian minister Ralph Waldo Emerson (1803–1882) visited Britain in 1832. She was able to meet him and to spend time with him and with Thomas Carlyle (1795–1881), and to sharpen her own views against theirs. When she left soon after this for her two-year trip to the United States, Martineau was able to rely on a host of Unitarians, in and around Boston and elsewhere, to help arrange the travel plans and speaking engagements that made it possible for her to study firsthand the problems then facing the young country.

THE ARMINIAN CURRENT IN AMERICAN UNITARIANISM

A second version of Unitarianism was now emerging in New England—this time from within the Congregationalists, the name the Puritans had adopted as a symbolic statement of their decentralized organization and locally based authority. Their more liberal "Arminian" wing was threatening to split from the original Puritan main body in order to join the Unitarian movement that had been flourishing since its initial establishment in Maine. Here we encounter once more the Arminianism referred to earlier. By this time it already had a lengthy history in the American colonies, but always as a minor, liberal current within Congregationalism.

Continuing in the tradition of its Dutch founder, American Arminianism, like Socinianism, was strongly anti-Trinitarian. The chief difference between the two streams of thought was that Socinianism tended to emphasize scientific empiricism as the major source of knowledge while Arminianism relied on a metaphysically based rationalism. It was grounded in the argument from design which, unlike that of an interfering God, could be accommodated to the discoveries of Isaac Newton in physics and to the work of John Locke in psychology. The nineteenth-century Arminians appreciated Locke, as well, for having been the first to make the critical distinction between the Gospels and the Epistles in the *New Testament* which, they felt, reinforced their anti-Trinitarian position. In the previous century, their movement had also found support in the biblical criticism of German theologians such as J.G. von Herder. Its American proponents also welcomed Gotthold Lessing's concept of ongoing revelation and made it a central feature of their world view.

THE UNITARIAN CONTROVERSY

By 1805 the new theology had become so popular within the American intellectual elite that the Harvard School of Divinity elected an Arminian president, in the person of Reverend Henry Ware. The times were ripe for an open joining of forces between these liberal Congregationalists and the Unitarians with whom they seemed to have so much in common. In 1812 the process was set in motion when the New England Unitarians gained their most influential leader in the person of William Ellery Channing (1780–1842). Channing, an Arminian in philosophy and Congregationalist minister of the Federal Street Church in Boston since 1803, had become aware of a growing controversy within his denomination regarding the preaching of Unitarian ideas in their pulpits. Channing happened to agree with these ideas himself. He criticized Congregationalism for its lack of openness to what he viewed as the "intrinsic moral sense" in human nature (Mendelsohn 1985: 61). His famous Baltimore Sermon of 1819 drew a clear line between Unitarianism and Calvinism and opened the way for a vote within every congregation on whether or not the Congregationalists would join the Unitarians. One hundred and twenty-five crossed over—including all but one of the churches in Boston (Scott 1964: 111). In May, 1825, the American Unitarian Association was formed with the mandate to promote Unitarianism and provide fellowship for the local churches throughout America. An immediate result was the recognition of Harvard as a Unitarian institution (C. Wright 1954: 280). Indeed, according to Harriet Beecher Stowe, by that time:

> All the literary men of Massachusetts were Unitarian. All the trustees and professors of Harvard College were Unitarian. All the elite of wealth and fashion crowded Unitarian churches. The judges on the bench were Unitarian, giving decisions by which the peculiar features of church organization, so carefully ordained by the Pilgrim fathers, had been nullified. (C. Wright 1954: 29)

Given such origins, it is not surprising that the Boston-dominated wing of the denomination encountered by Martineau on her visit had tended, from the start, to be somewhat more spiritualistic and conservative—where theology was concerned—than was the earlier, more naturalistically oriented branch of Unitarianism pioneered by Priestley and his followers. The latter was the version that spread to the American Midwest and the Western United States and to Western Canada: the version out of which humanist Unitarianism was to develop from the mid-1880s on. The Unitarian movement in Eastern Canada, on the other hand, tended to remain within a more Christian-influenced tradition. This was no doubt related to the fact that it originated with the establishment of the Montreal church in 1845 (as the Canada Presbytery of the Remonstrant Synod of Ulster) with the Irishman, John Cordner, as minister; and that it was supported during its formative years by the more conservative elements in New England (Hewett 1978: 34).

THE TIDE OF TRANSCENDENTALISM

In this same period, however, a large number of the New England Unitarians were proving to be in tune with yet a third current of thought: the transcendentalism that was then surging to popularity in American philosophy. This was somewhat surprising, given that the rationalist arm of Arminianism had accepted, at least in part, the empiricism of John Locke. By the time Martineau arrived among the Unitarians of Boston, she discovered that transcendentalism—with its belief in the primacy of a private and unknowable intuition—was rapidly displacing New England's former Arminian tradition of rationalism coupled with faith in continuing revelation. She was probably not surprised, however, having previously met and conversed with Ralph Waldo Emerson, the former leading Unitarian minister who was the major proponent of that view in the United States. The new philosophy had been introduced to the denomination by Emerson, who had studied Kant and the European Romantic Idealists and taken from them a mystical perspective on religion. He maintained that all the greatest truths are given as facts of consciousness, and are not to be derived from evidence or reason.

One of the Unitarians introduced to Martineau during her visit was the well-known transcendentalist, Margaret Fuller. The two women had little in common. Martineau, with her philosophy of scientific naturalism, abhorred Romanticism in all its poses, and was particularly distrustful of the Germanic influence in philosophy that seemed to have captured the American psyche. Her attitude toward Romanticism is demonstrated by the following story. An American Unitarian woman (no doubt of transcendentalist persuasion) probed Martineau's feelings at viewing Niagara Falls for the first time. "Did you not long to throw yourself down and mingle with Mother earth?" she rhapsodized. "No," was the terse response (quoted in Sanders 1986: 133).

At about this time Harriet was writing of those Unitarians fascinated with transcendentalism and various forms of pantheism, "All these claim to be philosophers, and scientific . . . while . . . wandering wide of the central point of knowledge . . . each in his own balloon, wafted in complacency by whatever current he may be caught by, and all crossing each other . . . hopeless of finding a common centre" (Martineau 1877b, I: 27). In her *Society in America*, she accused such people of weaving a rainbow arch of transcendentalism which, although intended as a means of comprehending the "whole," was all too "sadly liable to be puffed away in dark vapour with the first breeze of reality; scholars are thus labouring at a system of mental philosophy on any but the experimental method" (Martineau 1837, III: 197–8). Concerning Margaret Fuller specifically, she commented, "While she was living and moving in an ideal world . . . discoursing in public about the most fanciful and shallow conceits which the transcendentalists of Boston took for philosophy, she looked down on persons who acted" (Martineau 1877b, I: 381). Martineau was more tolerant concerning the foibles of Emerson himself—possibly because the two had, from the start, developed a strong personal liking for each other. He was later to write to her, "Joy that you exist. Honour to your spirit, which is so true and brave" (Wheatley 1957: 157).

MARTINEAU'S INFLUENCE

We should not forget that the religious connection worked both ways. Martineau had a lasting impact on American Unitarianism through her published articles and books (especially *Demarara*, a volume in the *Illustrations of Political Economy* that dealt with the economics of slavery). Also significant was the opportunity for her ideas to be disseminated among the young student ministers studying at Harvard at the time of her American visit, one of whom was the subsequently influential social activist, Theodore Parker (1810–1860). Although Parker's world view was shaped largely by the influence of Emerson, we can never know how much he was also affected by Martineau's ideas. He was later to claim that ". . . what was associated with Christianity was merely transient; . . . what was eternal was the moral element in religion" (Commager 1947: 75). And as for miracles, ". . . Parker had only pity for those who sought in the aberration of nature some divine revelation; nature itself was the supreme miracle" (*Ibid*.: 83).

Probably equally important for the history of American Unitarianism was the fact that Martineau chose to take a courageous stand with those who were trying to put forward the Abolitionist cause against slavery. Here she was forced to depart from many of her hosts. William Ellery Channing, with whom she was staying in Boston, was one of only six Unitarian ministers in the entire country who had spoken out against slavery. At the time of her visit, most concerned American Unitarians were still committed to the Liberian colonization scheme. The issue of slavery had never once been raised in Congress, and the majority of her Unitarian acquaintances assured her it never would be.

Martineau expressed her disappointment with the lack of liberal religious thought in America. She had expected to find, in a society formally devoted to freedom of belief, much speculation about the possibility of a religion founded on nature's laws—at least within the Unitarian fold. Instead, she had found "laws framed against speculative atheists, and general approbation directed against those who would embrace natural religion" (Martineau 11837, III: 226–7).

In later years, Martineau decided that her scientific world view of evolutionary naturalism had moved her far beyond the toleration limits of her former denomination. Clearly she was defining that religion in terms of the perspective of her younger brother James, by then a prestigious Unitarian minister. In 1851 he had published a hurtful review of a book written by Harriet in collaboration with Henry Atkinson, in which he blamed Atkinson's influence for her loss of faith. This must have been a crushing indication to her of how far apart they had drifted philosophically (Wheatley 1957: 310). It is one of those ironic contingencies of life that the Reverend James Martineau happened to represent the extreme opposite perspective to the scientific one introduced by Priestley in the continuum of views within Unitarianism at the time. James held to a vaguely "Romantic Idealist" theistic position with strongly mystical leanings. He thought no particular doctrine such as that of the trinity (or, conversely, of the *unity* of God) should be required of the church's followers (Wilbur 1953: 383–4). He even objected to the name of Unitarianism, because of its implication of specificity in belief. James taught that God was ". . . not One Person, he is not One at al . . . ." (Parke 1957: 73), but is, rather, Infinite Mind. Of Priestley's ideas he said:

> However fascinating the precision and simplicity of the Necessarian theory in its advance through the fields of physics and biological law, it meets with vehement resistance when it attempts to annex human nature and to put it under the same code with the tide and trees and reptiles. (*Ibid*: 74)

One can readily understand how Martineau might have concluded that a religious movement whose British wing was moving rapidly back into a liberal Christianity with a mystical anti-science stance, and whose American wing was dominated by a mystical transcendentalism, was no longer a congenial spiritual home for her.

One of Martineau's expressed objectives in writing her autobiography was to explain her "progression from Unitarianism to secular enlightenment" (Weiner 1983: x). Looking retrospectively at her Unitarian years she wrote, "The marvel remains how they now, and I then, could possibly wonder at the stationary or declining fortunes of their sect,—so evidently as Unitarianism is a mere clinging, from association and habit, to the old privilege of faith in a divine revelation, under an actual forfeiture of all its essential conditions" (Martineau 1877b, I: 31). In her autobiography, she disclaimed her earlier Unitarianism "*in toto*, and that by no twisting of language or darkening of its meanings," she declared, "can I be made out to have anything whatever in common with them about religious matters" (*Ibid*.: 120).

HUMANIST UNITARIANISM

It is doubly ironic that, at this very time (although probably unknown to Martineau), a vastly different current of thought was arising within the Unitarian movement in the Midwest and Western regions of North America. Transcendentalism had begun to face a new challenge from within the denomination. By 1866, when Emerson became the first president of the Free Religious Association (which, in many ways, represented the leading edge of Unitarian thought) the movement already had a solid core of ministers who were as scientific and naturalistic in philosophy as was Martineau—and as concerned as she had been about the anti-empiricism inherent in transcendentalism. These Unitarian humanists, along with Felix Adler (the founder of the American Ethical Societies), disagreed not only with Emerson's ideas but with the still-prevailing liberal Christian viewpoint as well.

Martineau did not live to witness it, but this group eventually grew in size and came to wield considerable weight within the Association and the denomination at large. Humanist Unitarianism expanded rapidly just before the turn of the century—mainly in the West (C. Wright 1954: 110–14). By then ministers with that perspective were turning for support to the nearest American Ethical Society (a religious movement based similarly on reason and science) as well as to the Western Conference of the American Unitarian Association, which they had come to dominate. Another source of humanism came from within the Icelandic immigrant communities in the Midwestern states and Canadian provinces. These people had been accustomed to a far more liberal form of Lutheranism than they encountered on arriving in North America, and many became attracted to Unitarianism as a result. In 1891 the humanistically oriented First Icelandic Unitarian Church was established in Winnipeg. In 1902 the Western Icelandic Unitarian Association was formed, uniting congregations throughout North Dakota, Minnesota, and Manitoba (Hewett 1978: 130–33). The liberalizing trend that had been initiated by the Priestley empirical tradition, influenced in the direction of humanism by interaction with the Ethical Culture Societies and furthered by the Icelanders, continued into the middle decades of the twentieth century. At that time fully one-fifth of all American congregations, and practically all Western Canadian ones, were acknowledged as humanist. By then, however, Harriet Martineau had been long forgotten, and an updated philosophical basis for humanism had emerged in North America.

During the early decades of the twentieth century, the ideas of the great American philosopher of naturalism, John Dewey (1859–1953), lived in the religious programs of Unitarian church schools. Dewey's Pragmatism was, in large part, an extension of Martineau's (and Comte's) pioneering work in the philosophy of social science. It can be argued that Pragmatism merely clarifies the way in which the older Positivism can be applied to the social realm in a non-reductionist fashion. Dewey explained that all the materials and events capable of being experienced by the senses are equally real or "existential," but that "each is entitled to its own characteristic categories, according to the questions it raises and the operations necessary to answer them" (Dewey 1929: 216). The distinction between the physical and social sciences, he pointed out, "is one of methods of operation, not kinds of reality" (*Ibid.*: 217).

Dewey's comments on religion echo Martineau as well. His book, *A Common Faith*, stresses the difference between those *experiences* most people throughout history have called *religious* and those *cultural institutions* known as *religions*. A religious experience, he said, implies a spiritual attitude having no source in the supernatural, one which can be applied to all facets of living. Religions, on the other hand, are specific, organized responses to life grounded in world views focusing on holy spirits, dogma and ritual. Dewey argued for faith in ideals built by humans and tested by the consequences of living by them throughout our history—and for recognizing them as such. He hoped that this would eventually replace traditional faiths in humanly created supernatural *explanations* and *justifications* of humanity's ideals. He considered ideals to be real aspects of the culture, both because they exert powerful influences upon us, and because they have their roots in the entire historical experience of humankind (Dewey 1934: 85–7).

In describing what was happening within American Unitarianism at the time, a historian later told how ". . . humanism swept through the denomination, becoming the most vital theological movement since Transcendentalism. Advocating science against supernaturalism, democracy against tyranny, reason against superstition, experience against revelation, humanists plowed new ground among Unitarians, eventually achieving parity with the liberal Christian position" (C. Wright 1982: 11–12). In fact, the Humanist Manifesto of 1933 was prepared and signed chiefly by Unitarian ministers. Its concluding comment sounded a theme so congenial to the spirit of Harriet Martineau that one can almost hear her saying the words. "Man," it began "is at last becoming aware that he alone is responsible for the realization of the world of his dreams, that he has within himself the power for its achievement" (Kurtz 1973: 10). This was the credo (although expressed in more inclusive language) that had guided her life. She would have been pleased to know that it had also shaped the Unitarianism of Western North America throughout the entire first half of the twentieth century.

Nonetheless, the longer tide of history may yet support the wisdom of Martineau's judgment that she had outgrown the Unitarian church. In 1960 another current joined the movement in the United States. The new current was Universalism, a similarly liberal stream of religious thought, but one emphasizing universal salvation and the essential goodness and autonomy of the individual rather than reason and empiricism. This movement also contained a strong humanist component, led by one of the greatest humanist thinkers and writers of the twentieth century, Kenneth Patton, a Universalist minister. However, the prevalence of mystical elements within Universalism may have contributed to the fact that, during the later decades of the twentieth century, transcendentalism and its various New Age and postmodernist offshoots have all but overwhelmed the new amalgamated denomination. Naturalistic humanism has been relegated to a minor and rapidly fading theme in the Unitarian chorus of today, as their theological schools turn out ministers who have never encountered scientific humanist philosophy and have never heard the name of Harriet Martineau. Sadly, where her influence is concerned, the Unitarian connection is indeed a disintegrating thread.

Near what she thought to be the end of her life, Martineau referred approvingly to Comte's doctrine "that theology can be extinguished only by a true science of Human Nature, and that this science is as yet barely initiated" (Martineau 1877b, II: 73). In 1855, deathly ill, but still years before her death in 1876, she hopefully expected that "the last of the mythologies is about to vanish before the flood of a brighter light" (*Ibid.*: 123). Recently, Edward O. Wilson (1998: 238–51) argued that, as we face a new millennium, the decisive battle of ideas will be between transcendentalism and empiricism. If this is indeed the case, one can only marvel at the prescience of Harriet Martineau in recognizing, so long ago, the fundamental nature of this issue. A Unitarian might even note that, for an atheist, she had a remarkable "gift of prophecy"!

CHAPTER THREE

Making Lemonade:

Harriet Martineau on Being Deaf

Mary Jo Deegan

I FIRST HEARD THE IDIOM "WHEN LIFE HANDS YOU A LEMON, LEARN TO MAKE lemonade" when I was co-editing my book on *Women and Disability* (Deegan and Brooks 1985). Life hands a woman a great big lemon when she has a disability, and making lemonade is more than a saccharine cliche in this context. I deliberately choose the concept of "lemon" and reject the concept of "challenge" in reference to the loss associated with a physical disability. This choice also reflects Martineau's perspective on disability. Making lemonade as a disabled woman is a tough and life-affirming decision. I prefer the concept of "making lemonade" to either "coping" or "adjusting" because these latter terms suggest ceding aspects of human joy and affirmation. The contemporary progressive literature on disability emphasizes that society, and not individuals, must change. The disability movement emphasizes a civil rights activism that alters the more psychological models. This movement has not been successful in changing employment of the disabled person, but it has radically changed some aspects of public access (see Deegan 1985, 1987, 1997a). Note that in this essay I use the terms "hearing impaired," "hearing loss," and "deaf." Martineau, of course, used "deaf." Martineau also wrote about "deaf mutes" who comprised a relatively large population in the 1800s compared to today. It is highly appropriate, then, that the topic of this chapter is Harriet Martineau who made world-class lemonade as a nineteenth-century woman with a severe hearing impairment.

When Martineau was twelve years of age, she was handed the first of many lemons: a discernable hearing loss. (This was one of several important losses during her youth, including the deaths of her nephew and brother in 1824, her father in 1826, and her fiancé in 1827 (Hoecker-Drysdale

1992: 24–5). The collapse of the family business in 1829 led to the family's rapid decline in income and social status (Hoecker-Drysdale 1992: 29–30). Martineau's responses to these events could be examined as further examples of "making lemonade.") At age twelve, she noticed she needed to sit near the front of a large classroom to adequately hear the teacher (Martineau 1877b, I: 55). This was only a minor inconvenience initially, but her hearing problems worsened appreciably over the next three years. She finally acknowledged the seriousness of her increasing deafness when she was fifteen years old, in 1817 (Martineau 1877b, I: 69).

Martineau also suffered from a loss of taste and smell but she rarely mentioned these other disabilities. She pithily summarized this range of disabilities in this way:

> Life is a long, hard, unrelieved working-day to us, who hear, or see, only by express effort, or have to make other senses serve the turn of that which is lost. When three out of five are deficient, the difficulty of cheerful living is great, and the terms of life are truly hard. (1877b, I: 57)

Since Martineau focused on her loss and problems associated with her deafness, and even that was only briefly discussed, I focus here on the impact of her hearing impairments.

Martineau wrote about the devastating changes precipitated by her deafness in scattered places throughout her corpus, but there are only a few notable writings on deafness: in a brief section and a few references in her experiential *Autobiography* (see especially, Martineau 1877b, I: 55–9, 69, 140, 153, 247, 491–2, and 536–7); in her 1834 dramaturgical "Letter to the Deaf"; in epidemiological and disability studies in a section of *Retrospect of Western Travel* (1838c: 128–54); in two articles on physical disability she published in 1854; and in her sociological fiction including here a short story on a deaf child (1853a). Martineau (1836a, 1854b) also wrote on mental disabilities, a related but distinct topic. I concentrate here on sensory impairments. These pieces and some references in her published correspondence are analyzed here to document how Martineau made lemonade out of her gendered disability. Deafness profoundly shaped all her experiences, ideas, and methods, however, so I am only examining a small portion of a very large pitcher of lemonade.

In this chapter, I demonstrate how Martineau analyzed being a deaf woman autobiographically and experientially to develop a concept of stages of response to the traumatic loss of partial hearing by a socialized person. On several occasions (e.g., 1834: 249; 1877b, I: 56; 1854a), she compared this form of hearing loss to the very different processes of being born without hearing or being totally deaf. She also devised an occupational strategy of becoming a sociologist as her way of making lemonade, and as a sociologist she formulated her observations and experiences into a brilliant dramaturgical analysis of how the hearing impaired make lemonade in social interactions with others (e.g., Goffman 1959, 1963, 1967). Martineau wrote her "Letter to the Deaf" as an "affectionate sister" (1834: 265) thereby becoming a founder of a sisterly standpoint theory (e.g., Dorothy Smith 1987) that is also precedent-setting. Finally, Martineau wrote about disabilities, both physical and mental, and was one of the earliest sociologists to study disability (and, with Florence Nightingale, the sociology of medicine as well—see Lynn McDonald, this volume).

MARTINEAU'S AUTOBIOGRAPHICAL REFLECTIONS

The Stages of Adjustment

Martineau wrote in 1834, that her deafness had moved "from being an almost intolerable grievance, [to] so much less of one, to myself and my friends" (1834: 248). She thought her response to her deafness was unusually well adapted and emerged from her experiences over time. Thus she articulated her experiential analysis of her stages of adjustment resulting in her re-integration of self and society, anticipating G.H. Mead's (1934) theory of the flexibility of the self and its emergence from social interaction.

1. Denial

Martineau's deafness occurred at an age when she had conquered communication skills, developed a self, and completed most of her formal schooling. This was fortunate in the sense that she received an adequate education and did not suffer from being thought dull or inattentive which were typical judgments of deaf children's behavior in the classroom (1877b, I: 56). Her able-bodied socialization, however, made her painfully aware of what she was losing as her hearing diminished. Her early denial of this impairment was partially due to the ambiguity of her loss and to its social painfulness.

2. Shame

Martineau's social pain arose from her sense of being flawed and a burden to others. Before her hearing impairment became apparent, Martineau was already a young girl flooded with feelings of shame and guilt resulting in extreme shyness and conscientiousness. Deafness exacerbated these traits and had the potential of justifying her withdrawal from human interaction. Martineau clearly reflected in 1834 that "nine-tenths" of her early "miseries arose from false shame" (1834: 249).

Shame and denial often accompanied one another resulting in maladaptive behaviors such as the futile pretense of having the ability to hear. Martineau observed that recently impaired deaf persons fear that "people are taking advantage of us in what they say" (1834: 250). Perhaps they are laughing at us, or they only want a merry companion and will not share the pain of disability, or they are making us too conspicuous (1834: 251). Trying to move beyond pain and denial, however, was a difficult and often confusing step.

3. Floundering

These early stages of denial and shame were followed by a time of disorder. Responding to a traumatic loss of hearing requires new habits and patterns of social interaction as well as the reconstruction of the self. Obtaining these new social patterns without guidance is fraught with perils and important consequences. The required changes were often unknown, isolating, and forced upon an unwilling person. Thus, a period of irritation and irascibility ensued (1834: 250).

During Martineau's period of adolescent adjustment, her parents allowed her considerable time to read, even at the dinner table. This was partially a response to her difficulty in participating in conversations she could not hear (Arbuckle 1983: x), but it also made Martineau a highly well-read person. At this time, when Martineau was awash with the changes initiated by her deafness, she found particular comfort in religious reading. *The Bible*, in particular, was always a solace and she recalled being absorbed in reading Milton's *Paradise Lost* during one of her "frequent fits of ear-ache" when she was seventeen years old and confused (Letter, to Anna Jameson, 15 June 1841, in Martineau 1990: 60).

4. Acceptance

After several years of denial, shame, and floundering, Martineau began to accept her disability and adapt to it. She developed a set of new responses called out by her disability and others' behaviors that she later codified into "rules" that she shared in her "Letter to the Deaf," that I discuss more below. Martineau's acceptance of her deafness meant she acquiesced to future, numerous daily adjustments. For example, her difficulties to hearing in chapel remained a pressing issue to Martineau. On 20 October 1932 she wrote an acquaintance, Eliza Flower, of her concern to sit in the one spot in the chapel where she could hear best. Martineau (1990: 37) asked Flower to secure this seat or one comparable for her in anticipation of her particular needs. Thus Martineau's acceptance finally resulted in her moving from a narrow focus on her deafness to a life with broad interests and a network of friendships.

5. Integration or "Making Lemonade"

Martineau's final adaptation to her deafness arose from her purposeful changing of her daily habits, the structure of her self (Mead 1934), and her choice of life-work. Deafness became part of Martineau's being, a given state in her everyday life. She did not "cope" or "adapt" or "respond to a challenge" as many contemporary scholars in disability posit as ideal behavior, a point to which I return later. Martineau made a positive life choice to be cheerful, active, and as capable a person as she could be. She lived without mixing anger or bitterness into her lemonade. She was thereby freed from the social pain of her loss to become one of the most remarkable women of her century.

I extensively discuss Martineau's sociological ideas and methods in response to her deafness below. Here I want to stress that she lived an integrated and happy life when she became a woman who was deaf and highly skilled in social observation and labor. For example, in 1839, the still overly conscientious Martineau (1990: 56) wrote Thomas and Jane Carlyle that "I hope it is no sign of disease to enjoy being quite alone as I do—& to deaf people the commonest intercourse is very laborious." Catherine Macready received a similar reflection in Martineau's (1990: 56) New Year's message of 1841 that contained the following confidence on Martineau's life and preference for solitude: "Besides, I really suffer less when mistress of my whole force, & can do most when my trumpet lies still for weeks together." After Martineau made peace with her disability, her career choices and options flowed from this integrated self. Martineau's achievements occurred, moreover, in a context where the cause of her deafness was ambiguous and unexplained. This undefined cause of her affliction was another source of adjustment and social change.

6. Making Lemonade and The Uncertain Stages of Impairment

Martineau established a new self, a deaf self, after her traumatic injury, but this does not mean that Martineau did not want to hear again. Part of her acceptance of her disability, then, included a search to end it.

The nature of and reasons for Martineau's hearing loss are difficult to determine today. For example, R.K. Webb (1960: 6) speculated that Martineau suffered from otosclerosis (which could be accommodated easily today with a hearing aid). Whatever the root cause of her deafness, we can only speculate, as did Martineau herself. Because of the uncertain cause and diagnosis, Martineau sometimes blamed herself for her deafness and hypothesized that it was psychosomatic. For example, Martineau (1990: 60) thought her childhood penchant for endurance and glamorizing suffering was a cause of her deafness. I do not believe Martineau always felt this way, but she did feel this way when she thought she was dying and struggling to find a meaning for her life in 1841.

On another occasion, she tried cigar smoking as a way to increase her hearing. James Payn (1884) recalled the incident in this way:

> No one who knew her would suspect her of anything "fast" or unfeminine, but, under the advice of some scientific person or another, she tried smoking. I had the privilege of providing her privately with some very mild cigars, and many and many a summer night have we sat together for half an hour or so in her porch at "The Knoll" smoking.

Although he recalled that "she fancied it had a beneficial effect upon her hearing," Martineau recalled it as being far less efficacious.

She noted on 22 February 1845 another bizarre attempt to cure her deafness. On this occasion, Martineau wrote Richard Monckton Milnes that [Samuel] Greg and [Elizabeth] Wynyard tried "double mesmerizing." Whatever this treatment was, it led to "a considerable improvement" in her hearing for a few days (Martineau 1990: 107).

Martineau (1834: 359) tried another undefined process called "galvanism" which allowed her to recover her "hearing for a few weeks" followed by "a nervous fever" and greater deafness afterward. Martineau (1834: 259–60) found her temporarily improved hearing provided an invaluable lesson by allowing her to see how she caused others to adjust to her disability.

Martineau's deafness interacted with her other illnesses, as well. Thus she wrote her dear friend Fanny Wedgwood on 22 April 1858 that she was slowly recovering from five weeks of "almost total deafness, and failure of sight" (Martineau 1983: 164). Such a loss must have been extremely frightening and her recovery of her damaged senses uncertain.

Martineau, however, was more optimistic in her description of the degree of her hearing impairment than Thomas Carlyle who wrote his mother in 1836 that Martineau was "deaf almost as a post" (Arbuckle 1983: xix). Martineau could hear with her ear trumpet, but this was clearly sometimes hard on her and her conversational partners. These problems could sometimes be resolved and transcended, nonetheless, by becoming a sociologist.

BECOMING A DEAF SOCIOLOGIST

Martineau's sociological labor occurred after the integration of her deafness into her everyday life and the restructuring of her "self." This was an ongoing achievement, nonetheless, and her "making lemonade" both allowed her to become a great sociologist and to continue to grow as a woman with a disability. Her choice of career, methodology, and topic selection were all influenced by her deafness and each of these factors is examined here.

Career Choice

On 19 September 1829, Martineau (1990: 19) wrote W.J. Fox that she would have followed her sisters' careers as governesses "if I had not been incapacitated for the office by great & increasing deafness, which obliges me to depend on my pen alone." Her habit of reading widely and constantly as she grew increasingly deaf in adolescence, moreover, generated a deep knowledge beyond her years and her gendered socialization. This habit of reading continued throughout her life and created a wide breadth of ideas.

Methodology—Objective and Observational

Martineau was extraordinarily accomplished as a methodologist and this was partially due to the integration of her deafness into her total life and observations. On 9 August 1844, Martineau (1990: 99) mentioned this union of deafness and the self in a letter to Elizabeth Barrett [Browning], noting that her deafness made her "liable to run all into one faculty—observation." This tendency is noticeable in all deaf people, but Martineau's impaired smell and taste narrowed her sensory input more than having only a hearing impairment.

Martineau (1834: 257) learned the habit of observing behavior, social interaction, dress, custom, and so forth, during the periods "when we (the deaf) have nothing else to do." This habit would provoke self-consciousness in those being scrutinized if the observer could hear, but this behavior is acceptable for the deaf.

Ironically, Martineau became the greatest of listeners because of her deafness. As she expressed it: "I carry a trumpet of remarkable fidelity: an instrument, moreover, which seems to exert some winning power, by which I gain more in *tête-à-têtes* than is given to people who hear general conversation" (Martineau 1837, I: xvii-xviii). People who spoke to her through her ear trumpet, in turn, focused their talk on her rather than a larger audience. This minimized distractions and interruptions in comparison to other forms of conversation.

Hearing limitations are, nonetheless, a disability to a researcher. Thus she could not overhear casual conversations in public places and she did not participate in group interviews and discussions. To remedy this deficiency, she instructed her assistant, Louisa Jeffrey, to listen to conversations everywhere she went and make reports to her (see Michael R. Hill's chapter, this volume).

Martineau, moreover, employed observation, census data, and written essays by the disabled to assess the performance of institutions serving this group. This triangulated, objective information generated an empirical basis for her work that could be identified and assessed by others.

Methodology—Subjective and Experiential

As I noted already, Martineau's deafness shaped and altered her self. She became attuned to her own reflections and observations more than she would have if she had had the use of all her senses. Simultaneously, she relied more on "objective" indicators of reality since her participation with others' talk and explanation was limited by her disability. She, more than able-bodied observers, needed these outside signs of behavior and meaning to confirm her perceptions.

She used her lived experience, moreover, to take the role of the other who was suffering from a disadvantage, whether that loss was physical, social, or mental. Thus Martineau not only observed others, she was able to understand their response because of her own life experiences. Sydney Smith once made light of Martineau's positive response to her deafness with the quip that she was writing a book "to prove that the only travellers who are fit to write books must be both deaf and blind" (Martineau 1877b, I: 186). Although Martineau was not overly self-absorbed, she was empowered by her response to deafness. Thus, she not only observed others, she also combined these experiences with her sociological imagination to create sociological fiction.

Martineau's Fictional Analysis of Deafness

In one fictional account, "The Deaf Playmate's Story," Martineau's protagonist is a young lad who becomes deaf while he is a schoolboy. Before his deafness is diagnosed, he slides from the top place in his class to one of the last places. He almost loses his best friend because neither of them can understand the other's behavior, and the deaf child's family is not a refuge at this time of confusion. They, too, are a source of misunderstanding and anger. Here Martineau drew on all her adolescent experiences and transformed them into a particularly powerful methodology: sociological fiction, akin to her 1832–1834 work in *Illustrations of Political Economy* (and for discussion of a similar skill and methodology in the work of Charlotte Perkins Gilman, see Deegan 1997b).

Topic Selections

Martineau's focus on others, their problems, and the potential to resolve them, was tied to her mature response to her own losses and their amelioration. Thus Martineau studied poverty, overcrowding, morals, manners, city life, social interaction, foreign countries, and slavery as ethical and intellectual puzzles that she could rationally understand and communicate to others (Hoecker-Drysdale 1992). Her study of the sick-room, illness, disease, and disability emerged directly from her encounter with deafness and a flawed body. This relation is evident in her "Letter to the Deaf," analyzed below.

LETTER TO THE DEAF, 1834

Martineau's (1834: 248) "Letter to the Deaf" is a major formal writing on the sociology of being deaf. She incorporated both her lived experience and her analytical skills to create this essay which she wrote as a "duty" to others who were deaf. Her standpoint theory was directed to those in her fraternity of the deaf.

Categorizing and Defining Deafness

Martineau's letter began with her self-reflection on her hearing impairment. When she was floundering to accept her deafness, Martineau turned to an admired, older, deaf woman who had lost her hearing at five years of age. They corresponded for a period of time and then Martineau wrote her a sonnet alluding to their shared infirmity. Her friend firmly informed her that they held very different perspectives on deafness and society because of their different ages at the onset of their disabilities. Upon reflection, Martineau (1834: 249) recognized that "She has suffered the most privation, and I the most pain," because her friend was cut off from everyday interactions more than Martineau was, but Martineau experienced a more devastating response to her loss. In an important methodological point, Martineau (1834: 250) protected her friend's anonymity because her friend was only one of several deaf women she knew.

Despite the differences within the deaf population, Martineau addressed her letter to all deaf people who could benefit from her insights and observations.

The Dramaturgical Presentation of the Deaf Self

After Martineau's initial stage of false shame or the type of "embarrassment" involving "a loss of face" (Goffman 1967), she began to rationally approach her new self and situation by planning a different everyday life (Martineau 1834: 250). This resulted in a series of observations and rules on the genesis of a new self.

This dramaturgical reconstruction must often occur alone: able-bodied others cannot help and may even hinder progress by too much sympathy

(Martineau 1834: 250). By confronting and not avoiding a disability, the hearing impaired, advised Martineau (1834: 250), can "forget our infirmity, from hour to hour" thereby moving it to a less central feature of the self.

The deaf, wrote Martineau (1834: 250), quite ruthlessly, can become "unscrupulous about truth, inquisitive, irritable, or morose" as a result of their hearing loss. These behaviors emerge because the hearing impaired do not control social interaction and lose an ability to understand what is going on in social interaction. The deaf person may want to withdraw from this intolerable situation and be left alone and "temporary misanthropy" emerges (1834: 251). These are not personality traits but responses to the situation generated by being deaf.

The most fundamental step in reconstructing the self is "To give the least possible pain to others" (1834: 251). Before the habit of acting on this principle is established, however, total observation of and attention to others is necessary. This review begins with a rational assessment of "our case" or situation and decisions must be made concerning "what we will give up" or struggle to retain (1834: 252). These plans and decisions restore a sense of control to the disoriented deaf person, and physicians can assist in this process by assessing the degree of loss and prognosis. Some things must be given up; for example, eliminating one's participation in making and hearing music.

The deaf person must also make others "let go" of the past self who was able-bodied. Forcing others to accept this new definition of the situation is facilitated when a person announces "I am very deaf" so any ambiguity about the disability is removed. A disabled person who talks about the infirmity changes the situation.

Another major principle is that the deaf must never give up society. "Social communication must be kept up through all its pains, for the sake of our friends as well as for our own," admonished Martineau (1834: 253). Society must be sought, not avoided. All companions, a timid one, a shouter, or a friend, must be accepted at this stage (1834: 253–4).

Over time, the newly deaf person created their own role in social situations, deciding how much to talk or listen. Again discussing embarrassment, Martineau (1834: 254) noted that "we must submit to be unusually insufficient, and sometimes ridiculous" but this stage passes. Soon the new situation is redefined to include both deafness and everyday trust in social interactions.

The period of confusion and sense of isolation can result in a disagreeable countenance, and this changes a pleasant everyday situation to one where the face signifies displeasure with others. A friend told Martineau that she often looked like she wanted to be left alone, sighed loudly, and twisted her fingers. These new habits emerged from her shame and floundering to respond to the new situation. She needed, therefore, to consciously replace these habits by a smile and the presentation of a pleasant self. This created a new rule of interaction: "turning every sigh into a smile will help you over a multitude of difficulties, and save you, at length, the trouble of thinking about either smiling or sighing" (1834: 255). Martineau was clearly talking about habit formation and not about being a hypocrite or smiling even when one is upset. Her new habits were unintentionally presenting a false and angry self because she was no longer clear about the definitions of self and situations.

Another of Martineau's (1834: 255) rules was "never to ask what is going forward." Martineau again harshly judged the irritating deaf person who always wants to know what was said, what is happening, and so on, so that even the most trivial facts are repeated. Martineau (1834: 257) filled her time when she could not understand what was happening by observing others.

Martineau's (1834: 257) next rule was "always to wait to be addressed." Similarly, she advocated giving "up all undertaking and occupations in which we cannot mark and check our own failures." If you cannot know how well you are acting, such as a deaf person who is singing, then "No one can judge for you" (1834: 257). A related recipe (Schutz 1971) advocated "letting go" of lost skills as less painful that struggling to keep what is lost (Martineau 1834: 258). A "hearty acquiescence" with infirmity, moreover, allowed cheerfulness and optimism to take root (1834: 259).

An equally important principle, however, was to safeguard and keep what was still possible: "we must struggle for whatever may be had, without encroaching on the comfort of others" (1834: 259). Using hearing aids, such as a trumpet, helped in this struggle. Many deaf people avoided such devices considering them useless in crowds or uncomfortable for the deaf or others. Martineau dismissed these ideas as mere excuses to be discarded. If she "should wear a fool's cap and bells" to make her friends more comfortable, she would do it (1834: 261).

Another rule of struggle was "to seize or make opportunities for preserving or rectifying our associations, as far as they are connected with the sense which is imperfect. Hunger and thirst after all sounds that you can obtain" (1834: 261). Connecting sounds with other stimuli or actions, "catching every breath of sound," and going to places filled with sound such as Parliament could be part of the fight to renew or make new sense associations (1834: 262).

Martineau (1834: 263) firmly rejected the nonsense that nothing is lost with a disability or that new strengths of the remaining senses compensated for this loss (contrary to Sydney Smith's teasing jest, above). She did stress, however, the importance of gathering "knowledge from whatever we see and touch, and to digest it into wisdom during the extra time which is our privilege" (1834: 263). One unaffected skill was the ability to think abstractly and this could be refined and strengthened. This benefit could combine with increased time to meditate and reflect (1834: 264). Observation and knowledge could lead, in turn, to greater knowledge and growth of self (1834: 264; see also Mead 1934).

As a result of applying these rules, Martineau (1834: 265) indicated that by 1834 she "suffer[ed] little or no pain" from her disability. Although she was mortified occasionally by some loss due to her disability, "we [deaf people] can never get beyond the necessity of keeping in full view the worst and the best that can be made of our lot" (1834: 265). She learned to make lemonade "under a great disability" and "a great privation" (1834: 265) and became one of the greatest sociologists of her century.

THE COMPARATIVE STUDY OF DISABILITIES

Martineau (1838c: 128–54) expanded her categories of physical disabilities in a section of *Retrospect of Western Travel*. She then used these institutional observations to make theoretical statements later in a series of two, unsigned, articles she published in Charles Dickens' *Household Words* (for authorship attributions, see Lohrli 1973). These writings collectively analyze the epidemiology of different disabilities; the educational and institutional response to them, primarily in the USA; her observations of these programs in her travels; and her examination of characteristic behaviors associated with different types of disabilities. This work was clearly the foundation for disability studies, an academic specialization that garnered increasing legitimacy in the USA in the 1980s (Deegan and Brooks 1985).

Institutional and Pedagogical Observation in the U.S.A.

People who were born deaf or became deaf at a very young age (before forming a self) were usually unable to speak or to be socialized during Martineau's era. This distinct group may comprise the "Deaf" today, a group with a distinct language, socialization, education, and institutional structure (Davis 1995). Thus Martineau reported the lack of such a social group, and her historically located observations need to be read in this context.

Her analyses of deaf mutes began with their historical ostracism, including Aristotle's assertions that they were a brutish group (Martineau 1838c: 129). This rejection was followed by a romanticized view of their natural and pure spirit, and this latter conviction was equally unacceptable (Martineau 1838c: 130–2). To counter these extreme positions, Martineau visited a series of institutions serving this population in the USA and England.

She first visited the "Pennsylvania Institution," founded in 1821. It served seventy-four persons, evenly divided by sex, and employed six deaf mute assistants. In 1830 there were 730 deaf mutes in Pennsylvania where 694 of them were whites and 36 were "persons of color" (Martineau 1838c: 136), so this institution included approximately ten percent of the entire group. Here she observed everyday interactions and occupational training. She also collected several essays written by the deaf mutes. Although most of the essays were not well conceived, she found that two of them were well done.

Next, Martineau (1838c: 135) visited the "New York Institution" (also called the "New York Asylum"), founded in 1830, accompanied by several women including two deaf mutes. One hundred forty deaf mutes (out of a population of 1066 in New York) lived here. She observed that some of the inmates were not totally deaf, but the teachers discouraged the use of ear trumpets and did not welcome Martineau's (1838c: 139) observations. Martineau was highly dissatisfied with the staff's response to her insights and tried unsuccessfully to have friends continue her inquiries after she left. Martineau (1838c: 142–3) also criticized the teaching methods there, although she did collect one thoughtful essay written by a student.

Neither of these institutions was as grim as her visit to the "Deaf and Dumb Asylum," because she found a young man there who was also blind. Martineau (1838c: 154–5) compared his minimal socialization to that of similar people in the "Deaf and Dumb Institution" of Genoa, Italy, who elicited her greatest sympathy and compassion at their losses.

For Martineau (1838c: 143), she found that the teaching and institutionalizing of the blind was "a far more cheering subject." She discovered some English educators opposed the teaching of braille (or similar system), but Martineau wholly endorsed it. She bought six copies of four books and a United States atlas that she wished to use in an experiment to test their efficaciousness in broadening the minds and skills of the blind (1838c: 144–5). The "New England Institution in Boston" treated their clients as "human beings who come to be educated" (Martineau 1838c: 147). She observed that training in exercise, good carriage, and manners is extremely difficult but not impossible. She then visited the "Philadelphia Asylum for the Blind" where she delighted in their musical skills. She did not explain how she was able to hear them, however, since she usually stressed how she had given up music (1838c: 152).

The epidemiology of blindness varied widely throughout the world, and she reported the following distribution of the blind: 1 in 300 in Egypt, 1 in 800 in Middle Europe; 1 in 1000 in North Europe (Martineau 1838c: 149). Although she praised the generous spirit of Americans, she recommended more philosophical and pedagogical development on the subject of disability and greater medical training and intervention to prevent disabilities from occurring.

Theoretical Analysis of Different Categories of Disability

These institutional visits and assessments were useful in Martineau's examination of the socialization and education of "Deaf Mutes" (1854a) and the blind (1854c). In these theoretical pieces, Martineau also drew on her experiential knowledge of deafness. Although she made many similar points in the work discussed above, her ideas were more organized in the later articles. Martineau (1877b, I: 55) always believed that the education of the disabled was abysmal, and stated categorically in her autobiography: "I have never seen a deaf child's education well managed at home, or in an ordinary school." She tried to improve this situation through her pedagogic analyses.

1. Deaf Mutes

Her first article confronted the severe physical and social constraints on "deaf mutes." She began by noting that the size of the population was severely underestimated because individuals usually know of only a small number of deaf mutes and erroneously extrapolate from their personal experience to estimate the total number of people with this condition. Before advancing her estimate, however, she made the point that even if there were only a small number their importance would reside in their unusual social and physical condition. This is an important methodological point, learning about the usual from the unusual, that was stressed by ethnomethodologists in the 1960s (see, for example, Garfinkle 1967).

Martineau estimated from the 1840 census that there were approximately 14,000 deaf mutes in England (1854a: 134). This group lived in families that were profoundly effected by this member, including the social cost of the latter's tantrums, anger, demands, and lack of social feeling. Martineau, therefore, recommended that deaf mutes live with other deaf mutes instead of with their families. In this institutional setting, deaf mutes could communicate with others for the first time and enter a society of equals. The recommendation would be supported by the Deaf today (Davis 1995).

Able-bodied people assumed that the best setting for deaf mutes was with other able-bodied people, but this ethnocentric bias was based on ignorance of the social pain of always being an outsider and, according to Martineau's observations, having inferior skills in comparison to others. Martineau dismissed people who romanticized deaf mutes and suggested they spend some time with this group as a remedy to this nonsense. Five years spent in this task would reveal "the arrogance and violence of their tempers, the childishness of their moods, and the astounding ignorance of the commonest things" (1854a: 136).

2. Partial Deafness

Martineau then compared this population with the totally and partially deaf. The totally deaf, she believed should also attend their own schools, and this remains a controversial belief in deaf education today (see, for example, Davis 1995). Martineau supported the learning of sign language there because this allowed deaf children to communicate and enter into social discourse. Schools for the deaf, therefore, normalized the entire group and provided the best environment for the totally deaf child.

The partially deaf, however, were betwixt and between the able-bodied and the deaf. Learning at home was therefore the preferred method for this group. Mothers could observe the deficiencies in their child's behavior, correct and teach their offspring both unstintingly and lovingly, try to check moroseness and social withdrawal, and provide a role model for ideal social interaction with the child (Martineau 1854a: 137–8). Most families vacillated between overindulgence and harshness, anger and over-tolerance, but it was the family's duty to avoid causing more problems for their deaf member.

3. Blindness

In her final article on blindness, Martineau (1854c) compared the more favorable response to the blind with the far less favorable reaction to the deaf. She explained that the blind were far more similar to able-bodied people than the deaf because: (1) blindness could be understood unambiguously, (2) the blind partake in everyday interactions, (3) they learn social manners and meanings, (4) they can read and write through braille or similar systems, and (5) their other senses, especially touch and hearing, can provide information that is lost through blindness.

The deaf, however, have an ambiguous disability and its consequences are hard to comprehend. The deaf are excluded from many everyday interactions and are limited systematically in the skills needed to learn social manners and meanings. Although they may develop the ability to read and write, their lack of social training and understanding inhibits their understanding of what they read and write. Finally, other senses can help provide information lost through hearing impairments, but social grace and interaction are acquired primarily through social interaction. Deafness, like being both deaf and mute, structurally circumscribed the opportunities to establish and form a self (Mead 1934).

In these articles, Martineau clearly drew on her own experiences with disability, her philosophical and sociological skills, and her commitment to education, science, observation, and rationality. She placed disability in a social context and did not treat it as an individual affliction. In this way, she established a sociological image and language for disability that remains insightful and useful today.

ASSESSING MARTINEAU'S DEAFNESS—AUTOBIOGRAPHICALLY AND AS THE FOUNDATION FOR THE SOCIOLOGY OF DISABILITY

Martineau cannot be understood as a person or sociologist unless her deafness is included as part of her autobiography, knowledge, and methodology. She reveals her honesty, courage, innovativeness, and endurance in her reaction to and integration of this disability. Her contribution to disability studies, however, is of even greater moment.

Contemporary North American disability studies have been dominated by the popular value of individualism and the stress on psychological adaptation to a distinct bodily problem. Social programs to respond to disability are often premised on an individual fitting and accepting these values and models of behavior. There are, as a result, very few sociological theories of disability. Erving Goffman's (1963) study of "stigma" as a flawed identity is one of the few exceptions to this dearth of understanding. Many sociological theorists who do discuss physical disability, including Goffman, erroneously categorize it as social "deviance" from the normal body and style of interaction.

Martineau's rules for social interaction, admittedly often conservative and nonconfrontational, fill a lacunae in sociological knowledge that is sorely lacking today. Her brilliant, rational approach to deafness as a problem in social interaction that can be confronted, ameliorated, or resolved by admitting certain physical limits on ongoing life is creative and on the forefront of sociological analysis.

Although Goffman (1963) documents and discusses many of the problems arising from a spoiled social identity, his approach to this situation did not result in positive solutions or recipes for action (Deegan 1975, 1978b). Martineau, in contrast, offers many solutions and rules for normalizing social interactions. She revealed how social problems can be caused by deafness and presented her lived solutions from a gendered standpoint. Her technique for discussing the dramaturgy of deafness remains an indispensable tool for contemporary sociologists and scholars in disability studies.

Martineau's gendered analyses, moreover, clearly place her in the forefront of the study of women and disability. This population is one of the most understudied, misunderstood, and invisible of all women's groups (Deegan 1987, 1997a; Deegan and Brooks 1985). Although many scholars in women's studies give lip-service to the devastating effects of disability, significantly more efforts go into understanding the intersection of race, class, and gender than in focusing on gender and disability, a topic that is usually associated with problems in occupation, employment, education, and aging (Deegan 1997a).

Martineau's autobiography can be studied as an experiential and epistemological analysis of the intersection of class, gender, and disability for a British woman in the nineteenth century. Since Martineau is sometimes dismissed as a neurotic, white, middle class, privileged woman, it is important to see that she achieved her high status after she conquered and confronted her multiple disadvantages. Her radical approach to understanding these problems led then and now to a frequent misunderstanding and misapprehension of her work. Martineau "made lemonade" with elan and brilliance and in the process revealed how this is a social and not a physical accomplishment.

CONCLUSION

Harriet Martineau was a keen social observer who studied social facts over half a century before Émile Durkheim. The latter is widely and falsely credited with creating this methodological emphasis in sociology. Martineau firmly advocated rational thought combined with empirical scientific procedure, which was a product of Enlightenment philosophy. Although these were often popular ideas in England and Europe in the nineteenth century, few women wrote about this social phenomenon (McDonald 1994). She was also truly unique in her reflexive use of experiential and biographical data, presaging in particular, the rueful insight of W.E.B. Du Bois in 1903 that as an African-American sociologist he studied the problem of American race relations and he personally experienced it. In this chapter I have examined the impact of Martineau's deafness; her methodological response to it; her autobiographical and dramaturgical reflexivity; her sociological fiction; her epidemiological and institutional analyses of disability; and her specific analyses of different disabilities.

Martineau's creative reaction to the lemon of traumatic deafness was much more than "coping" or "acceptance" of her disability, she became one of the most important intellectuals of her century and a founding figure in the discipline of sociology. Her phenomenal achievements are also more than another "super-crip" story that is used to blame less socially successful disabled people for the social discrimination and physical losses they endure.

Martineau's making lemonade is a process open to everyone when they are handed one of life's lemons. In other words, everyone faces big problems over the lifecourse and learning to respond to them with humor, insight, compassion, and intelligence is a noble and fascinating part of the human condition. It is a universal challenge and potentially a universally inspiring story, the very grounds of cultural myth and meaning.

Martineau's making lemonade also has a particular meaning for women who are hearing impaired as adults because she addresses their unique problems. Thus Martineau holds the preeminent position as the first female sociologist to analyze the interaction of gender and disability. She wrote this from a woman's standpoint and as a person with a disability. Martineau's analysis of being a deaf female combined an empirical, experiential, and rational standpoint, a position that is often falsely interpreted by contemporary, post-modern theorists as oppositional to women's standpoint theory (McDonald 1994). Thus, Martineau's social ideas remain central to contemporary issues.

CHAPTER FOUR

A Methodological Comparison of Harriet Martineau's *Society in America* (1837) and Alexis De Tocqueville's *Democracy in America* (1835–1840)

Michael R. Hill

IT IS COMMONPLACE IN AMERICAN INTELLECTUAL CIRCLES TO CITE ALEXIS DE Tocqueville's (1835–40) *Democracy in America* as an insightful work by an astute foreign observer who carefully assayed the character of American politics and social institutions. Year after year, Tocqueville's *Democracy in America* receives, by far, many more citations in *Social Sciences Citation Index* than does Harriet Martineau's (1837) *Society in America*. Few essays on "democracy" appear in popular outlets such as *The New York Times*, *U.S. News & World Report*, and *Newsweek* without including an homage to Tocqueville and his presumably well-founded insights. At the same time, Harriet Martineau's instructive and once well-known analysis, *Society in America*, is today largely uncited and unappreciated by most mainline scholars and popular pundits alike.

The neglect of Martineau, relative to Tocqueville, is perplexing to feminist sociologists. For example, Mary Jo Deegan (1991: 13) argues that:

> [Martineau] is one of the major founders of sociology as a legitimated area of study. Her preeminence in this regard is equal to, if not greater than, that of any man in her era, including the relatively overpraised Comte and de Tocqueville.

Shulamit Reinharz (1992: 49) contends that Martineau's:

> *Society in America* deserves to be studied as one of the earliest feminist ethnographies and as a profound contribution to the understanding of U.S. women's lives.

And, Lynn McDonald (1994: 171) observes that:

> Tocqueville's *Democracy in America* is richer in quotable quotes than *Society in America*, but Martineau's book is in many respects wiser. Both authors give moving accounts of the misery caused by slavery. Both saw it as a fundamental violation of the American Constitution and thus destined to disappear. But Martineau was the more astute in recognizing the separate issue of racism, relating the discrimination freed blacks faced in the urban north. Generally speaking, where there are differences in findings between Tocqueville and Martineau she, with the benefit of hindsight, turns out to have been accurate. While, for example, the French aristocrat judged political participation to have been extensive, she saw apathy and indifference. She treated the high level of church attendance in America as a sign of conformity, from fear of dissent. Tocqueville was dead wrong on the status of women, a subject she discussed at length and with excellent judgment.

If these and similar critiques are correct, and I believe they are, relative to Tocqueville, the time has arrived for mainstream theoreticians and textbook writers to demonstrate a more robust grasp of Martineau's work. The average sociologist apparently needs Joe R. Feagin's (forthcoming) stirring wake-up call, not only to pay attention to Martineau, Jane Addams, W.E.B. Du Bois, and other early sociologists, but also to comprehend their frequent *superiority* to many of the white male sociologists, such as Tocqueville, who are traditionally and frequently trotted out for honorific citation. In this light, this chapter therefore issues a direct methodological challenge to one of sociology's sacred cows: Alexis de Tocqueville.

Specifically, Martineau's data in *Society in America* are *methodologically superior* to those gathered by Tocqueville for *Democracy in America*. A straightforward test is required, the import of which should be understood even by sophomores in undergraduate research methods classes. As professional sociologists, we presumably value the idea that social analysis must be based on solid empirical research rather than ideological convenience. Thus, if Martineau's methodology is demonstrably superior, then her critical observations of American life must be recommended over those propounded by Tocqueville. Intellectually and scientifically, there is no acceptable alternative conclusion within mainstream sociological epistemology (Hill 1984). This chapter offers a comparison of the methodological procedures against which Tocqueville's and Martineau's theoretical insights must ultimately be tested if their works are to be proffered and promulgated as empirically-grounded social scientific knowledge.

ACCESSIBLE SOURCES

Below, this chapter compares and contrasts the methodological dimensions of Martineau's U.S. studies relative to Tocqueville's more widely-known work. This comparison is made possible by a surprisingly large volume of readily available empirical evidence. It is important, from a sociology of knowledge perspective, to note that the empirical basis on which to build a comparative methodological analysis of Martineau's and Tocqueville's American studies is not obscure: it is not for lack of evidence that Martineau has been unheralded whereas Tocqueville is more often celebrated. The relevant evidentiary materials have been ignored rather than embraced by those who champion and structurally reproduce Tocqueville's vision of American life.

Martineau was a prolific writer whose works wait, ready for sociologically-informed analysis, in myriad university libraries across the English-speaking world. Her preeminent inquiry into American institutions, *Society in America*, was quickly supplemented by a second and equally important empirical work titled *Retrospect of Western Travel* (Martineau 1838c). Unfortunately, *Retrospect* is even less cited today than *Society in America*. The empirical procedures employed in making and recording her American observations are carefully detailed in her (1838b) methodological handbook, the first in the social sciences: *How to Observe Morals and Manners*. For relevant biographical data, her *Autobiography* (1877b) is a useful reference. Gayle Graham Yates' edition of Martineau's (1985) writings on women is directly pertinent to the further consideration of women's issues. Two of Martineau's fiction works are notably germane to her analysis of New World slavery, specifically: her didactic antislavery tale, *Demerara*, in the *Illustrations of Political Economy* (Martineau 1832–4, no. 4) and her (1841) celebration of Toussaint L'Ouverture, the Black Haitian revolutionary, in *The Hour and the Man*. For a list of other major works in Martineau's prodigious corpus, see Joseph Rivlin's (1947) detailed bibliography of her separately published works.

Documentary riches of the type more often found only in obscure archival deposits (Hill 1993) are, in this case, widely available for scholarly study and assessment. Three volumes of Martineau's (1983, 1990, 1995) correspondence have been published, as well as a collection of the letters of James Martineau, Harriet's clerical brother (Drummond 1902). Selections from Harriet's hard-to-find newspaper articles from the *Daily News* are also available (Martineau 1994). The recently released microfilm edition of Martineau's papers at Birmingham University (Adam Matthew Publications 1991), together with the online finding aid for the Reinhard S. Speck collection in the Bancroft Library at the University of California, Berkeley, provide an additional wealth of easily accessible materials.

Modern scholarship on Martineau is increasing, although predominantly within the fields of literature and women's studies programs. There are several full-length studies of Martineau as a literary figure, of which Valerie Pichanick's (1980) *Harriet Martineau: The Woman and Her Work, 1802–76* is perhaps the best known current example, but which, like its predecessors and more recent successors, seriously misunderstands the nature of sociological research and exposition. For analyses of Martineau's skill and accomplishments as an empirical researcher, we must turn to the social sciences.

In reference to Martineau's American studies, Seymour Martin Lipset (1962) provided a useful introduction to *Society in America* in his one-volume abridgement of that work (an enduring edition handsomely reprinted by Transaction Publishers in 1981), and to which John Cawelti (1963) provided an insightful critique. It was my pleasure to chronicle the methodological characteristics and scientific logic of Martineau's sociological worldview in my introduction to Transaction's sesquicentennial edition of Martineau's *How to Observe Morals and Manners* (Hill 1989). Katherine Bullock (1992) presents a critical reexamination of *Society in America* and Susan Hoecker-Drysdale (1992) usefully surveys the sociological dimensions of Martineau's work as a whole, including her American studies. The published record addressing Martineau's substantive social scientific observations in North America may be relatively smaller, but it is not obscure.

The materials required to explicate Tocqueville's methodological procedures are likewise widely available in university libraries. Tocqueville's (1835–40) most noted work, *Democracy in America*, is seen usefully in the context of Gustave de Beaumont and Tocqueville's (1833) joint monograph, *On the Penitentiary System in the United States and Its Application in France*. The latter work was the original justification for Tocqueville's trip to the U.S. Other relevant sources include Tocqueville's (1831) American notebooks (published as *Journey to America* in 1959) and his complete works (*Oeuvres Complètes*, published in French in 1967 and containing several volumes of Tocqueville's letters). Beaumont's (1835) sentimental antislavery novel, *Marie*, parallels Martineau's more theoretically-steeped offerings in the genre.

Tocqueville's niche in the patriarchal pantheon is secured by numerous full-length studies, of which George Pierson's (1938) is the best known standard work. Among sociologists, Irving Zeitlin (1971) approached Tocqueville with a critical edge and selections from Tocqueville's (1980) writing have been enshrined in the University of Chicago's institutionally prestigious Heritage of Sociology series. Taken together, the sources cited above provide a wealth of empirical documentation by which Tocqueville and Martineau can be instructively and critically compared.

POINTS OF COMPARISON

There is a clear basis for placing Martineau and Tocqueville side-by-side for comparative scrutiny. Both were foreigners who traveled to the U.S. in the early 1830s: Tocqueville ventured from France, Martineau visited from England. Both traveled extensively in the United States. The geographic routes they took from city to city, state to state, are nearly identical, with the exception that Tocqueville took a long detour into French-speaking Canada. This high degree of spatial congruence is impressive and, so far as their routes in the United States are concerned, they both had opportunities to see much the same thing.

During their respective travels, both interviewed and talked with leading citizens, including presidents, judges, legislators, esteemed writers, and others with noted reputations. Both traveled with companions: Tocqueville with Gustave de Beaumont, Martineau with Louisa Jeffrey. Both Tocqueville and Martineau wrote lengthy, social scientific analyses based on their visits to the U.S. Martineau and Beaumont both wrote fictional accounts of slavery in the New World. But, whereas Tocqueville and Martineau were both widely read during their era, only Tocqueville is read extensively today. On the surface, one might conclude that—whereas Martineau's *Society in America* is arguably similar in many ways—Tocqueville's *Democracy in America* has simply weathered the test of time, that Tocqueville's work is the better of the two. Close inspection shows, however, that the latter conclusion is untenable when their respective methodologies are compared. As social science *per se*, Martineau's work is methodologically superior to Tocqueville. When their research methods are attentively compared, any similarity between these two intercontinental travelers quickly disappears.

POINTS OF CONTRAST

Despite the apparent similarities between Tocqueville and Martineau, the record documents significant differences in their backgrounds, purposes, and methods. These points of contrast reveal serious relative deficiencies in the methodological techniques used by Tocqueville. In all, Martineau and Tocqueville can be contrasted on at least eight major methodological points.

Contrasting Backgrounds

Martineau differed in terms of social class, maturity, and experience. Martineau, an Englishwoman born in 1802 to middle-class parents, was thirty-two years old when she debarked at New York to begin her tour of the United States in 1834. Martineau came to the U.S. as a successful, well-known writer. She was a knowledgeable and experienced political economist, and she admired and embraced an inclusive conception of democracy. By comparison, Tocqueville, a Frenchman born in 1805 to an aristocratic family, was twenty-six years of age when he arrived at Newport in 1831. In contrast to Martineau, Tocqueville came from a privileged background and was an inexperienced and obscure young man searching for ways to launch his career. His concept of democracy was perversely elitist.

Contrasting Purposes

Martineau and Tocqueville came to the U.S. for different purposes. In 1834, Martineau had just completed two years of intensive writing, specifically: the monthly, book-length installments comprising the *Illustrations of Political Economy*. She sought a trip for rest and relaxation. Martineau planned tentatively to make Europe her destination and then a friend, Lord Henley, intervened, pleading:

> Whatever else may or may not be true about the Americans, it is certain that they have got at principles of justice and mercy in their treatment of the least happy classes of society which we should do well to understand. Will you not go, and tell us what they are? (Martineau 1877b, I: 203; see also Martineau 1837, III: 179–80)

Martineau (1877b, I: 331) accepted this philanthropic charge, noting that "the reasons he urged were of course prominent in my mind during my travels."

Martineau traveled without expressly intending to produce a book on America, and she declined advances from eager publishers who pressed her to write such a book. She entertained the idea, but did not want to be encumbered by a firm obligation. Martineau told one publisher, "I would not say that I certainly should not write a book on my return" (*Ibid.*: 329). She left open the future possibility of writing about her travels, insisting on a free hand in collecting data and making observations. She wrote:

> I went and returned entirely free from any kind of claim on me, on any hand, for a book. I can truly say that I traveled without any such idea in my mind. I am sure that no traveller seeing things through author spectacles, can see them as they are; and it was not till I looked over my journal on my return that I decided to write "*Society in America.*" (*Ibid.*: 330)

"My first desire was for rest," she wrote (*Ibid.*), but it was "rest" framed in Martineau's inimitable peripatetic manner:

> I believed it would be good for me to "rough it" for a while, before I grew too old and fixed in my habits for such an experiment.

Thus, Martineau sailed to the U.S. for two years of "roughing it," to relax, to gather information on social welfare practices for Lord Henley, and to systematically see the U.S. through something other than "author spectacles."

By contrast, Tocqueville and Beaumont traveled to the United States as a premeditated ploy to bolster their political careers. They arrived with investigation and publication as primary concerns. Before their departure from France, they sought and obtained government authorization to prepare an official report on American penal practices, resulting in Beaumont and Tocqueville's (1833) *On the Penitentiary System in the United States and Its Application in France*. Beyond this official purpose, however, they toyed with the idea of writing about life in the U.S. Authorities generally agree, however, that the plan to write *Democracy in America* did not crystallize until well after Tocqueville returned to France.

In sum, Tocqueville came to the U.S. sponsored by the French government and prepared to view American penal institutions through the very "author spectacles" that Martineau judged anathema to objective observation. Martineau entered the U.S. primed to see things "as they are." She entertained the possibility of writing a book about the U.S., but kept publishers at arm's length to ensure her independence. Tocqueville went to the U.S. to report specifically on prison conditions. His idea to prepare a larger institutional analysis took shape only after his return to France. Compared to Martineau, Tocqueville was simultaneously too focused (i.e., on prisons) and too much the dilettante to write accurately about American society as a whole.

Methodological Preparation

Martineau arrived in the U.S. armed with a remarkable set of methodological guidelines that she drafted during the month-long voyage across the Atlantic (Hill 1989). This she later expanded into her methodological treatise on *How To Observe Morals and Manners*. The core data collection principles Martineau advocated have a strongly positivist character. She concentrated on the observation of things, by which she meant physical artifacts, official records, and other traces of institutionalized behavior and social organization. "The grand secret of wise inquiry into Morals and Manners," she wrote, "is to begin with the study of THINGS, using the DISCOURSE OF PERSONS as a commentary upon them." Interviews, conversations, and informants had secondary importance to Martineau. She wrote: "To arrive at the facts of the condition of a people through the discourse of individuals, is a hopeless enterprise. The plain truth is—it is beginning at the wrong end" (Martineau 1838b: 73).

Prior to her arrival, Martineau read widely about the U.S. while at the same time reserving judgment:

> I went with a mind, I believe, as nearly as possible unprejudiced about America, with a strong disposition to admire democratic institutions, but an entire ignorance how far the people of the United States lived up to, or fell below, their own theory. I had read whatever I could lay hold of that had been written about them; but was unable to satisfy myself that, after all, I understood anything whatever of their condition. As to knowledge of them, my mind was nearly a blank; as to opinion of their state, I did not carry the germ of one. (Martineau 1837, I: x)

Methodologically, she wrote: "It is taken for granted that the traveller is informed before he sets out, respecting the form of Government and general course of Legislation of the nation he studies" (Martineau 1838b: 192). Whereas Tocqueville later relied heavily on secondary sources in the subsequent execution of *Democracy in America*, Martineau's reading was a requisite preparatory step.

There is no record that Tocqueville developed a systematic proposal for data collection. His preparation consisted primarily of obtaining letters of introduction from influential persons in France. In the field, he concentrated on obtaining interviews with persons he considered knowledgeable about American life and institutions. Methodologically, Tocqueville took as primary the very data that Martineau relegated to secondary status.

Documentation and Record Keeping

Martineau and Tocqueville both kept travel journals during their U.S. tours, but only Martineau thought beforehand about the problems of recording data. She recognized the necessity to record observable facts, to be sure to note the things that are most easily forgotten, to make daily entries, and she understood the dangers of generalizing on the spot (Martineau 1838b: 232–39).

Unfortunately, and to the best of my knowledge, Martineau's notebooks have not survived. Indeed, she may have destroyed her notes to protect her informants, as Martineau (1837, I: xix) assured her confidential informants that their identities would "remain private." In later life, Martineau commanded all her correspondents to destroy such of her letters that they had retained. Hence, it is consistent to assume that Martineau may have intentionally destroyed her field notes. Tocqueville's (1831) journals, however, have been published and are replete with speculative generalizations—and worse. At first look, his journals appear to be verbatim transcripts. But, when recording one interview, Tocqueville noted unreflexively, but revealingly: "I have only taken in this conversation what accorded with all the notions I had already received" (Pierson 1938: 302). George Pierson (1938: 302) surmises that "this procedure was characteristic with Tocqueville, whenever he had begun to make up his mind about a question." In many cases, at least, Tocqueville apparently only recorded what he expected to hear.

Time in the Field

Martineau spent nearly two years (i.e., twenty-three and a half months) in the U.S. Tocqueville's tour lasted only approximately nine months, and a significant part of this time was spent in French Canada, visiting Montréal and Québec. Martineau took a considerably longer, more in-depth look at American social life. Travel in the 1830s was no easy matter, making Martineau's accomplishment all the more adventurous and remarkable.

Research Assistants

Martineau and Tocqueville both engaged traveling companions, but where Martineau enjoyed the services of what today would be called a "research assistant," Tocqueville traveled with an older schoolmate. Martineau, concerned that her partial deafness would prove problematic—and not wanting to travel alone as a woman—eventually chose Louisa Jeffrey to assist her (Wheatley 1957: 148). Of this companion, Martineau (1877b, I: 331) wrote:

> I was singularly fortunate . . . a lady of very superior qualifications, who was eager to travel, but not rich enough to indulge her desire, offered to go with me, as companion and helper, if I would bear her expenses. She paid her own voyages, and I the rest; and most capitally she fulfilled her share of the compact. Not only well educated but remarkably clever, and above all, supremely rational, and with a faultless temper . . . she toiled incessantly, to spare my time, strength and faculties. She managed the business of travel, and was for ever on the watch to supply my want of ears,—and, I may add, my defects of memory.

Jeffrey traveled specifically as Martineau's assistant and personal companion, investing her efforts toward the success of Martineau's investigations.

Tocqueville was accompanied by Gustave de Beaumont, also of aristocratic origin and a school chum two years Tocqueville's senior. Tocqueville and Beaumont were young colleagues, off to see the world together. In contrast, Jeffrey collected data under Martineau's direction, extending the scope and range of Martineau's inquiries. Tocqueville, on the other hand, did not have the helpful service of a dedicated assistant. Rather, he traveled with a friend who shared his own aristocratic presumptions, ambitions, and linguistic limitations.

Liabilities

Tocqueville and Martineau both collected data at a disadvantage, but with very different consequences. Martineau, as noted above, was partially deaf. Tocqueville and Beaumont, on the other hand, spoke but limited English even though Tocqueville concentrated on discourse as a data source. Martineau acknowledged her disability and its direct impact on data collection. Indeed, the reality of her hearing loss may well have led her to stress the epistemological priority of observation over discourse (I am indebted to Shulamit Reinharz for suggesting this insight). She noted, however, the increased willingness of informants to share confidences with her when she used an ear trumpet as a hearing aid:

> I carry a trumpet of remarkable fidelity: an instrument, moreover, which seems to exert some winning power, by which I gain more in *téte-à-tétes* than is given to people who hear general conversation. (Martineau 1837, I: xvii–xviii)

Martineau turned her disability to advantage (as Mary Jo Deegan further explicates in Chapter Three, this volume). Martineau was acutely aware that she could not overhear casual conversations in public places. To remedy this deficiency, she instructed her assistant, Jeffrey, to listen to conversations everywhere she went and to make reports.

Martineau and Jeffrey were English and spoke the same language as the vast majority of U.S. citizens. This, to Martineau (1838b: 67) was an obvious requisite:

> Nothing need be said on a matter so obvious as the necessity of understanding the language of the people visited. Some familiarity with it must be attained before any thing else can be done.

Tocqueville and Beaumont were much less prepared: both were native French speakers and their fluency in English was deficient. Just prior to their departure to the U.S., they rated their linguistic skills as functionally no better than what today we might call "restaurant" English. Whereas Martineau could not easily overhear conversations in the street, she reaped a windfall of unexpected and informative confidences when she used her ear trumpet, and she sent her assistant to fill the gaps in her information by reporting on conversations heard in public places. Tocqueville and Beaumont, by contrast, were severely limited in their ability to understand spoken conversations in English, particularly during the early stages of their relatively shorter journey.

Informant Bias

Tocqueville concentrated on discourse as a source of data, and thus it is crucial to examine the nature of his informant pool. Table 4.1, below, lists the names of the informants with whom Tocqueville recorded detailed conversations, typically in a question and answer format. The striking point is that *all* of Tocqueville's primary informants were *male*. If Tocqueville had extended conversations with women, he did not consider them sufficiently important to record. Tocqueville's (1831: 141) American journals include only *one* conversation with a woman, and it is reported here in full:

> Coming back I go into the house of one of the French people. His wife like an Indian woman, working at a mat. A red child by her side. I ask her if she is French.—No.—English?—No.—What blood? She answers me lowering her head: a savage.

This represents the sum total of Tocqueville's recorded data from women about women or any other matter.

Tocqueville's conversations with male informants are also flawed by extreme class bias. He interviewed not just any men, but purposefully sought those he considered to be "the most enlightened" people. Table 4.2, below, shows that Tocqueville interviewed primarily men from the professional, upper-middle, and upper classes.

Further, Tocqueville was especially pleased to encounter informants who spoke French. For example, Tocqueville (1831: 171) recorded an interview in New Orleans with a lawyer "who speaks French, an advantage we have come to appreciate during our travels." A consequence of seeking French-speakers undoubtedly intensified his reliance on well-educated, upper-class informants, and when he turned to native French speakers like himself he necessarily received Francophone distortions of the culturally dominant Anglo society.

Martineau concentrated on observable data. Nonetheless, she sought and included interview data in her published reports. Unlike Tocqueville, her informants included persons of all classes, people of color, and both sexes. She noted methodologically:

> The Discourse of individuals is an indispensable commentary upon the classes of national facts which the traveller has observed. . . . He must seek intercourse with all classes of the society he visits,—not only the rich and the poor, but those who may be classed by profession, pursuit, habits of mind, and turn of manners. He must converse with young men and maidens, old men and children, beggars and savans, postilions and potentates. He must study little ones at their mothers' knees, and flirtations in ballrooms, and dealings in the market-place. He must overhear the mirth of revellers, and the grief of

Table 4.1. Named Principal Informants in Tocqueville's American Notebooks

1. Mr. ——— (a farmer)
2. Mr. ——— (a land owner)
3. Mr. ——— (a lawyer)
4. Mr. ——— (a recorder)
5. Mr. ——— (a trader)
6. Mr. Adams
7. Mr. Barclay
8. Mr. Biddle
9. Mr. Channing
10. Mr. Clay
11. Mr. Coolidge
12. Mr. Charles Carroll
13. Mr. James Carroll
14. Mr. Coxe
15. Mr. Cronche
16. Mr. Cruise
17. Mr. Curtis
18. Mr. Dallas
19. Mr. Danny
20. Mr. Dens
21. Mr. Drake
22. Mr. Duponceau
23. Mr. Dwight
24. Mr. Everett
25. Mr. Finley
26. Mr. Gilpin
27. Mr. Gray
28. Mr. Guillemin
29. Mr. Houston
30. Mr. Howard
31. Mr. Hyde
32. Mr. Ingersoll
33. Major Lamord
34. Mr. Latrobe
35. Mr. Lieber
36. Mr. Livingston
37. Mr. Lynds
38. Mr. MacIlvaine
39. Mr. MacLean
40. Mr. Maxwell
41. Mr. Mazureau

42–43. Messrs. Mondelet.

44. Mr. Morse
45. Mr. Mullon
46. Mr. Neilson
47. Mr. Poinsett
48. Mr. Quiblier
49. Mr. Quincy
50. Mr. Richard
51. Mr. Richards
52. Mr. Riker
53. Mr. Robertsvaux
54. Mr. Schermerhorn
55. Mr. Serurier
56. Mr. Smith
57. Mr. Sparks
58. Mr. Spencer
59. Mr. Stewart
60. Mr. Storer
61. Mr. Trist
62. Mr. Tuckerman
63. Mr. Vaughn
64. Mr. Wainwright
65. Mr. Walker
66. Mr. Wells
67. Mr. Williamson
68. Mr. Winthrope
69. Mr. Wood

Source: Tocqueville (1831)

Table 4.2. Occupational Annotations of Principal Informants in Tocqueville's Non-Alphabetic American Notebooks

Note: Tocqueville typically annotated the records of his interviews, noting the occupation and reputation of his principal informants. The following list comprises the annotations from Tocqueville's (1831) non-alphabetic notebooks. The annotations are presented without the associated names to focus the reader's attention on the occupations and social strata from which Tocqueville drew his informants. The severe bias toward professional, upper-middle, and upper class males is evident by inspection.

"a judge"
"a district attorney"
"a distinguished man of law"
"a Catholic priest"
"a well-educated man of good sense"
"a good-hearted and enlightened cleric"
"a very zealous Protestant clergyman"
"a planter from Georgia"
"a distinguished Boston literary man"
"president of Cambridge University" [sic., i.e., Harvard]
"a senator from the State of Massachusetts"
"a young German exiled for his liberalness, who has become known in the United States by his work entitled *Encyclopaedia Americana*"
"former United States Minister in Spain and a distinguished writer"
"the former President" [of the United States—Adams]
"the celebrated preacher and the most noteworthy writer in the America of today"
"Son of the Lt. Governor of Massachusetts and a member of the legislature"
"Franklin's disciple, and an old man very much respected in Philadelphia"
"Mayor of Philadelphia and a man who seems to be much regarded in this country"
"the author of several well-considered books, and well known for his learning"
"a distinguished Baltimore doctor"
"a Catholic priest and vice-president of the College of St. Mary at Baltimore"
"last survivor of the signatories of the Declaration of Independence"
"President of the Bank of the United States, is one of the most distinguished men in this country"
"was for a long time the American Ambassador to Mexico, and has the reputation of being a very outstanding man"
"the leading lawyer in Cincinnati"
"most of these gentlemen [with whom Tocqueville spoke at a dinner] belonged to the old families of Maryland"
"a criminal judge"
"a very distinguished young lawyer in Ohio"
"judge of the Supreme Court of the United States"
"the leading doctor in Cincinnati"
"one of the greatest merchants of Louisville"
"a farmer"
"a trader"
"one of the leading lawyers in Louisiana"
"French Consul at New Orleans"
"a well-known New Orleans lawyer"
"a lawyer from Montgomery"
"former French minister in the United States"
"a government official, a Virginian and a very talented man"
"a senior official in the State Department"

> mourners. Wherever there is speech, he must devote himself to hear. (Martineau 1838c: 223–4)

The contrast between Martineau's inclusive interviews and Tocqueville's elitist strategy is especially striking in their respective investigations of prison conditions in the U.S.

Beaumont and Tocqueville (1833) studied prison conditions in the U.S. and co-authored a monograph on the topic, but Tocqueville talked only to wardens and overseers, never to prisoners. Martineau also visited American prisons, but took specific steps to interview prisoners in private—in their cells without guards present (Martineau 1838b, I: 123–39). Although Martineau emphasized discourse as a commentary on observable social patterns, she clearly understood—in ways that Tocqueville apparently could not imagine—the importance of talking to prisoners as well as wardens if one wanted to understand the character of the fledgling U.S. prison system.

Martineau's access to women and domestic scenes stands in sharp contrast to Tocqueville's disputations with elite males. "I am sure," she wrote:

> I have seen much more of domestic life than could possibly have been exhibited to any gentleman travelling through the country. The nursery, the boudoir, the kitchen, are all excellent schools in which to learn the morals and manners of a people: and, as for public and professional affairs,—those may always gain full information upon such matters, who really feel an interest in them,—*be they men or women*. (Martineau 1837, I: xvi, emphasis added)

In sum, the pools from which Martineau and Tocqueville drew informants differed significantly. Tocqueville's informant pool was narrowly patriarchal and aristocratic whereas Martineau's was far more representative of class, race, and gender, and included public and professional settings as well as backstage domestic scenes.

CONCLUSION

Martineau's methodological procedures were thoughtfully planned, reflexive, and surprisingly modern. As a seasoned political economist, she was more experienced than Tocqueville and spent more time (by a factor of nearly three) gathering data in the U.S. In comparison to Tocqueville, her methodological techniques were multifaceted (i.e., triangulated), philosophically rationalized, and systematically more rigorous. Martineau concentrated on direct observation, supplemented by interviews, to examine the "fit" between the reality and rhetoric of American democracy.

Martineau eschewed the ethnocentric temptation to contrast U.S. society with English institutions. Instead, she compared:

> . . . the existing state of society in America with the principles on which it is professedly founded; thus testing Institutions, Morals, and Manners by an indisputable, instead of an arbitrary standard. (*Ibid.*: viii)

And, she was humbly cognizant of the enormity of her empirical task:

> It is in the highest degree improbable that my scanty gleanings in the wide field of American society should present a precisely fair sample of the whole. I can only explain that I have spared no pains to discover the truth . . . and invite correction, in all errors of fact. (*Ibid.*: viii)

Martineau's *Society in America* is a remarkably sophisticated, reflexive sociological study. If we argue seriously on methodological grounds, Martineau clearly deserves a permanent place in the social scientific canon.

Tocqueville, by comparison, is a major methodological disappointment. Whereas Martineau understood the intricate interactions between rhetoric and reality, Tocqueville did not. Lacking a logical plan of inquiry, Tocqueville's data collection procedures allowed rhetoric to wag the tail that eventually resulted in his *Democracy in America*. In the U.S., he spoke primarily to elite, white, male informants; recorded only what he wanted to hear; and failed to make systematic observations of concrete social patterns across the crucial divisions of race, class, and gender. His plan to write *Democracy in America* took shape only after he returned to France, and by then it was too late to make the necessary systematic observations or obtain input from a cross-section of informants.

Where Martineau read as much as she could before going abroad, Tocqueville relied heavily on books and documents sent to him from the U.S. after his return to France rather than on data collected via systematic, first-hand observation. (Interestingly, Martineau's work was brought to Tocqueville's attention during the long interval between the appearance of his first volume in 1835 and the completion of *Democracy in America* in 1840, but he refused to read it). Methodologically, Tocqueville relied in large part on the very type of discursive rhetoric that Martineau sought to test and question through direct empirical observation. *Democracy in America* may indeed be a well-written political tract, but as empirically-grounded social science its well-accepted status as a classic must be seriously reconsidered.

Martineau prefaced *Society in America* with an anonymous comment from the *Edinburgh Review* on the difficulty of exposing intellectual fraud in traveler's reports:

> . . . and so, with a few flowing strokes, [the writer] completes a picture, which, though it may not resemble any possible object, his countrymen are to take for a national portrait. Nor is the fraud so readily detected; for the character of a people has such a complexity of aspect, that even the honest observer knows not always, not perhaps after long inspection, what to determine regarding it. (Martineau 1837, I: v–vi)

For too long, the American intellectual establishment has readily accepted *Democracy in America* as a cogent, empirically-based portrait of American institutions, even though, methodologically, "it may not resemble any possible object." And, as the long record of scholarly adulation of Tocqueville is evidence, such frauds are apparently not readily detected. American society, as the unknown essayist in the *Edinburgh Review* would undoubtedly agree, has an extraordinary "complexity of aspect," and it was Martineau, not Tocqueville, who sought with integrity and methodological rigor to discover the degree of correspondence between the reality and the rhetoric of social institutions in the United States.

Tocqueville purported to write on "democracy" in the U.S., but he did so from the perspective of a privileged, white male at a time when only propertied white men had the franchise. His methodological choices simply confirmed his elite perspective. Martineau, by contrast, embraced a far wider conception of democracy. Hence, methodologically, she pursued empirical strategies that allowed her to see the structural effects of white male privilege on the disenfranchised sectors of American society. In the long run, it is Martineau's more inclusive, progressive conception of democracy, not Tocqueville's, that is institutionalized today in voting rights for women, people of color, and the economically dispossessed.

CHAPTER FIVE

The Meaning of "Things": Theory and Method in Harriet Martineau's *How to Observe Morals and Manners* (1838) and Émile Durkheim's *The Rules of Sociological Method* (1895)

Patricia Madoo Lengermann
Jill Niebrugge

CONVENTIONAL UNDERSTANDINGS OF SOCIOLOGY'S HISTORY TELL OF A founding generation of male thinkers—typically identified as Comte, Spencer, and Marx—whose major achievements are understood as naming the field, affirming the possibility of a science of society, and constructing broad general mappings of human social life. These conventional accounts leave it for a second generation of male sociologists—typically identified as Durkheim, Weber, Simmel, and Park—to begin to draw formal disciplinary parameters for the field and to elaborate a methodology for the new science of sociology. Among these thinkers, the work of Émile Durkheim (1858–1917) in his methodological statement, *The Rules of Sociological Method* (1895), and his application and extension of that statement in the empirical study, *Suicide* (1897), is seen as an exemplar of this new precision about the nature and purpose of sociological inquiry. But when we add Harriet Martineau (1802–1876) to the history of sociology, we find that in the first generation, present and active in the creation of sociology, we have a sociologist who perceived that a primary project for the establishment of a science of society was the explication of the field's epistemology and methodology as well as a statement of the field's subject and purpose. Martineau undertakes this project early in her career as a sociologist, in two linked studies: her should-be-classic methodological statement, *How to Observe Morals and Manners* (outlined in 1834 and published in full in 1838), and her first full-fledged empirical application and extension of that statement, *Society in America* (1837).

This chapter is a comparison of Martineau's (1838b) *How to Observe Morals and Manners* and Durkheim's (1895) much later *The Rules of Sociological Method*. We make this comparison following an idea suggested by Arthur Stinchcombe (1982) in "Should Sociologists Forget Their Mothers and Fathers?"—which regrettably discusses only sociology's "fathers." Stinchcombe (1982: 3) argues that one among many contemporary uses of classic texts is to help us identify the field's "fundamental ideas" and see how later writings "modify an idea nearer to the main trunk . . . addressing questions that the great minds of the past have addressed." In our comparison, we have the ironic situation that since it is Durkheim's work that has been accepted as the classic and Martineau who must be introduced, we compare her work to his—although, as will emerge below, hers is in every sense the classic statement of fundamental ideas about methodology in the history of sociology to which his ought to be related as branch to trunk—if we may extend Stinchcombe's metaphor. We use the strategy of comparison to explore similarities in fundamental ideas between the two theorists; to point to equally significant differences; to establish that in Martineau we have the beginning of a feminist tradition and a critical tradition in social theory (as surely as in Durkheim's work we have a development of functionalist and scientistic sociology), and to show that highly important work by women has been written out of the record of sociology. In the organization of this paper our discussions of Durkheim are necessarily brief, for those descriptions serve a heuristic purpose as a backdrop against which the elaboration of Martineau's theory and method may be developed. And always our purpose is not to disparage Durkheim but to acknowledge Martineau.

GENERAL SIMILARITIES AND DIFFERENCES

Our essay begins with a remarkable coincidence or similarity in wording between Martineau and Durkheim. Writing in the mid-1830s in *How to Observe Morals and Manners*, Martineau (1838b: 73–4) takes as her fundamental methodological principle that:

> The grand secret of wise inquiry into Morals and Manners is to begin with the study of THINGS, using the DISCOURSE OF PERSONS as a commentary upon them.
>
> Though the facts sought by travellers relate to Persons, they may most readily be learned from Things. . . . The voice of a whole people goes up in the silent workings of an institution; the condition of the masses is reflected from the surface of a record. The institutions of a nation,—political, religious, or social,—put evidence into the observer's hands as to its capabilities and wants which the study of individuals could not yield in the course of a lifetime. The Records of any society, be they what they may, whether architectural remains, epitaphs, civic registers, national music, or any of the thousand manifestations of the common mind which may be found among every people, afford more information on Morals in a day than converse with individuals in a year.

Somewhat later Durkheim (1895: 14, 44–5) argued that:

> The first and most fundamental rule is *Consider social facts as things.* . . . Social life consists, then, of free currents perpetually in the process of transformation and incapable of being mentally fixed by the observer, and the scholar cannot approach the study of social reality from this angle. But we know that it possesses the power of crystallization without ceasing to be itself. Thus, apart from the individual acts to which they give rise, collective habits find expression in definite forms: legal rules, moral regulations, popular proverbs, social conventions, etc.

These two passages are simply the most striking among many parallels in phrasing and in concern between Martineau and Durkheim, sufficient to establish a common ground of concerns that sociology must address. Both are concerned with the problem of ethnocentrism and the need for disciplined mental training to overcome it. Martineau (1838b: 34) writes that, "The observer who sets out with a more philosophic belief, . . . escapes the affliction of seeing sin where he sees difference." Durkheim warns against observers "who start with the idea that our morality is the only morality." Both are concerned with the question of what Martineau calls morals and Durkheim, collective representations, by which both mean the socially generated ideas that guide individual conduct in a society. Both seek to establish social science as at once a science like chemistry or geology and yet as a study distinct in its own right. Martineau writes (1838b: 13–15):

> The observer of Men and Manners stands as much in need of intellectual preparation as any other student. . . . But . . . [e]very man . . . thinks that eyes, ears, and memory are enough for morals, though they would not qualify him for botanical or statistical observation. . . . No wise man blushes at being ignorant of any science which it has not suited his purposes to study. . . . No linguist wrings his hands when astronomical discoveries are talked of in his presence; no political economist covers his face when shown a shell or a plant which he can not class; still less should . . . the natural philosopher . . . be ashamed to own himself unacquainted with the science which, of all the sciences which have yet opened upon men, is . . . the most difficult in its application . . . the science of Morals . . . .

Durkheim (1895: 3) writes that social phenomena can be distinguished from "biological phenomena, since, they consist of representations and of actions" and from "psychological phenomena, which exist only in the individual consciousness and through it." Both are interested in defining the subject and purpose of sociology and both seek to describe methods for its study.

Yet while having so many concerns in common, they so often arrive at different conclusions; their eyes light on the same issue but their minds trace a very different pattern. Thus, repeatedly, the reader of the two works finds statements that seem—indeed, are—strikingly parallel at one level; but going on to the next lines in each passage, or the next layer of development, the reader is struck by how differently Martineau and Durkheim interpret the original concern. Having agreed at one level that the subject matter and purpose of sociology is the scientific study of collective ideas, they diverge at the next level of development. Martineau sees the subject and purpose as the tracing of a people's morals and manners to assess how much those promote the greatest relative human happiness. Durkheim sees that subject and purpose as the quest for the universal structural components of societies to be discovered through a process of abstracting from all the evidence of human social life. Both agree on the importance of "objectivity" or "impartiality" on the part of the observer. Durkheim seeks this in the observer's "distancing" from the flux of individual events in social life and through selecting as "things" for study those which exist most independent of any individual manifestation. Martineau argues that impartiality can only be achieved when parochialism of judgment is overcome, but that the observer must develop a sympathetic or empathetic understanding of a people's ongoing daily life, selecting "things" that illuminate the meanings of this quotidian reality. Although on many occasions they look at the same "things"—e.g., legal records, popular sayings, religion, crime, suicide, relations between the metropolis and the province—Martineau looks at these in terms of her standard of general human happiness which she sees as dependent on moral autonomy or freedom from domination; Durkheim looks at these same things as indicators of the degree to which social structures promote the societal integration of both people and institutions. Durkheim views society as an organism; and discussing this organicism, Jennifer Lehmann (1993: 2) argues that "Durkheim's organicism is metaphorical only in the sense that all theory is metaphorical." Martineau does not see society as anything but itself; her theory is remarkably free from metaphor though not from simile and imagery. Both theorists contemplate the fact of differences among societies. Durkheim responds to difference by seeking to establish an evolutionary typology in terms of what he identifies as universal traits of societal organization, most especially the intensity of the division of labor. Martineau begins with a belief that in all societies people share certain moral ideas—approval of charity in some form, condemnation of tormenting another without reason, etc.—and certain basic human needs for food, clothing, shelter, domestic affection, the marking of birth and death. The task of the sociologist is to define the differences in the way people meet these basic needs and express their basic moral sense.

Finally, we should note that the two works, *How to Observe Morals and Manners* and *The Rules of Sociological Method* have come to occupy very different places in the historical reconstruction done so far of sociology. Martineau has typically been remembered in the history of sociological theory as the translator of Comte. For example, Park and Burgess (1921) in the book that became "the green bible" of American sociology students for a generation, *Introduction to the Science of Sociology*, begin by citing from Martineau's translation of Comte, crediting her in a footnote. Park and Burgess (1921: 1) say of Comte: "Comte did not, to be sure, create sociology. He did give it a name, a program, and place among the sciences." While that claim may surely be made, Park and Burgess could as easily have looked to Martineau and written: "Martineau did not, to be sure, create sociology. She was using the name as early as 1837, and she did give it a program, and a place among the sciences and a purpose in society." In the last decade this pattern of non-recognition has changed as several important statements by sociologists have emphasized her significance for sociology (Deegan 1991; Hill 1989; Hoecker-Drysdale 1992, 2000; Lengermann and Niebrugge-Brantley 1998, 2000a, 2000b; McDonald 1994, 1998; and Reinharz 1992—among others).

Martineau wrote the first draft of *How to Observe Morals and Manners* on shipboard in 1834 as she sailed to America to do two years of field research for what became *Society in America* (1837) and *Retrospect of Western Travel* (1838c). Originally intended as a chapter in a single volume on observation in the natural and social sciences, Martineau expanded her discussion in 1838 to meet her publisher's wish for a series of volumes on "How to Observe" in various sciences—the first volume being *How to Observe Geology*. Hill 1989 gives a good account of how Martineau came to undertake this volume. The book did not fare well. In 1838, there was not yet an established social science community waiting as an audience (the British Association for the Promotion of Social Science was not formed until the mid-1850s). Martineau was writing for a general public that had been wildly receptive of her first work, *Illustrations of Political Economy* (1832–4). But where the *Illustrations* offered social science—in this case, political economy—in the form of a series of moral and lively tales, as Hill observes, "her 'how to' manual asked readers to become active rigorous, moral observers. This prospect of hard work may have dampened its reception" (Hill 1989: lv). Her sense of this general audience is most reflected in the text in Martineau's use of the term "the traveller"—as well as "the student of society," "the student of morals" or "the observer"—travel being the social experience in which she could most imagine the average person consciously acting as social scientist. *How to Observe* went out of print rapidly and has been available primarily in research libraries until Hill's editing of the sesquicentennial edition published by Transaction in 1989. It attracted occasional scholarly comment by social scientists (see, for example, Deegan 1991; Hill 1989, 1991; Hoecker-Drysdale 1992;

Lengermann and Niebrugge-Brantley 1996, 1998; Lipset 1968; Reinharz 1992; Rossi 1973; Terry 1983).

By contrast, *The Rules of Sociological Method* had a ready audience, for Durkheim was working to establish sociology as a university program and the social science movement was well under way in Britain, the United States, France, and Germany. Durkheim's place in sociology is as one of what Mike Gane (1988: 1) in a book-length study of *The Rules* calls "the 'founding fathers' of modern sociology . . . the trinity: Marx, Weber and Durkheim . . . . Translations and commentaries of Durkheim's writings, at first only a trickle, have become an inundation." *The Rules of Sociological Method* is a standard reading in sociological theory and is well-excerpted in Anthony Giddens' widely used *Émile Durkheim: Selected Writings* (Durkheim 1972). *The Rules* is often presented paired with *Suicide* (1897) the empirical study usually interpreted as Durkheim's test of its methodology. (Disputing this interpretation, Gane argues that Durkheim reverses his methodology by creating his typology of suicide in order to organize his data rather than arriving inductively at the typology through the data. Our point is that *Suicide* and *Society in America* as applications of a formal methodology expand and refine ideas in the methodological statements. For Durkheim, it should be noted that in *Suicide* he is true to his major methodological principle—to consider social facts as things).

WHY "THINGS"?

The passages with which we began—on the importance of looking at things or treating social facts as things—occupy similar positions in the argument of both works. Both Martineau and Durkheim open their works by trying to define the particular quality in human life that the sociologist seeks to study (and both do so in the first fifteen pages). Both then move to stress the need to find "things" that will serve as social indicators of those issues each has defined as sociology's subject matter. Martineau devotes most of *How to Observe* to identifying and discussing those "things" which she judges are the best social indicators; in this regard, her achievement is holistic in scope. Durkheim, writing for a consciously professional audience, is schematic in his suggestion of things, moving from a discussion of things to a concern with how to classify and explain the social facts one has found.

A first way to understand the relationship between the two thinkers is to consider why each considers the finding of "things" so critical to the method of sociology. The answer to this lies in their understanding of the subject and project of sociology. For Martineau, the subject of sociology is what is "'fixed and essential'" in the "morals and manners" of a people. Although Martineau does not always hold firmly to a distinction between morals and manners in her analysis, she is clear in her intent: morals are people's expressed convictions about goodness, right and wrong; manners are their daily interactions—which may follow those convictions, violate them, or rework them. She explains, "Manners have not been treated of separately from Morals . . . . The reason is, that manners are inseparable from morals, or at least, cease to have meaning when separated" (1838b: 222). She sees the morals and manners of any people originating in their responses to universals of the human condition—"a necessity for food, clothing, and shelter; and everywhere some mode of general agreement how to live together . . . everywhere [one will] find birth, marriage, and death; and therefore domestic affections" (*Ibid.*: 24).

In defining the project of sociology, she asks, "What results from all these [universal] elements of social life does [the sociologist] mean to look for?" (*Ibid.*: 24). She answers that the project of sociology must be to see how a people develop morals and manners both to manage these universals and to produce the great end of all social life, human happiness:

> That man should be happy is so evidently the intention of his Creator, the contrivances to that end are so multitudinous and so striking, that the perception of the aim may be called universal. . . . There are . . . a host of obstacles to the express recognition of, and practical obedience to these great principles; but they may be discovered as the root of . . . morals in all countries. There are impediments from ignorance, and consequent error, selfishness, and passion . . . but yet all men entertain one common conviction, that what makes people happy is good and right, and that what makes them miserable is evil and wrong. This conviction is at the bottom of practices which seem the most inconsistent with it (*Ibid.*: 36–7).

Martineau's language here as elsewhere reflects her position as an intellectual heir both of the Enlightenment and of the American and French Revolutions (a position she shares in sociology most strikingly with Comte, although their reactions to this heritage are very different). Her seeming liberality in arguing for human happiness as the end of society and social arrangements actually has quite clear limits which become evident in her descriptions of the social indicators—the things—to be looked at in analyzing a society. She should not be read as offering a call to bacchanalia and indulgence—although she does believe in leisure and pleasure as well as work as sources of human happiness. For her, a system of social arrangements is conducive to human happiness to the extent that it allows individuals to act as autonomous moral and practical agents motivated by an active "Idea of Liberty" (*Ibid.*: 187) and willing to oppose domination.

Martineau stresses that people may work out different, but potentially equally satisfactory, ways of social co-existence. She argues that while there is a universal moral sense, its particular form will vary from society to society. On the one hand, "some influences act upon the minds of all people in all countries. . . . For instance, to torment another without any reason, real or imaginary, is considered wrong all over the world. In the same manner, to make others happy is universally considered right" (*Ibid.*: 35). On the other hand, the social scientist is

> not to conclude unfavourably about the diet of the multitude because he sees them swallowing blubber, or scooping out water-melons, instead of regaling themselves with beef and beer. He is not to suppose their social meetings a failure because they eat with their fingers instead of with silver forks, or touch foreheads instead of making a bow. He is not to conclude against domestic morals, on account of a diversity of methods of entering upon marriage. (*Ibid.*: 25)

Her first rule for the observer confronting this diversity is that morals and manners should be evaluated in terms of their relation to human happiness. Her second is that the observer must be aware that "every prevalent virtue or vice is the result of the particular circumstances amidst which the society exists" (*Ibid.*: 39). One of the great achievements of sociology is to trace the circumstances leading to a particular moral or manner. But even where that is not possible, the sociologist must remember that people acquire their moral sense through the society in which they are raised: "every man's feelings of right and wrong, instead of being born with him, grow up in him from the influences to which he is subjected" (*Ibid.*: 34–5). This does not mean a standardized moral sense develops among all the people in a given society; what Martineau rather sees is that "the people of each age or country, having grown up under common influences, think and feel sufficiently alike to live together in a general agreement as to right and wrong" (*Ibid.*: 109). This general agreement has limits; human reason can always lead some individuals to a higher morality than that common to their society:

> While all nations were ravaging one another as they had opportunity, there were always parents who did not abuse their physical power over their children. In the midst of a general worship of power, birth, and wealth, the affections have wrought out in individual minds a preference of obscurity and poverty for the sake of spiritual objects. Amidst the supremacy of the worship of honour and social ease, there have always been confessors who could endure disgrace for the truth, and martyrs who could die for it.—Such individual cases have never been wanting. . . .
>
> . . . there is reason to anticipate that the age may come when the individual worship of spiritual supremacy may expand into the national; when a people may agree to govern one another with the smallest possible application of physical force; when goodness shall come to be naturally more honoured than birth, wealth, or even intellect. . . .

> Meantime, it is the traveller's business to learn what is the species of Moral Sentiment which lies deepest in the hearts of the majority of the people. (*Ibid.*: 111–13).

With this explicitly stated understanding of sociology's subject and purpose, Martineau's chief reason for seeking "things" as social indicators is to solve the problem of representativeness or sampling in looking to what is "'fixed and essential'" in any particular society.

> Which of us would undertake to classify the morals and manners of any hamlet in England, after spending the summer in it?
>
> If it be thus with us at home, . . . what hope of a trustworthy judgment remains for the foreign tourist . . . ? He looks at all the people along his line of road, and converses with a few individuals from among them. If he diverges, from time to time, from the high road,—if he winds about among villages, and crosses mountains, to dip into the hamlets of the valleys,—he still pursues only a line, and does not command the expanse; he is furnished, at best, with no more than a sample of the people; and whether they indeed be a sample, must remain a conjecture which he has no means of verifying. (*Ibid.*: 15–16)

If Martineau could have been assured that she could talk to everyone, she would have done that and drawn her generalizations accordingly.

For Durkheim the need for "things" is not simply or primarily one of representativeness or sampling—though he shares that concern. It is to avoid the error, which he sees as prevalent in sociological thinking, of confusing the ideas that people in a society have about their society with the actual structures that pattern social life: "We must, therefore, consider social phenomena in themselves as distinct from the consciously formed representations of them in the mind; we must study them objectively as external things, for it is this character that they present to us" (Durkheim 1895: 28). Even if he could speak to all the people, Durkheim would not choose to do so, because he is not interested in their meanings—understood as psychic, subjective experiences—but in social structure.

> But in reality there is in every society a certain group of phenomena which may be differentiated from those studied by the other natural sciences. When I fulfil my obligations as brother, husband, or citizen, when I execute my contracts, I perform duties which are defined, externally to myself and my acts, in law and in custom. Even if they conform to my own sentiments and I feel their reality subjectively, such reality is still objective, for I did not create them; I merely inherited them through my education. How many times it happens, moreover, that we are ignorant of the details of the obligations incumbent upon us, and that in order to acquaint ourselves with them we must consult the law and its authorized interpreters! (*Ibid.*: 1)

In developing this analysis, Durkheim argues that "the social" possesses three critical interrelated qualities—externality from the individual, constraining impact on individual, and collective origin. In making these points, he emphasizes that the social fact is "capable of exercising on the individual an external constraint," that it exists "independent of its individual manifestations" and that it "is general because it is collective (that is, more or less obligatory), and certainly not collective because it is general" (*Ibid.*: 13, 9).

In her insistence that the purpose of sociology is to understand how a society's morals and manners promote or fail to promote human happiness, Martineau establishes a foundation both for a feminist sociology and a critical sociology. It is a measure of the direction taken by mainstream sociological theory that the idea that sociology should be concerned with the production of human happiness can perhaps seem "naive" because it violates what has been imposed as the fundamental principle of value-neutrality.

THE STANCE TOWARD THINGS

At the heart of both works is what Martineau (1838b: 23) describes as the fact—and Durkheim seems to see as the problem—that, according to Martineau:

> There are two parties to the work of observation on Morals and Manners—the observer and the observed. This is an important fact which the traveller seldom dwells upon as he ought; yet a moment's consideration shows that the mind of the observer—the instrument by which the work is done, is as essential as the material to be wrought. If the instrument be in bad order, it will furnish a bad product, be the material what it may.

Durkheim (1895: 14–15) agrees with this basic idea and sees the instrument—the mind of the sociologist—as often in bad order because of poor epistemology and methodology: "Instead of observing, describing, and comparing things, we are content to . . . proceed . . . from ideas to things, not from things to ideas. . . . It is clear that this method cannot give objective results."

For Durkheim, the solution is for the social scientist to establish an appropriate distance between the scientific activity of constructing an analytic understanding and the collective understandings in place in the society. This distancing is to be accomplished, in part, by the creation of concepts different from those used in everyday life: "In the present state of knowledge, we cannot be certain of the exact nature of the state, of sovereignty, political liberty, democracy, socialism, communism, etc. Our method should . . . avoid . . . all use of these concepts so long as they have not been scientifically established" (*Ibid.*: 22). A second way to accomplish distancing is by selecting for study those social facts which exist most independently of any individual instance:

> [I]f the points of reference themselves are variable, if they are perpetually shifting in relation to each other, there is no common standard, and the scientist has no means of distinguishing between those impressions which are external and those that are subjective. So long as social life is not separated from the individual or particular events which comprise it, and has no separate existence, it will present this dilemma. . . . *When, then, the sociologist undertakes the investigation of some order of social facts, he must endeavor to consider them from an aspect that is independent of their individual manifestations.* (*Ibid.*: 44–5)

Martineau, like Durkheim, seeks an impartial standard for the observer and is all well aware of the problems that confront the observer who brings to bear only his/her own understandings of a practice. But she sees impartiality as only one part of the problem—though a real one. Because the great ends of human association are the production of the most happiness for the most people, "impartiality" does not mean "value-neutrality" to Martineau, nor even objectivity as Durkheim seeks it. It means the repair to the rational standard of whether a given social practice is significant in producing happiness for a people and whether that practice indeed occasions the greatest relative amount of happiness for that society.

> Every element of social life derives its importance from this great consideration. The external conveniences of men, their internal emotions and affections, their social arrangements, graduate in importance precisely as they affect the general happiness of the section of the race among whom they exist. Here then is the wise traveller's aim,—to be kept in view to the exclusion of prejudice, both philosophical and national. . . . To test one people by another, is to argue within a very small segment of a circle; and the observer can only pass backwards from the point of truth. To test the morals and manners of a nation by reference to the essentials of human happiness, is to strike at once to the centre, and see things as they are. (Martineau 1838b: 25–6)

The sociologist cannot make a link between the morals and manners s/he observes in a society and their realization of human happiness without some understanding of what those morals and manners mean to the people who practice them. The quality of mind most essential in the observer, for Martineau, then, is not *distance* but *sympathy*—a skill which distinguishes the student of society from "the student of geology or general statistics." The student of society who lacks sympathy, writes Martineau, is "like one who, without hearing the music, sees a roomful of people begin to dance" (*Ibid.*: 55). She believes that it is impossible to understand a group's (or individual's) norms without sympathy:

> Without . . . rules, men could not live together, and they are also necessary to the repose of individual minds. . . . A life without purpose is uncomfortable enough; but a life without rules would be a wretchedness which, happily, man is not constituted to bear. The rules by which men live are chiefly drawn from universal convictions about right and wrong . . . . When sentiment is connected with these rules, they become religion; and religion is the animating spirit of all that is said and done. If the stranger cannot sympathize in the sentiment, he cannot understand the religion; and without understanding the religion, he cannot appreciate the spirit of words and acts. (*Ibid.*: 54–5)

Thus, Martineau and Durkheim offer us two opposite prescriptions for the study of society: Durkheim advises distancing and Martineau advises the development of sympathy as the only way to interpret conduct that may be widely at odds with what one is conditioned to oneself.

THE DELINEATION OF THINGS

These different understandings direct Martineau and Durkheim to study different—though not totally different—"things"—as social indicators. Despite their differences they find many of the same "things" significant: suicide, religion, statistical rates, population size and density, crime, the division of labor, the relation of metropolis and province. Durkheim has the advantage of improved governmental collections but Martineau clearly endorses the importance of such data and uses it when she can get it. Both feel they must not only describe but explain the things they identify as social indicators. Durkheim (1895: 128) seeks general rules of explanation, arguing forcefully that "*A given effect has always a single corresponding cause*" and that "It would be incomprehensible if the most widespread forms of organization would not at the same time be, *at least in their aggregate*, the most advantageous" (*Ibid.*: 58). Martineau does not seek general rules but rather attempts to establish causal connections among a people's circumstance, their morals and manners, and their general happiness. She seems to see the possibility of multiple causes producing what seems to be the same outcome, stressing that people find a variety of ways to handle the arrangements of living together so as to produce happiness. As a woman, aware of women's universal subordination, she does not feel that the fact that a practice is everywhere makes it necessarily right or "advantageous"—indeed, she would surely ask, "Advantageous for whom?"

Durkheim has two chief criteria for selecting things: (1) their existence independent of individual instances and (2) their possessing the quality of compelling individuals to act in certain ways. He recommends generally looking at "legal and moral rules, popular aphorisms and proverbs, articles of faith wherein religious or political groups condense their beliefs, standards of taste established by literary schools, etc. None of these can be found entirely reproduced in the applications made of them by individuals, since they can exist even without being actually applied" (*Ibid*.: 7). He notes that "It is this principle that we have applied in studying the diverse forms of social solidarity and their evolution, through the medium of the legal structure which reflects them" (*Ibid*.: 45–6). Further, he not only takes "things" as present in the society, he also in a sense creates them through his use of statistical method; he discovers statistical regularities in the accounts in official documents and these become for him things which can be scientifically manipulated through methods like "concomitant variation" (correlation). Interestingly, he is also particularly taken with three related social facts, only one of which has the objectivity he longs for—(1) population size, (2) what he calls "dynamic density," and (3) the complexity of the social structure. By "dynamic density" he means "not . . . the purely physical concentration of the aggregate, which can have no effect if the individuals, or rather the groups of individuals, remain separated by social distance [but] . . . the social concentration, . . . the number of individuals who are actually having not only commercial but also social relations, i.e., who not only exchange services or compete with one another but also live a common life" (*Ibid*.: 113–14). When he looks at complexity of social structure, he moves to invoke the evolutionary metaphor of a continuum of simple to complex societal types or "species":

> If . . . we understand the most simple society that has ever existed, to make our classification we should have only to follow the way these simple societies form compounds and how these compound societies combine to form more complex wholes. . . . The definite meaning of the term 'simplicity' can be no other than that of a complete absence of parts. . . . The '*horde*' . . . corresponds exactly to this definition. It is a social aggregate which does not include, and has never included, within itself any other more elementary aggregate, but is directly compose of individuals. . . . [T]he horde is thus the protoplasm of the social realm and, consequently, the natural basis of classification. (*Ibid*.: 80, 82–3)

Yet, touchingly, at the end of his chapter on "Rules for the Observation of Social Facts," Durkheim admits of his own method:

> No doubt, in proceeding thus, we leave the concrete data of collective life temporarily outside the realm of science; and yet, however changeable and unstable it may be, its unintelligibility need not be assumed. In order to follow a methodical course, we must establish the foundations of science on solid ground and not on shifting sound. We must approach the social realm

> where it offers the easiest access to scientific investigation. Only subsequently will it be possible to push research further and, by successive approximations, to encompass, little by little, this fleeting reality, which the human mind will never, perhaps be able to grasp completely. (*Ibid.*: 46)

Martineau would agree with many of the particulars that Durkheim recommends—she wants mortality, birth and marriage rates; she recommends the study of popular songs, literature, religion, suicide. But she often pursues these for somewhat different reasons from Durkheim. For instance, her plea for statistics is as strong as any in sociology, but it is framed in the context of a critical theory aimed at the production of human happiness.

> The Health of a community is an almost unfailing index of its morals. No one can wonder at this who considers how physical suffering irritates the temper, depresses energy, deadens hope, induces recklessness, and, in short, poisons life. The domestic affections, too, are apt to languish through disappointment in countries where the average of death is very high. There is least marriage in unhealthy countries, and most in healthy ones,—other circumstances being equal. . . .
>
> A faithful register of births, marriages, and deaths, is wished for by enlightened philanthropists of all advanced countries, far more as a test of national morals and the national welfare, than as a matter of the highest social convenience. . . .
>
> The comparative ages of the dead will indicate to him not only the amount of health, but the comparative force of various species of disease; and from the character of its diseases, and the amount of its health, much of the moral state of a people may be safely pronounced upon. The proportion of marriages to births and deaths is always an indication of the degree of comfort enjoyed, and of the consequent purity of morals. . . . (Martineau 1838b: 166–70)

And she has different reservations about certain types of data. For instance, she has less faith in what the laws of a society can tell the observer who

> must remember that neither the composition of the government, nor the body of the laws, nor the administration of them is an evidence of what idea of liberty at present is among the people, except in a democratic republic, where the acts of government are the result of the last expression of the national will. Every other representative system is too partial for its legislative acts to be more than the expression of the will of a party. . . . (*Ibid.*: 192)

Where Durkheim's concern with objectivity moves him toward distance and hence toward secondary data, Martineau's concern with a critical assessment of relative happiness moves her toward an empathetic understanding of the meanings of a people and this she feels requires not only texts or secondary data but *direct observation*. Advising how to get information about the level of health in a society, Martineau calls for both types of data: "There are two principal methods by which he may obtain the knowledge he wants,—by examining civic registers, and by visiting burial-grounds" (*Ibid.*: 168). She repeatedly returns to burial grounds as typical of the kinds of "monuments" that may represent the voice of a people:

> [The observer] will find no better place of study than the Cemetery,—no more instructive teaching than Monumental Inscriptions. . . .
>
> "De mortuis nil nisi bonum" is the universal agreement of mourners. It follows that epitaphs must everywhere indicate what is there considered good.
>
> The observer must give his attention to this. Among a people "whose merchants are princes," the praise of the departed will be in a different strain from that which will be found among a warlike nation, or a community of agriculturists. Here one may find monumental homage to public spirit, in the form of active citizenship; there to domestic virtue as the highest honour. (*Ibid.*: 113, 115–16)

She explores the way "discourse" itself may be observed as a "thing."

> [The observer] must seek intercourse with all classes of the society he visits. . . . He must study little ones at their mothers' knees, and flirtations in ball-rooms, and dealings in the market-place. He must overhear the mirth of revelers, and the grief of mourners. Wherever there is speech, he must devote himself to hear.
>
> One way in which discourse serves as a commentary upon the things he has observed is in the exhibition of certain general characters of its own, which are accordant with general facts he has registered. . . . In one country less regard is paid to truth in particulars, to circumstantial accuracy, than in another. One nation has most sincerity; another more kindliness in speech. One proses; another is light and sportive. One is frank; another reserved. One flatters the stranger; another is careless of him: and the discourse of the one is designed to produce a certain effect upon him; while that of the other flows out spontaneously, or is restrained, according to the traveller's own humour. (*Ibid.*: 223–4)

Unlike Durkheim, Martineau does not feel that "the concrete data of collective life [must be left] temporarily outside the realm of science." Those data, in regard especially to "manners," have to do with coming to understand the quotidian features of people's lives. She understands that in social science accounts the daily aspects of life must be presented through what literary critics call "texture"—that quality of a text which is left after the paraphraseable argument has been removed. In her opening advice to look to "things," Martineau offers a list rich in texture of some of the particulars, the evidence of daily life, that should be observed by the student of society.

> In cities, do social meetings abound? and what are their purposes and character? Are they most religious, political or festive? If religious, have they more the character of Passion Week at Rome, or of a camp-meeting in Ohio? If political, do the people meet on wide plains to worship the Sun of the Celestial Empire, as in China; or in town-halls, to remonstrate with their representatives, as in England; or in secret places, to spring mines under the thrones of their rulers, as in Spain? If festive, are they most like an Italian carnival, where everybody laughs; or an Egyptian holiday, when all eyes are solemnly fixed on the whirling Dervishes? Are women there? In what proportions, and under what law of liberty? What are the public amusements? . . . .—In country towns, how is the imitation of the metropolis carried on? Do the provincials emulate most in show, in science, or in the fine arts?—In the villages, what are the popular amusements? Do the people meet to drink or to read, to discuss, or play games, or dance? What are the public houses like? Do the people eat fruit and tell stories? or drink ale and talk politics? or call for tea and saunter about? or coffee and play dominoes? or lemonade and laugh at Punch? . . . (*Ibid.*: 74–5)

This list is refined in the chapters of Part II which it introduces; the breadth of her discussion of the texture of daily living is suggested by the table of contents for Part II (*Ibid.*: viii-ix):

PART II. What to Observe
- CHAP. I. Religion
  - Churches
  - Clergy
  - Superstitions
  - Suicide
- CHAP. II. General Moral Notions
  - Epitaphs
  - Love of Kindred and Birth-place
  - Talk of Aged and Children
  - Character of prevalent Pride
  - Character of popular Idols
  - Epochs of Society
  - Treatment of the Guilty
  - Testimony of Criminals
  - Popular Songs
  - Literature and Philosophy
- CHAP. III. Domestic State
  - Soil and Aspect of the Country

Markets
Agricultural Class
Manufacturing Class
Commercial Class
Health
Marriage and Women
Children
CHAP. IV. Idea of Liberty
Police
Legislation
Classes in Society
Servants
Imitation of the Metropolis
Newspapers
Schools
Objects and Form of Persecution
CHAP. V. Progress
Conditions of Progress
Charity
Arts and Inventions
Multiplicity of Objects
CHAP. VI. Discourse

She sees, as she explores the routine of everyday life, the ways that a society's total circumstance—its geography, its geology, its relation to strong or weak neighbors, its climate, etc.—affects morals and manners. She illustrates this principle by a textured description of the ways circumstance influence morality, as in her comparison of Holland with other societies:

> It is amusing to the traveller in Holland to observe how new points of morals spring up out of its swamps, as in the East from the dryness of the deserts. To injure the piles upon which the city is built, is at Amsterdam a capital offense; and no inhabitant could outgrow the shame of tampering with the vegetation by which the soil of the dykes is held together. While Irish children are meritoriously employed in gathering rushes to make candles, and sedges for thatch, "the veriest child in Holland would resent as an injury any suspicion that she had rooted up a sedge or a rush, which had been planted to strengthen the embankments." Such are certain points of morals in a country where water is the great enemy. . . . In Holland, a malignant enemy cut the dyke, as the last act of malice; in Arabia, he fills up the wells. (*Ibid.*: 157–8)

The heart of Martineau's analysis is her concern with the production of human happiness which she sees as dependent on three tendencies in a people's morals and manners, which we could almost speak of as their support of "liberty, equality, fraternity." But her treatment is not a clichéd restating of a revolutionary slogan but an anticipation of concerns that will be central to feminist sociology: resistance to domination, moral agency, material equity, and inclusivity. She focuses throughout her analysis on indicators that address this cluster of concerns; for example, she is consistently interested in the class system in a society, the relative freedom of opinion and expression, the status of women, the relation between metropolis and province, the practice of charity.

In her chapter on "The Domestic State," Martineau analyzes social class conditions that produce or preclude human happiness. She argues specifically that practical material conditions—what people must daily do to earn their livelihoods, and how successful they are at it—is a determining "circumstance" of morality. She posits that a certain standard of material sufficiency is essential to any morality:

> . . . nothing remains to be learned of the domestic morals of people who are plunged in hopeless poverty. There is no foundation for good morals among such. They herd together, desperate or depressed; they have no prospect; their self-respect is prostrated; they have nothing to lose, there is nothing for them to gain by an effort that they can make.—But it is needless to speak of this. When we treat of the domestic morals of any class, it is always presupposed that they are not in circumstances which render total immorality almost inevitable. (*Ibid.*: 159)

It follows from this that in the morals and manners of practical affairs those societies will be happiest which provide both an equitable distribution of goods and "in which every man who has power in him may attain all to which that power is a requisite" because this "cannot but enhance the importance of each in the eyes of all; and the consequence is a mutual respect and deference, and also a mutual helpfulness which are in themselves virtues of a high order, and preparatives for others" (*Ibid.*: 49). What we would understand today as "the income distribution profile of a society," she treats as a direct indicator of the potential for human happiness. She formulates this in the principle: that happiness is much affected by "whether the society is divided in Two Classes, or whether there is a Gradation" (*Ibid.*: 193). She elaborates:

> Where there are only two, proprietors and labourers, the Idea of Liberty is deficient or absent. The proprietary class can have no others desires on the subject than to repress the encroachments of the sovereign above them, or the servile class below them: and in the servile class the conception of liberty is yet unformed . . . .
>
> There are two pledges of the idea of liberty in a community:—the one is the mingling of the functions of proprietor and labourer throughout the

> whole of a society ruled by a representative government; the other is the graduation of ranks by some other principle than hereditary succession. (*Ibid*.: 193–4)

She understands that access to material well-being is affected not only by class but by gender and by ethnicity. Pursuing this idea, she recommends looking particularly at the status of women and of servants. She uses the relative autonomy of women as a clear test of a society's liberty in regards to allowing the individual to work out the best use of her or his powers.

> The traveller everywhere finds woman treated as the inferior party in a compact in which both parties have an equal interest. Any agreement thus formed is imperfect, and is liable to disturbance; and the danger is great in proportion to the degradation of the supposed weaker party. The degree of the degradation of women is as good a test as the moralist can adopt for ascertaining the state of domestic morals in any country. (*Ibid*.: 178–9)

The major way women are kept subservient is by being denied any agency outside marriage, any practical way to support themselves independently. These restrictions on women's autonomy, in turn, corrupts the marriage union.

> At present, society is undergoing a transition from a feudal state to one of mutual government; and women, gaining in some ways, suffer in others during the process. . . . The charge of their own maintenance is thrown upon large numbers of women, without the requisite variety of employments having been opened to them, or the needful education imparted. . . . The unfavourable influence of these results upon the happiness of domestic life may be seen at a glance.
>
> Domestic morals are affected in two principal respects [by this lack of occupation for women]. Where feminine occupations of a profitable nature are few, and therefore overstocked, and therefore yielding a scanty maintenance with difficulty, there is the strongest temptation to prefer luxury with infamy to hardship with unrecognized honour. Hence arises much of the corruption of the cities. . . .
>
> The other way in which domestic morals are affected by the scope which is allowed to the powers of women, is through the views of marriage which are induced. Marriage is debased by being considered the one worldly object in life,—that on which maintenance, consequence, and power depend. (*Ibid*.: 180–2)

She explores the effects of ethnicity in her discussion of servants: "The treatment and conduct of domestics depend on causes which lie far deeper than the principles and tempers of particular servants and masters . . . . In England the old Saxon and Norman feud smolders, (however unconscious the parties may be of the fact,) in the relation of master and servant" (*Ibid.*: 196). She expands the issue of domestic service to look at the ethnic tensions in Ireland and on the racial tensions in the United States, where she sees the presence of slavery having a deeply corrosive effect on attempts to establish service by contract between domestic and employer.

Moral autonomy turns not only on access to material resources but also on freedom of thought. In analyzing freedom of opinion, Martineau advises the sociologist to look at a host of indicators—the presence of the feudal temper, the cultural hegemony of the metropolis, the presence of newspapers, the provision of free education, the relation between police and citizenry, and "the objects and form of Persecution for Opinion in each country" (*Ibid.*: 206). We can illustrate her thinking through two very contemporary concerns—cultural hegemony and the control of public opinion.

Writing about the relation between the metropolis and the province—which we could today think of as that between "core" and "periphery" (Wallerstein 1974)—Martineau theorizes that:

> Where there is least freedom and the least desire of it, everything centres in the metropolis. Where there is most freedom, each 'city, town, and villa,' thinks and acts for itself. In despotic countries, the principle of centralization actuates everything." (Martineau 1838b: 199)

If we take Martineau's (1838b: 199–200) acknowledgment that, "The traveller will find that 'Paris is France,'" we see again how she and Durkheim can view the same "thing" very differently. He interprets the difference between Britain and France as an absence of integration in the former: "Roads, railroads, etc. can serve for commerce better than for fusion of populations, of which they are only a very imperfect index. Such is the case in England, whose physical density is greater than that of France, but where the coalescence of social areas is much less advanced, as is proved by the persistence of local spirit and regional life" (Durkheim 1895: 115). Martineau, in contrast, sees the regional vitality of England as a sign of its respect for individual liberty. As indicators of the control or freedom of public opinion, Martineau looks to a society's newspapers—not to the content of any one but rather to the degree of freedom of expression that seems present in them. She stresses that all freedom of expression—whether in newspapers or some other form—is relative, always there is some restriction: "Persecution for opinion is always going on among a people enlightened enough to entertain any opinions at all" (Martineau 1838b: 206). She finds that America presents a most interesting example of this persecution because there it is done by the "will of the majority":

> The absence of an aristocratic or a sovereign will impels men to find some other will on which to repose their individual weakness, and with which to

> employ their human veneration. The will of the majority becomes their refuge and unwritten law. The few free-minded resist this will, when it is in opposition to their own, and the slavish many submit. This is accordingly found to be the most conspicuous fault of the Americans. Their cautious subservience to public opinion,—their deficiency of moral independence—is the crying sin of their society. (*Ibid.*: 48–9)

In her analysis of the practice of charity as a measure of the progress of a society, we have perhaps the best insight into Martineau's understanding of the relation among moral agency, the rejection of the principle of domination, material equity, and inclusivity. She asserts that charity is a universal human moral sense—though it differs widely in form. What Martineau wishes to see in charity is the true "fraternal spirit" in which "the helpless are now aided expressly on the ground of their helplessness,—not from the emotions of compassion excited by the spectacle of suffering in particular cases, but in a nobler and more abstract way" (*Ibid.*: 211). She establishes a typology of forms of charity that may characterize a people and argues that the highest form is that which seeks to empower the individual, to make the individual an autonomous agent able to make her/his own way in the world.

> The lowest order of charity is that which is satisfied with relieving the immediate pressure of distress in individual cases. A higher is that which makes provision on a large scale for the relief of such distress; as when a nation passes on from common alms-giving to a general provision for the destitute. A higher still is when such provision is made in the way of anticipation, or for distant objects; as when the . . . freeing of slaves, the treatment of the insane, or the education of the blind and deaf mutes is undertaken. The highest charity of all is that which aims at prevention rather than the alleviation of evil. . . . In short, it is a nobler charity to prevent destitution, crime, and ignorance, than to relieve individuals who never ought to have been made destitute, criminal, and ignorant. (Martineau 1838b: 216–17)

Martineau's analysis of charity, like many of her analyses, employs a device that Durkheim specifically identifies and dwells on—typology. But where Durkheim seeks a universal and evolutionary typology for societies in general, Martineau seeks simply to establish what seem to her to be the possibilities for variation in a given social indicator of morals and manners. For instance, she classifies religions as ascetic, licentious, or moderate—but does not tie those to a system of evolution of the whole society; she classifies types of suicide—"in the largest sense . . . the voluntary surrender of life from any cause" (*Ibid.*: 103–108)—in terms of the duty to group which might impel them, the religious sense of escape that might make them preferable to life, the sense of personal honor which demands it. In her analysis of suicide or religion or charity, Martineau is willing to take reported instances (in sufficient numbers) and build a typology based not on evolution but most typically on the *sentiment*, the moral sense, which impels the behavior.

In her choice of the things—evidences drawn from daily life and from the lives of women; in her reporting of those things so as to leave the detail—the texture of that life—as part of the report; in what she seeks to draw from those things—a knowledge of the moral sense of a people, Martineau stands as an exemplar of the feminist and interpretive traditions in sociology as surely and as worthily as Durkheim stands for the positivist and functionalist.

MARTINEAU'S PLACE IN THE HISTORY OF SOCIOLOGY

If feminist sociology is to claim its full place in sociology, it is important that scholars—feminist and non-feminist—appreciate that it has a history in sociology and, as importantly, a history in sociological theory. The absence of classical feminist theory from the accounts of the history of sociology has significance as a problem in the politics of knowledge and gender and for sociological theory itself. Approaching it as a problem in the politics of knowledge and gender, we note this fundamental fact: the scholarship represented in this volume is not an isolated effort; over the last twenty-five years, published work recovering the history of women in sociology has increased (e.g., Broschart 1991a, b; Collins 1990; Costin 1983; Deegan 1978a, 1981, 1983, 1988a, b, c, 1991, 1995, 1996, 1998, 1999, forthcoming a, b; Deegan and Hill 1987, 1997; Deegan and Podeschi forthcoming; Deegan and Rynbrandt 2000; Deegan and Wahl forthcoming; Fish 1981, 1985; Fitzpatrick 1990; Hill 1988, 1989; Hill and Deegan forthcoming; Hoecker-Drysdale 1992, 1996, 1998, 2000; Honegger and Wobbe 1998; Hutcheon 1996; Lemert 1995; Lengermann and Niebrugge-Brantley 1996b, 1998, 2000a, b; McDonald 1993, 1994, 1998, forthcoming; Reinharz 1992, 1993; Rosenberg 1982; Rossi 1973; Sydie and Adams forthcoming; Terry 1983; and Thompson and Deegan 1981, among others), and numerous additional papers have been presented at regional, national, and international sociological meetings. Yet despite this labor, most women founders like Martineau remain largely absent from the institutionalized considerations of the history of sociological theory.

The general failure to affirm the history of feminist theory in sociology is another way that institutionalized patriarchy continues to grip the profession. The history of sociology is typically told as a history of its canon, understood as its major theories and theorists; those theories are almost exclusively presented as the creation of white, privileged class men. The chief way that new recruits to the profession are socialized to a sense of sociology is through the theory texts that tell the story of its history. Only one theory text currently acknowledges the presence of women as theorists in the founding and classical generations (Ritzer 1996); another acknowledges the presence of women only as activists but explains their disappearance from the record of sociology as being due to their *not* having produced "the theoretical schemes [which] tend to be more permanent, since they are more easily passed along to subsequent generations through intellectual networks" (Collins and Makowsky 1998: 297); another, which offers a chapter on feminism and readings from Dorothy E. Smith, sees feminism as "not a strong or widespread movement until the 1960s" (Farganis 1996). As of August 2000, there had not been a single article on the sociology of any of the women sociologists of the founding and classical generations in *The American Journal of Sociology*, the *American Sociological Review* or in *Sociological Theory*. At the 1997 ASA Theory Section mini-conference on "Theory as a Vocation," the first session dealing with "Past Exemplars" focused exclusively on Weber, Simmel, Parsons, Merton, and Shils. The 1998 Theory Section mini-conference on "The Method of Theory" has sessions on "Methods for Constructing Postulates from Starting Ideas" and "Methods for Deriving Predictions from the Postulates"—phrasing which tends to be not simply descriptive but prescriptive as to what constitutes an acceptable theoretical voice.

And the women, of whom Martineau is among the first, speak theory in a different voice, one reason perhaps they are not seen as "past exemplars." By "voice" we mean the relation established through the text among author, audience, and subject. The women's voice, as opposed to that of a "canonized" male theorist like Durkheim, is embodied rather than generalized, engaged rather than abstracted, specific rather than universal, accessible rather than arcane, connected rather than distanced, critical and ameliorative rather than "value-neutral." It is important to realize that Martineau and the other women founders, writing at the moment of the creation of sociology, had a freedom to experiment with ways of doing theory that later institutionalized practices for doing theory make undiscernible to all but the most daring. The omission of classical feminist theory from the history of sociology is, thus, a problem not only for feminist theory but for sociological theory itself—because theorists like Martineau offer alternative, potentially regenerative ways of doing theory, ways that connect theory and life.

CHAPTER SIX

"Words on Work": Harriet Martineau's Sociology of Work and Occupations—Part I: Her Theory of Work

Susan Hoecker-Drysdale

MARTINEAU IS A PIONEER IN USING THE PRISM OF WORK TO RENDER A spectrum on society through the sociological study of the division of labour, the meaning of work, disparities in work, and alienation and inequality in the industrial setting. My inquiry addresses the two fundamental dimensions of Martineau's concerns: First, work as subject, work as agency, that is, work as the essence of self, as vocation, as fundamental to "being and living" in the world. Martineau's philosophy of work creates the foundation for the organization of her personal life and is pivotal in her entire sociological perspective. Her early religious tales and essays (Martineau 1823a, 1831a, b, c, 1832a) reflected a Calvinist work ethic and an insistent sense of moral duty. Second, work as scientific object, that is, work as an object of study and analysis, developed in her empirical and descriptive investigations of the Victorian division of labour and the transformations in occupations and industries within the increasingly industrialized, specialized, stratified, and gendered circumstances of production in England and America. This is discussed in Chapter Seven, this volume.

As early as her writings in the *Monthly Repository* in the 1820s, she takes up matters of mental work, intellectual and scientific work, in a series "Essays on the Art of Thinking" and a number of moral essays, including essays on ". . . the Proper Use of the Retrospective Faculty" and ". . . the Proper Use of the Prospective Faculty" (Martineau 1822a, b). These essays concern the constructive use of memory and historical understanding to facilitate effective practical action and hope for the future. The importance, and indeed responsibility, to gain some knowledge of economic and social systems is expressed in an essay "On the Duty of Studying Political

Economy" (1831d). These philosophical tracts express Martineau's lifelong conviction that all human beings have a responsibility to develop and inform themselves in order to increase benefit to themselves and to society at large. This can be construed as the fundamental duty or work of the citizen, and at the very least expresses the centrality of agency and action in Martineau's perspective. Work took on first moral and then sociological dimensions, so that it became, for her, synonymous with autonomy, emancipation, and selfhood.

The present discussion explores aspects of the first dimension of Martineau's study of work, that is, work as subject, and presents her philosophy of work and self, work and society, and work and political status. The immediate concern is to construct the framework of Martineau's philosophical presuppositions as she explores sociologically work as the subject/object.

It is important to recognize at the outset that for Martineau, no less than for Marx, Weber, Durkheim, Veblen, and Gilman, work constitutes the essential lens through which to view society. Martineau's implicit position is that work and work relations express as much about the culture and politics of a nation as about its economics. Like Saint-Simon, she envisioned a society of "work for each and order for all,"—however, a society born, not out of the structure and control of a central authority, but out of education, training, and information for its members. Indeed the problem of a meaningful fit between the population and the division of labour (Durkheim's problem of the "forced division of labour") was to be effected, in Martineau's view, through education and training.

Perhaps the best instance with which to demonstrate how she understands societal relations through the study of work is that of domestic service, a frequent subject of Martineau, whereby one can understand the norms of reciprocity and exchange, class, gender and race relations, cultural and political power, social control and exploitation, class values, and the degree of moral sympathy (Martineau 1838a).

Decrying the paucity of research on domestic service and the prevalence of social (male) stereotypes about and ignorance of the subject, Martineau investigates the causes of the rise of the system of domestic service by doing a historical/comparative analysis of England, Ireland, Scotland, and America, employing a typology of domestic service: (1) the slavery-patrimonial system guaranteeing maintenance; (2) employment by contract, which means freedom to work with no provision for maintenance; (3) the current system of domestic service which is "a compound of the other two systems quite opposite in their principles. It combines . . . the requisition of obedience and subjection to caprice of the first, and the uncertainty of maintenance of the last" (*Ibid*.: 413).

In identifying the roots of the nineteenth-century domestic system and the class estrangement it produced, she points to three historical causes: (1) The Norman conquest and the resulting "evil of arbitrary rank" which "created enmity between the classes of employers and employed" in England and "imposed a foreign aristocracy on a people reluctant to serve them" (*Ibid.*: 414). Service was exacted. (2) Asceticism (imposed upon workers in service) which makes the lives of the disadvantaged ever more wretched by such practices as employers forbidding spontaneous gatherings of the sexes and the abolition of the social life of workers. These are "to him [the worker], instead of books and thoughts, his intellectual exercise, his spiritual delight . . . take this from him, or throw restraint over it, or debase it for him, and you do what in you lies towards making him a machine, or a brute, or a fiend," leaving only the worries of providing for clothing and housing in harsh climates, etc. (*Ibid.*: 417–18). And (3), the growth of the commercial spirit (breeding selfishness, lack of trust, absence of traditions of service, social struggles). These developments create an alienation, a loss of trust in the old system of service, a loss of old loyalties and relationships. "The lottery of commerce is preferred to the sure gains of service" (*Ibid.*: 419).

Martineau uses the instance of domestic service to identify the transformations ushering in a modern, very different kind of society, in which the value of work declines and class conflicts are exposed in the alienation between employers and employees. Social relations are no longer reciprocal but instrumental. Those who do not live by manual labour cannot understand those who do. Middle-class women are excluded from useful work, while overworked working-class women, such as maids of all-work, are overrepresented in lunatic asylums.

In related articles, ("Modern Domestic Service" in *Edinburgh Review* (Martineau 1862), "Female Industry" in *Edinburgh Review* (1859b), in *Household Words* (see Martineau 1861: 158–65), *Daily News* leaders, etc.), she continues her analysis of society through the lens of work, looking particularly at women's work. Interested in exposing the problems, the myths, and conflicts related to work, and bringing remedies to bear, she reminds us that the days when women were supported by a father, brother, or husband, when marriage and motherhood were arranged and expected, and when women worked only in family establishments, are gone:

> From that time (the uprising of a middle class) to this, the need and the supply of female industry have gone on increasing, and latterly at an unparalleled rate, while our ideas, our language, and our arrangements have not altered in any corresponding degree. (Martineau 1859b: 153)

The study of domestic service, as Martineau shows, reveals some important truths about work in society: that certain kinds of drudgery remain hidden (Martineau 1838a: 409); that domestic service embodies the exploiters/exploited relationship (*Ibid*.: 409–10); that reciprocity and exchange are critical in social relations but not currently cultivated (*Ibid*.: 421), and that in the waning of traditions, tensions and isolation of the classes simmer toward eruption. Class reconciliation is now hindered by the reserve and unsociableness of the national character [England] which is a product of these developments (*Ibid*.: 415, 419).

> Offenses are brooded over which might be explained away; anger becomes treachery through concealment . . . with no promise of an intermission of offense . . . As it is, with the reserved tempers of the English, the score mounts up, and it is left to future generations to pay the awful reckoning. (*Ibid*.: 419)

Martineau develops a class analysis about the state of domestic service relations and indeed about work relations in general in England. In an 1862 article, "Modern Domestic Service," she does a comparative study of domestic work and factory employment (Martineau 1862: 414–15) and shows that, based on the criteria of freedom, dress, sociability, relations between the sexes, life interests, and independence, factory employment is highly preferable:

> There are few of the employed class who would not prefer a herring and potatoes in a room of their own to the choicest meals in the servants' hall. (*Ibid*.: 414)

The example of domestic service demonstrates how Martineau employs empirical inquiries of specific work situations to expose conditions in society as a whole. The strategy both interacts with, and is sustained by, a number of presuppositions/observations about work and society deriving from her research and reflections. Here then are some of these grounding principles.

THEORETICAL PROPOSITIONS REGARDING WORK AND THE SELF

Human Work Is an Essential Aspect of Being and Living in the World as a Human Being

Work is necessary for survival. All human beings want and need useful work. High value is given to work, that is to say, that meaningful work is living, a theme which we find not only in Martineau, but also in Marx (1844), Veblen (1898, 1914), Gilman (1898, 1903, 1915), and of course

Weber (1904–5). All wrote specifically on work as human activity which reflects the will, motivation, values, and sense of worth.

For Martineau, the question of "what to do with one's life" is a matter of choosing to exercise one's capacities, in the circumstances, to the utmost. She traces this process for herself in the *Autobiography* and concludes: "I had now, by thirty years of age, ascertained my career, found occupation, and achieved independence, and the rest of my life was provided with its duties and interests. Any one to whom that happens by thirty years of age may be satisfied, and I was so" (Martineau 1877b, I: 137).

Thus, for example, the problematic of the Hareem for Martineau was the enforced idleness which violates the basic human urge or need to work, as seen in the desire or necessity of *species being* to labour, in Marx (1844), and the instinct of workmanship of Veblen (1898, 1914). The pursuit of wealth and status, accompanied by idleness, notably in America in the 1830s, was a major obstacle to the self-actualization of, at least the privileged, members of that society. The underclasses and the enslaved are not able to produce a world which reflects themselves, which is a source of contemplation. They are Marx's, and Martineau's, alienated beings.

Work Manifests and Facilitates Agency; It Expresses the Self; Work Is Self-realization

It forms the nexus of self and society. It allows the exercise of personal capacities and facilitates development, at the same time that it expresses certain basic human rights—freedom, equality, self-fulfillment. Martineau's beliefs about work as the basis of life activity, perhaps work as a metaphor for life and as central in one's life course, derive largely from the influences of Calvinism and Necessarianism. She believes that although "the 'workings' of the universe are governed by laws which cannot be broken by human will . . . no action fails to produce effects, and no efforts can be lost. I have no doubt . . . that true Necessarians must be the most diligent and confident of all workers" (Martineau 1877b, I: 85–6).

Dealing with increasing deafness and other childhood difficulties engendered a diligence and persistence in everything she did. "Life," she wrote, "is a long, hard, unrelieved working-day to us, who hear, or see, only by express effort" (*Ibid.*: 57). But Martineau understood that her work defined her. Providing for herself "substantial, labourious and serious occupation," she had an extraordinarily clear view of her life and work.

> My business in life has been to think and learn, and to speak out with absolute freedom what I have thought and learned. The freedom is itself a positive and never-failing enjoyment to me, after the bondage of my early life. My work and I have been fitted to each other, as is proved by the success of my work and my own happiness in it. The simplicity and independence of

> this vocation first suited my infirm and ill-developed nature, and then sufficed for my needs, together with family ties and domestic duties . . . as every woman's heart requires . . . I am probably the happiest single woman in England. (*Ibid*.: 101–102)

Aware of class restrictions on useful and meaningful work for women, Martineau expresses the sense of release, of autonomy, regarding work, within the context of the family's financial disaster in 1829:

> I, who had been obliged to write before breakfast, or in some private way, had henceforth liberty to do my own work in my own way; for we had lost our gentility . . . but for that loss of money, we might have lived on in the ordinary provincial method of ladies with small means, sewing, and economizing, and growing narrower every year; whereas, by being thrown, while it was yet time, on our own resources, we have worked hard and usefully, won friends, reputation and independence, seen the world abundantly, abroad and at home, and, in short, have truly lived instead of vegetated. (*Ibid*.: 108)

She had barely escaped the shackles of the privileged classes which prohibited women's independent choices about work. These personal circumstances illustrated the more general point that "the worst kinds of aristocratic tyranny are found among women who do not work; they had it in their power to inflict more misery by their tyranny than their husbands can generally impose" (Martineau 1838a: 431). On the other hand, multitudes of women, delicately reared, had been thrown upon their own resources. "The blessedness of work, the heavenly fruits of toil, have been experienced by hundreds or thousands who, but for adversity, might now have been perishing, body and spirit, from *ennui*" (*Ibid*., 432). This, in turn, has consequences for domestic service, as such women become more responsible, sympathetic, and just mistresses who will "break up . . . the fatal persuasion of an opposition of interests between the employers and the employed" (Martineau 1838b: 432).

While often accused of exaggerating the value of domestic life and work, Martineau never assumes that they satisfy most women's needs for meaningful work. She believes that domestic competencies and good domestic practices are no substitute for paid work in the public or societal sphere. However, the opposite is also true; that is, an orderly domestic life is necessary to the life satisfaction of any worker. Knowledge of home nursing, cooking, cleaning, and hygiene, for example, were part of the necessary domestic skills.

Work is a Vocation

Martineau experienced work as a vocation on a personal level. She wrote:

> Authorship has never been with me a matter of choice. I have not done it for amusement, or for money, or for fame, or for any reason but because I could not help it. Things were pressing to be said; and there was more or less evidence that I was the person to say them. (Martineau 1877b, I: 188)

She goes on to describe the passionate drive, beyond her control, to convey ideas and understanding to others:

> If my life *had* depended on more leisure and holiday, I could not have taken it. What wanted to be said must be said, for the sake of the many, whatever might be the consequences to the one worker concerned. Nor could the immediate task be put aside, from the remote consideration, forever pressed upon me, of lengthening my life. (Martineau 1877b, I: 143)

One must of course respond to one's calling: ". . . an author has his lot pretty much in his own hands, because it is in his power to shape his habits in accordance with the laws of nature: and an author who does not do this has no business with the lofty vocation" (*Ibid*.: 144–5).

Martineau exhibits a firm resolve in describing work habits: "intellectual industry and intellectual punctuality are as practicable as industry and punctuality in any other direction" (*Ibid*.). Sitting down to work even "in the absence of inspiration," she would find herself "in full train" after a quarter hour (*Ibid*.). The discipline of vocation is manifested in a regular daily schedule in which she gives full priority to her work: "I never pass a day without writing" (serious writing in the morning, correspondence at night), and the systematic approach of background reading, note taking, outlining and structuring before writing, was a regime she followed from the days of her strenuous schedule in writing *Illustrations of Political Economy* onward. Hers was an example *par excellence* of a functionally rationalized work life.

With increasing clarity her work was the work of social science and of politics, whose separation she rejected. Science was to be useful, and her scientific work was intended for advocacy and reform, as well as for intellectual understanding. When she wrote from a particular viewpoint or attempted to influence political decision-making, she was accused of not being objective and of "meddling." By contrast, when men in the sociological tradition have combined science and action, it has been seen as the convergence of intellect and morality. Martineau's sense of vocation hinged upon duty: as a public educator particularly, she believed she had a duty to impart what she could to the public and to improve the ordinary individual's understanding of society. Vocation, for Martineau, required: involvement, commitment, dedication to the task, seriousness of endeavour, regular work habits, a strong belief in the significance of one's work.

Martineau assumes that work as vocation can, and hopefully will, become a reality for every individual. Vocation means not only a commitment to one's own development in one's work, but also, importantly, taking one's work seriously, as a duty to the larger social order. A typical example of work as vocation for women is to be found in nursing, an important new occupation which she analyzed and promoted in cooperation with her friend Florence Nightingale (see Chapter Eight, this volume).

> Who could imagine that all the time there is a vocation for women almost entirely neglected in this country;—an occupation combining the advantages which Adam Smith represents as alternatives—of social repute and pecuniary profit;—an employment undisturbed by any jealousy of men, congenial with all the best instincts of women, universally honoured, better paid than any other woman's work, except, as has been said, that of queens and of actresses! (Martineau 1865: 411–12)

Work and Life Are at Once Mental and Physical

Like Saint-Simon (1825), Marx (1844), Tristan (1843), Veblen (1898), and Gilman (1898), although much earlier than most of them, Martineau emphasized the dual nature of work. Work should employ both mental and physical capacities, but a balance can be struck by regular mental activities outside of work for manual workers, and by physical exercise and engagement in physical work for those who work by the mind. A perfect example of the former is found in Knight's *Guide to Service*, her *The Ladies' Maid* (Martineau 1838d), where she advocates that the lady's maid memorize poetry while sewing for mental improvement and self-enhancement (Logan 1999). Activities of leisure and culture should be encouraged among domestic servants. She recommends that households have reading rooms for servants and provisions for leisured hours with their friends, during which the mistress should take care of herself (Martineau 1862: 421). Of the latter, she concludes that women who do no physical work and get no exercise, will wither intellectually and lose their mental capabilities (Martineau 1837, III: 151–61). Finally, it should be recalled that Martineau both supported and lectured in the mechanics institutes and directed a considerable proportion of her writings toward the working-class reader.

In her letter published in *Mind Amongst the Spindles* (1844a), Martineau reflects on not only the orderly, disciplined organization of work and life among the young women textile workers of Waltham and Lowell, Massachusetts, but also the balance of the physical and mental aspects of their work. They were working-class women who toiled seventy hours a week, and managed to develop a community and a cultural life.

> The difference was in their superior culture. Their minds were fresh, and strong, and free by knowledge and power of thought; and this is the reason why they are not worn and depressed under their labours. . . .
>
> At Waltham, where I saw the mills, and conversed with the people, I had an opportunity of observing the invigorating effects of MIND in a life of labour. . . . [This could be emulated elsewhere], if people employed are so educated as to have the command of themselves and of their lot in life, which is always and everywhere controlled by mind, far more than by outward circumstances. (Martineau 1985: 161, 164)

Martineau was of course dedicated to the idea of an "educated" working class. She was enthusiastic about the *Guide to Service* books for workers' training, schools for the children of rural workers, night schools for working men and women, and literature, including her own, which would educate all classes (Martineau 1864c: 2).

Leisure Is As Essential to Life As Work

Martineau, as Karl Marx, is committed to the idea that leisure is as integral to one's life as work. More than that, like work, it is a basic human right, as she makes clear in *Society in America*, for example. Referring to William Godwin, whose ideas had considerable influence on Martineau, as the first advocate of leisure as a birthright, she emphasizes that

> leisure, some degree of it, is necessary to the health of every man's spirit. Not only intellectual production, but peace of mind cannot flourish without it. It may be had under the present system, but it is not. With community of property . . . the requisite amount of work would bear a very small proportion to that of disposable time. (Martineau 1837, III: 43–44)

Unfortunately, the nineteenth-century mercenary, competitive system makes leisure problematic for all who work, from professionals and merchants to the mechanic and farming classes.

> There must be something wrong in the system which compels men to devote almost the whole of their waking hours to procure that which, under a different combination of labour, might be obtained at a saving of three-fourths of the time. . . . No thinking man or woman, who reflects on the amount of time, thought, and energy, which would be set free by the pressure of competition and money-getting being removed,—time, thought, and energy now spent in wearing out the body, and in partially stimulating and partially wasting the mind, can be satisfied under the present system. (*Ibid.*: 48–9)

THEORETICAL PROPOSITIONS REGARDING WORK AND SOCIETY

The Meaning of Work as Societally-Defined Indicates the Character of a Society

As Martineau and her successors Thorstein Veblen and Charlotte Gilman show, gender inequities and the practices of slavery lead to the debasement of work. Work performed by subordinates is regarded as dirty and contaminating, to be avoided, indicative of inferior status. Therefore, work itself is demeaned and nourishes negative attitudes and practices which degrade and deteriorate social relations in society. There is little point in masters telling their servants that every one respects the industrious, while they themselves are seen to pay the most honour to the lazy and luxurious.

> There is no use in mistresses assuring their maids that there is great credit in humble usefulness, when they themselves, pining in idleness, will not touch their household burdens with one of their fingers. Men and maid-servants will go on to believe from what they see, rather than from what they are told. (Martineau 1838a: 431)

Should a mistress on the plantation or in an English household attempt the slightest task, even the servants will think that "the ladies are degrading themselves by doing useful things, which are 'servants' work'" (Martineau 1838a: 430). Occupations which should be considered honourable and responsible, teaching in particular, are entered only on desperation or on refusal of other work such as needle work, and are considered irksome, deserving only low wages. That female labor yields "scant reward . . . lies in the subordination of the sex" (Martineau 1837, III: 150). Martineau regularly draws attention to the fact that women's work is often harder than men's (Martineau 1859b: 154).

Martineau's observations of society in England and America yielded many examples of the association of idleness with high prestige and honour, on the one hand, and work with low status, stupidity, dirtiness, and perhaps unworthiness, on the other. Those who do not engage in useful work, and who have control over those who do, hold feelings of dislike or hatred toward the workers. This is most accentuated within the slavery system. So much so, she concludes, that hatred is a sign of the times:

> The word "hatred" is not too strong for the feeling of a large proportion of slave-holders toward particular slaves . . . . As long as the slave remains ignorant, docile, and contented, he is taken good care of, humoured, and spoken of with a contemptuous, compassionate kindness. But, from the moment he exhibits the attributes of a rational being,—from the moment his intellect seems likely to come into the most distant competition with that of whites,

> the most deadly hatred springs up;—not in the black, but in his oppressors. It is a very old truth that we hate those whom we have injured. (Martineau 1837, II: 152–3)

By comparison, in the older society, England, where idleness and honour seem irrevocably linked, the true value of work remains eclipsed.

> The probability is . . . that the struggle for a supposed state of privilege (authority and idleness) will continue till a crisis comes, which shall reveal that all this is no privilege at all, but a curse. (Martineau 1838a: 431)

Martineau's best world is one in which employer and employee work reciprocally: "[where] . . . mutual service is honourable, and not disgraceful" (*Ibid.*: 430). That is, work should be a mutual affair between employer and employee, part of community life, in which individuals express their relation to and responsibility toward one another. This is indeed an important part of the moral sympathy (Adam Smith 1759) which Martineau considered a critical element in civilized society (see Martineau 1836c, I: 179–91).

Total Appropriation of Another's Work Is Immoral and Damages the Worker and Society

The exploitation of others' work, as in slavery and sweatshop labour, and the appropriation of others' physical and intellectual exertions for the singular benefit of the employer are inhuman and destructive of individuals and society. While it is true that Martineau came to the defense of factory occupiers (i.e., owners) in the debate over the fencing of machinery, in the greatest debate she had with Charles Dickens (Martineau 1855) and that she wrote about "boys carelessly putting themselves in the way of the machine!!", she also writes about the ways in which workers become increasingly routinized by the machines (Martineau 1859b). Nevertheless, Martineau favours technology and is convinced that the welfare of the worker depends on his/her willingness to adjust to the increasing differentiation in the division of labour created by new machinery and new capital investments, as illustrated in her political economy tale, *The Hill and the Valley* (Martineau 1832–4, no. 2).

The consequent alienation and estrangement, loss of control over one's work, one's physical movements, and unhealthy work conditions were often a function of gender. "In Staffordshire potteries women paint without a rest for the hand because of male jealousy [of the workmen]" (Martineau 1859b: 170). She writes of the dreadful health of overworked "sempstresses" (Martineau 1837, III: 148) and the cruel physical effects of long hours of sewing (see her articles on female dress; Martineau 1859b; 1861); the exploitation of children working in the potteries whose physical well-being and very lives were endangered (following the report on *Children's Employment; Factories*, in 1863); and the need for a national education system. It must be noted, however, that perhaps because of her extreme optimism about technology and her defensiveness as a manufacturer's daughter, Martineau (e.g., 1994) sometimes tended to slight the horrifying evidence from industrial scenes.

Society Must Provide the Conditions for Freedom of Development in Work for Each Individual

Just as Marx crowns his future socialist society with the idea of the "free development of each leading to the free development of all," Martineau emphasizes the free development of members of society via a free work situation (Martineau, 1836c, II: 121–2; 132). In writing on women's work as reported in the Census of 1851 and a number of reports in the 1850s, Martineau emphasizes that three of six million Englishwomen work for subsistence and two of three are independent (sole supporters of themselves).

> With this new condition of affairs, new duties and new views must be accepted. Old obstructions must be removed; and *the aim must be set before us*, as a nation as well as in private life, *to provide for the free development and full use of the powers of every member of the community*. In other words, we must *improve and extend education* to the utmost; and then open a fair field to the powers and energies we have educed. This will secure our welfare, nationally and in our homes, to which few elements can contribute more vitally and more richly than the independent industry of our countrywomen. (Martineau 1859b: 173; my emphasis)

This is not simply a utopian dream for Martineau but a commitment to social progress, not only by advancing the material base, but by exercising progressive practices in work: training, education, equity, appropriate use of the skills of all, and establishment of organizations such as building associations and mechanics institutes to enable the mental and physical development of workers and empower them to meet their housing and health needs through community efforts.

The Division of Labour Develops According to the Natural Laws of Political Economy

Its development is not simply a function of population growth and concentration, technology and increased communication and transportation, as with Durkheim (1893: 200–25), but in addition, for Martineau, reflects the reality of private ownership and control in production and markets. She points out the implications of such practices as monetary speculation (which she always opposed as too risky and damaging to the economic welfare of others), patriarchal practices at work (e.g., in watchmaking (1859b: 168), potterymaking (*Ibid.*: 170), the exclusion of women from many venues such as the National Academy of Arts (*Ibid.*: 172), the practices of slavery (the most destructive, exploitative division of labour), gender inequalities (pay inequities and women's lack of control over their own wages (*Ibid.*: 160, 170, 171), discrimination (*Ibid.*: 155) and ghettoization, as in sewing machines work (*Ibid.*: 109), class differentiations and even ageism. These problems were omitted from Durkheim's analysis. She shows that machine technology genders the division of labour and works to exclude women from productive work, thus reserving high status, power and rewards for men (Martineau 1859b).

Just as Durkheim assumes the modern division of labour to be natural and normative and an essential factor in the cohesion of society, Martineau, particularly early in her career, asserts that society evolves in every respect according to the Laws of Political Economy. For both, there is a kind of natural inevitability in the occupational and industrial order, but also in the accompanying problem of the fit of people to the division of labour (Martineau 1838a: 405; Durkheim 1893). While both emphasize the importance of education, Martineau's proposals for education and employment specifically address the realities of gender, race, class and age (Martineau 1864a, b). Her critique focuses on gender discrimination in all types of work, from medicine to silver engraving (Martineau 1859a, 1861), the poor provision for the aged after their work years, a concern with race as a permanent hindrance to economic improvement (1837), and the critical need for individual (including women's) economic independence (1859a; 1837, II: 337ff.). These arguments precede Durkheim's analysis by three to five decades.

Machine Technology Facilitates Progress

It was axiomatic for Martineau that machines have the potential to take over arduous human tasks while expanding production and opportunities for employment. She would agree with Smith, rather than Montesquieu, that technology has the potential to create employment opportunities for all, especially for women, and that factories and manufactures make society orderly and regulated (i.e., rationalized). In Martineau's view, growth in the material base of industrial capitalism almost certainly improves life for all, but there are obstacles: gender and race inequities in opportunities (1859b: 166), costs in product quality with industrialization, and inept enforcement of state regulation.

Martineau, like Smith, is often seen as an apologist for and defender of bourgeois capitalism, and if we consider the key elements of bourgeois capitalism as outlined by Weber (1904–5), we would have to agree. She saw technology, a free marketplace, and a formally free labour force as necessary, if not sufficient, conditions of a progressive society. However, as her American studies show, it is the morals of economic and political practices— the quality of social relations and the degree of social responsibility in society—which ultimately matter. As with Adam Smith, therefore, we find in Martineau a critique and warnings about the consequences of industrial capitalism, particularly in these articles on work and in her political economy tales.

THEORETICAL PROPOSITIONS REGARDING WORK, RIGHTS, AND CITIZENSHIP

The Right to Work

Martineau asserted the right to work and the right to free access to particular forms of work by all members of society (the right not to be excluded on irrelevant grounds). In her studies of America, Martineau emphasizes the formal American values of freedom with respect to life, liberty, and the pursuit of happiness. According to Martineau, in the instances of both slavery and the subordination of women (systems of coercion), a basic human right was being violated: the right to work, to be free to choose one's work, which presumably makes possible the pursuit of the other values. Free human work is a right of blacks as well as whites, women as well as men, workers as well as owners. Her resistance to unions, especially in her early decades, was based on her belief in the right to work (especially for women, who were not then unionized). She anticipated that, in the circumstances of the time, women would be negatively affected by unionization of the labour force. In another instructive case, she lamented that, in the plantation system of the American South, the idea of human rights was reduced to "sufficient subsistence in return for labour" (Martineau 1837, II: 343).

In the area of work, Martineau points particularly to the problem of domination. Power over another's right to work constitutes absolute power over the other. The essential feature of slavery is that bondage, a sin against humanity, means denial of another's right to freedom of work and leisure. In addition to her critiques of slavery and all its dehumanizing characteristics, Martineau anticipates the future suffrage cry of "Work and Emancipation" in her linkage of women's subordinate political and social status with economic dependency and the denial of freedom to work in the public sphere (*Ibid*.: 150).

The Right to Work Is Linked to Citizenship

Just as society controls property and marriage rights, it controls the right to work, access to work, access to specific kinds of work, and to the terms of work. It is clear in *Society in America* that Martineau understood the interconnections of human rights, citizenship, and work.

> One remarkable effect of democratic institutions is the excellence of the work turned out by those who live under them. In a country where the whole course is open to every one; where, in theory, everything may be obtained by merit, men have the strongest stimulus to exert their powers, and try what they can achieve. (*Ibid.*: 352–3)

However, work and the systems of manufacture and commerce in America of the 1830s were essentially corrupted by the practices of slavery, racism, and gender discrimination. Contrary to popular opinion, women, according to Martineau, were not in the majority financially supported by men, but they were blocked from education and training and given few choices in employment. The rights of slaves were denied on every count and freed slaves did not enjoy full citizen's rights. Dignity, autonomy, and privacy were denied. Not only were social realities in conflict with the nation's political principles, but, to Martineau, American society's progress and indeed its very survival depended on giving full rights to the governed, to those who were not yet full citizens of the Republic.

Work and the Right to Relevant Education

The right to education—and the relevance of education for the development of individuals and the preparation for work—is corollary to citizenship and the right to work. This proposition is revealed in many contexts, as in Martineau's discussions in the 1850s of the need for a national educational system in England and in her earliest essays on the need for education for middle-class girls and boys (Martineau 1864a); on education as the vehicle for intellectual and moral competency, "an indispensable condition of the privileges of citizenship" in *Society in America* (1837, III: 163) and in *Household Education* (1849), and on the importance of public education in mass media and literature, guides to service, her fiction, works for the mechanics institutes, public libraries and workers' societies.

Role of the Democratic State

The democratic state has an important role in assuring fair, safe, and nondiscriminatory practices at work and must take into account the needs of the workers and the employers. Critical of "meddling" factory legislation and convinced by the Necessarian belief in embedded natural laws,

Martineau nevertheless recognizes that community commitment is required to enable women's access to work and education, the provision of education and training for all children, a healthy environment and good health practices, and even a prospering industrial state.

> We are only beginning to think of the claim of all workers,—that their work should be paid for by its quality, and its place in the market, irrespective of the status of the worker:—we are only beginning to see that the time must come when such artificial depreciation must cease, under the great natural laws of society . . . A social organization framed for a community of which half stayed at home, while the other half went out to work, cannot answer the purposes of a society, of which a quarter remains at home while three-quarters go out to work. This seems clear enough. (Martineau 1859b: 153)

Thus, for Martineau, the state, the society and the individual are tightly interconnected in terms of the issues of rights. The ways in which the polity and the economy work together determine the possibilities for the individual and his/her fate with regard to work and occupation. The rights of women, slaves, and other disempowered groups are denied insofar as their choices and possibilities for fulfilling work and financial returns are determined by forces entirely outside of themselves. The disparities between the absence of education and training and the "freedom to choose" one's work, to meet the imperatives of a democratic society, are especially glaring in America in the 1830s, but, as well, in the England of Martineau's entire lifetime.

CONCLUSION

In the course of writing over six decades on a great breadth of subjects, in myriad empirical reports and theoretical analyses, Harriet Martineau constructs a theory or philosophy of work, which both informs her empirical investigations and demonstrates how she uses the prism of work to render an analytical and critical spectrum on society.

CHAPTER SEVEN

"Words on Work": Harriet Martineau's Sociology of Work and Occupations—Part II: Empirical Investigations

Susan Hoecker-Drysdale

HARRIET MARTINEAU'S INVESTIGATIONS OF INDUSTRIES AND OCCUPAtions were conducted over several decades of growth and expansion in the British industrial economy. The present chapter focuses on Martineau's empirical studies in terms of what they reveal of the sociological dimensions of her research on occupations and industries. Her analyses of work and occupations appear in a number of genres, fiction and nonfiction, and include philosophical reflections on work as a human activity as well as studies of economic activities in a variety of cultures,—Britain, America, Ireland, and the Middle East. These empirical studies resonate with the presuppositions (outlined in Chapter Six, this volume) concerning the changing nature of work and the evolving division of labour in Victorian England, the new processes of machine production, the interface of science and nature, and the transformations in societal relations emanating from the workplace. A brief discussion of the British economy at the time will contextualize Martineau's studies.

NINETEENTH-CENTURY BRITISH INDUSTRY

Industrial capitalism was approaching its zenith in the 1850s when Martineau conducted a major study of Birmingham industries. The critical development of the new machine age had been the steam engine, which one estimate placed at 500,000 in Britain by 1850. Mechanization occurred first and most quickly in the cotton industry, as measured by the numbers of steam-powered spindles and looms. "By 1838 over four-fifths of English cotton mills were steam powered" (Mathias 1969: 133). Steam-driven mechanization spread quickly to other areas, particularly iron-making, printing, and threshing. Nevertheless, in these and many other processes of production, work continued in the traditional modes, much of it done by artisans, skilled and unskilled labourers, and families in homes and workshops. Moreover, aside from a few large industrial firms, the majority of workers at mid-century were employed in small mills and factories of fifty to two hundred employees. The degree of mechanization varied dramatically within industries such as textiles: high in cotton and worsted manufactures before 1850 and low in silk and linen industries (Berg 1980: 20–31). In some industries like the metal trades, work continued to be done largely by hand well into the second half of the century. Still other industries like leather manufacture, shoemaking, glove and hatmaking, and reinmaking involved largely skilled labour, which was changed less by mechanization than by transformations in the division of labour.

As Maxine Berg (1980: 29) points out, "mechanisation in early nineteenth-century Britain was a complex and uneven process: large parts of the country and many sectors of the economy were changing very slowly, and even in the most rapidly transforming areas there were many surviving legacies." The result was an industrial structure with establishments of various sizes and degrees of mechanization, but with an expanding and increasingly differentiated division of labour, new trades related to new products for consumption, shifting locations of the labour force, and increasing degrees of specialization within many occupations and trades. Nevertheless, traditional production in many industries remained strong well.

Agriculture continued to be a major player in the economy, even as it was changing, with new technologies on farms requiring skills rather than simply brawn. Rather than a simple, direct shift in the economy from agricultural to industrial production, agriculture sustained itself and contributed in the rural context to industrialization, through an improved supply of workers and families, food, community security, and new tools of food production. The family remained the major unit of production, whether on the farm or in the artisan workshop or factory, but the participation of women in the paid labour force increased with the development of greater specialization and centralized production in factories. Work assumed a gendered character: women were given repetitive, labour-intensive, often menial and burdensome, tasks in the factories, while men ran the machines which had eliminated much of the drudgery.

Industrial growth was an uneven and not necessarily progressive result of mechanization. The consequences of these "scientific and mechanical" changes for the members of society—labourers, their families, large and small business owners, women as well as men, and children who laboured—were increasingly controversial, precipitating first Luddism (1811–1816) and later Chartism (1838–1848) and strikes, as workers struggled to come to terms with the inevitable development of mechanized production in factories and on farms and with the decline in working conditions. Issues of health and safety, work hours, wages, child labour, education and training led to the increased need for, and controversy over, unions or "combinations" in most new or changed occupations and industries.

By mid-century markets and the new commerce were becoming international, rather than simply national, bringing concerns about the consequences of competition in international trade. It became clear that complex interconnections had developed among technology, labour, investment, production, trade and commerce (distribution and consumption). In the midst of these developments, the writings of Adam Smith (1759; 1776), Dugald Stewart (1829; 1854–60), and J.R. McCulloch (1824), as well as Karl Marx and Friedrich Engels (Marx 1844; Marx and Engels 1846, 1848), took on new intellectual and political significance in the emerging field of political economy.

MARTINEAU'S PERSPECTIVE ON WORK

Martineau had a strong interest for many years in the arenas of work, occupations, and industries and their social consequences. In Chapter Six we saw that the presuppositions underlying her perspective are rooted in her *belief in progress*, specifically the possibilities and opportunities for a better life for all, better working and living conditions, more consumer goods, an expansion of education for the working classes, children, and women, better health and health care, and therefore, increased longevity. She was interested in cultural, economic, and political enrichments for building more democratic societies. This meant, of course, the overcoming of certain distinctions and discriminatory practices related to factors of class and gender, and implied the enlargement of opportunities for subordinate groups: women, workers, racial minorities. Underpinning this belief is the conviction that progress *will* make these developments a reality. *A belief in the promise of technology* constitutes another central value in her perspective. She shares the cautious optimism of Smith and Malthus and even of Marx; for Martineau, like Marx, was able to envision a future where machines perform the monotonous routine tasks, leaving humans to pursue work and other activities toward self-development.

As a political economist and sociologist by practice, she carefully observed the new technologies and subsequent reorganization of production, and the proliferation and specialization of occupations as the division of labour expanded and became more differentiated. She elaborated on Western tendencies toward what Mannheim (1940) calls functional rationalisation in industry and the need for self-rationalisation in work, and frequently lectured the public on the desirability of a personal, self-regulated lifestyle, required, she believed, for any kind of occupational or economic success. At the same time, she examined the consequences of industrialized work and a specialized division of labour for workers and their families, for men, women, and children, recognizing that alienation and abusive working conditions had to be addressed.

MARTINEAU'S METHODOLOGY

Her Objectives

In her scientific studies of work and occupations Martineau pursues a number of implicit objectives: (1) to educate the public via detailed empirical descriptions of new occupations and industries in Birmingham, in England generally, and abroad, including historical background, the role of technological change and economics; (2) to analyze changes in the division of labour, the social structure of the workplace, and the challenges to nature precipitated by industry, frequently using Census data and government documents in addition to results of her own investigations; (3) to explore various occupations sociologically in descriptive, prescriptive, and relational terms; and (4) to critique and advocate, as she both reveals and deplores the work conditions and social situations of slaves and women, women's work deprivation, workers' rights, the exploitation of children, work and family life, safety, and health and physical well-being.

Indeed her studies can be seen as two-fold, centering around work and occupations, on the one hand, and investigations of industries, on the other. In conducting empirical studies in a variety of industrial, artisan, and domestic contexts, Martineau addresses *work as a scientific object.* Work defined more specifically as economic activity becomes the central topic in her *Illustrations of Political Economy* (Martineau 1832–4). In these fictional tales designed to educate the general reader on the principles of political economy, she explores the interrelations of labour, capital and technology, the critical importance of the changing division of labour and economic diversification, the exigencies of labour-management relations, the merits and disadvantages of unions, prices and wages, and money and free trade, among other themes. She positions her didactic stories within new industrial and agricultural situations to instruct the public on how to deal with changing economic realities. She evokes a nominalist model of society in which economic cooperation and the identity of interests are paramount.

In her monumental study of American society, *Society in America* (1837) Martineau dedicates one entire volume of three to the economy, including agriculture, transport and markets, manufactures, commerce, and the morals (social and cultural structures) of each. Both here and in *How To Observe Morals and Manners* (1838b), the economy and all its aspects are seen as fundamental in shaping the life and culture of a society. In turn, occupations and industries, including agriculture, are to be understood within the larger societal context. Martineau shows the interconnections with regard to: historical development and expansion of industry and trade, agriculture and manufactures, land and land use and capital, health and the rates of production, gender and the division of labour, and human rights and productivity. She analyses relationships within class structures, the injuries and contradictions of class, and the impact of vices and virtues (morals) generated within the economic system, specifically with regard to slavery, manufacture and commerce. In 1838–1839 Martineau published several mini-volumes on domestic occupations under the title of *The Guide to Service* as part of the "Industrial Series" being published by Charles Knight for the Poor Law Commission. From this period on, and throughout her writings, Martineau would weave the study of occupations into her studies of other societies, of capitalism and modernity, of economics and politics, of women's status and experiences, of education, and of history.

Genres

As we have seen, her studies are built upon the themes of the centrality of work and occupation for the individual and the foundational nature of the economy in defining the relation between the individual and social structures. Martineau effectively used both fiction and nonfiction to examine the topics of occupations, industrialization and the new economy. In her political economy tales (1832–4), individuals act out economic principles while specific characters represent particular occupations or serve as advocates for certain industries. Her analyses on work appear as well in her investigations from 1834 of American society, Ireland (1852, 1859c) and the Middle East (1848), her small volumes on various occupations for Charles Knight's *Guide to Service*, in her portrayals of the occupations of governess and physician through the protagonists in her most successful novel *Deerbrook* (1839a), and in her later investigations of occupations and industries for *Household Words* after 1851. As many other writers, Martineau fluctuated between publications based on "fact-finding" and writing "stories" (fiction) to convey her ideas on economy and society, turning from one to the other as she tired of one particular approach (see Martineau 1877b). She was generally equally at home and successful in both, if one can judge by the size and breadth of her readership.

Her "words on work" are directed toward workers and employers as she instructs them on mutual expectations for domestic efficiency and harmony; toward entrepreneurs as she takes up the issues of production, trade, working conditions, global production and exchange; and toward the general public whom she educates about the new economy. For example, the

Guide to Service series were comprised of handbooks, didactic primers of a sort, instructing servant and employer all aspects of domestic employment, including duties at work, desirable working conditions and treatment of employees, and the importance for both parties of meeting responsibilities. Similar studies of occupations appeared in her many articles in *Household Words*; her studies of industries provided detailed accounts of new manufacturing processes. In a number of journal articles Martineau reviewed studies of work; she critiqued their methods and findings, emphasizing factual issues and questions needing further examination (see Martineau, 1838a, 1859b, 1861, 1862). She included considerable sociological analysis of the structures and processes in these "modern" occupational and industrial contexts.

Methods and Analysis

In these diverse writings on work, she turns to empiricism—to such methods and techniques as direct observation, interviews, oral histories and life stories, use of official documents, census data and other sources of contemporary statistics, and historical records of all sorts. In addition to her historical and empirical approaches, she often analyses work and occupations and industrialization cross-culturally, either for comparative analysis or to show the global nature of the modern economy. She makes considerable use of typologies and a variety of classificatory schemes for analysing and comparing occupations, as will be seen in the discussion below. Martineau strove to obtain the most precise and useful data available and to base her analyses on her own observations and interviews as much as possible.

Industrial Studies

Soon after her return from America she agreed to Charles Knight's request to contribute to the *Guide to Service* series because it served the needs of public education and of social science, and, not incidently, the goals of the Poor Law Commission. Likewise, in 1851, having been strongly urged by Dickens to contribute to *Household Words* and having spent some time in Birmingham with her brother Robert, a highly respected brass founder, and his family, she proposed a series of articles on Birmingham manufactures (Martineau 1877b, II: 67): "a full, but picturesque account of manufactures and other productive processes . . . both for instruction and entertainment."

In her studies in Birmingham, Martineau selects industries which not only represent the new economy of production and trade, new use of raw materials, and new directions in consumer products, but which also demonstrate innovations in manufacture, new production technologies. In undertaking her investigation of Birmingham industries, as with her occupational studies, Martineau observed the principles of research which she had articulated in 1838 in *How To Observe Morals and Manners*. She systematically identified what she wished to study and why, what she wanted to know about the objects of investigation, how she would collect her data, and how she would analyze the material for her readers. With a maid, a sister, or a niece to serve as a research assistant (and an extra set of ears), Martineau set out to observe, interview, collect statistical data, and describe the major industrial scenes in Birmingham in two different periods in the winter of 1851. It is apparent from her articles published in *Household Words* from 1851–1854 that she followed an organized research protocol, exploring systemically the history, context, development, and current operations of these industries. In each case she studies the details of the production processes, later explaining them to the reader as fully as possible, as she analyzes the labour situation, wages, working conditions, gender and the division of labour, skill levels of the labour force, and the relation between factory production and the family's work-life. She notes the connections of these industries with other countries, in terms of raw materials and markets. Where possible she includes comparative or related data from other sources, in addition to her own empirical observations.

STUDIES ON WORK AND OCCUPATIONS

In addition to her studies of industry for such publications as *Household Words*, Martineau carefully examined a considerable number of traditional, new, and changing occupations. For each occupation, social roles and role behaviour were examined. Describing the details of work activity in each case, Martineau pointed out instances of (what we would now call) the overabundance of roles, as with the maid of all-work, nurses, and other women's occupations. She explored matters of social relations at work, job security, health and the quality of working conditions, the impact of occupation on families and family life, the changing nature of the class system as both effect and cause in the new occupational order, and gender relations, including population data, historical factors, and data on the consequences of technological change.

In these studies she makes use of occupational typologies to distinguish, for example, differences and similarities in various kinds of domestic work or teaching occupations. In the work sphere, she identifies types and categories of occupations to facilitate analysis and comparison of traditional occupations, changing occupations, and emerging occupations for women as well as men. In these studies, occupations were sites for understanding and analysing the increasingly differentiated division of labour and its consequences. The several categories of occupations included domestic service, agricultural occupations, service occupations, teaching, husbandry, seamstressing, emerging occupations as steel grinder and policeman, traditional professions-governess, baker, artist, and changing occupations-soldier, sailor, nursing. Within these occupations and industries (farming, fishing, textile manufacture, teaching, etc.) subtypes of occupations are identified, determined either by Census classifications or Martineau's own analysis. Often impatient with the difficulties of using Census data, she wrote a number of articles criticising the reporting system which tended to "lump" disparate occupational groups together, making analysis difficult. At the beginning of the nineteenth century, "the occupations of the residents were roughly set down,—as agriculture, manufacturing and trading, and neither" (Martineau 1854d: 341). Over a lifetime of work on occupations, Martineau gave much attention to women's occupations, in part because she herself was a woman earning her own living, and, in the main, because women's accessibility to acceptable work was so problematic in that era (Martineau 1859b: 151–73).

The Frame of Martineau's Studies

In analyzing the many aspects of the changing division of labour and the new technologies of production, Martineau reveals the possibilities and the opportunities which these new developments offer. At the same time, and no less importantly, she identifies their inherent and consequential problems. Displaying an astute sensitivity, her work can be seen as critical sociology, an interrogation of the effects of the dramatic economic transformations unfolding in Britain and in the Western world (see Polanyi 1944). We can identify the following problematic sociological dimensions of the emerging economy which comprise the foci of these studies: (1) the division of labour especially its organization or reorganization and the broad subject of working conditions, together with the new technologies of production; (2) the meaning of work as it results from these changes; (3) gender and class relations and work; (4) work and family life; and (5) nineteenth-century globalization and international trade.

THE DIVISION OF LABOR

The Organization of the Division of Labour

Predating Durkheim's proclamation in 1893 in his introduction of *The Division of Labour in Society* to "equip yourself to fulfill usefully a specific function" (Durkheim 1893: 4), Martineau declares that each individual must qualify her/himself to work in modern occupations. Although influenced by Saint-Simon's idea that each individual's place in society is determined by one's work and that each should have useful work to do, she rejects his authoritarian model. She contends that work and individual growth, as well as a progressive division of labour, are impossible when some of society's members are enslaved, indentured, neglected, or ignored (Martineau 1837, II: 293–369). Modern society, she believes, provides the possibility for greater freedom and positive control over one's work, but the modern worker must also accept responsibility for performing the work competently. Within the structures of an increasingly differentiated division of labour in nineteenth-century England, Martineau believed that each individual had rights and responsibilities, accruing to participation in modern society, through some means of education and training, and access to some kind of work. We have seen in Chapter Six that her theory of work included propositions regarding work and the realization of the self, work as a natural and necessary part of life in society, and work as the vital link between the free citizen and the state in a modern division of labour. And so, like Durkheim and Weber, she recognizes that the new division of labour is built upon the unit of the free individual and therefore less upon traditional groups of workers, composed of family members, traditional artisan groups, or members of the community.

Work in the emerging economy was being rationalized in many respects, as shown in many of her studies. The problem in the new division of labour is that work, in American society particularly, was increasingly split between head work and hand work, manual work being considered repulsive and to be avoided (*Ibid.*). However, she was optimistic that the honour of work would in the long run be sustained by that democratic culture. To be denied work, as privileged American women were at the time, she considered to be the gravest insult to intelligent individuals.

Martineau deals at length with the impact of technology in reorganizing work, the effects of time and place on the structure of work, and the increasing significance of elements of class and gender in changing the world of work. She sees an absolute necessity to resolve the problems of modern employment by, for example, clear contractual agreements between employer and employee and better employee preparation, training, and education for work.

Even given the impact of technology, the division of labour was in rather gradual transition, and therefore contained elements of the traditional as well as the emerging world of work. Nor had the structures of work become centred wholly around manufactures. She recognized, for example, the continuing importance of agriculture. "The first head of industry is always Agriculture" (Martineau 1859b: 154). Agricultural occupations, far from disappearing, are changing in Martineau's day due to technological innovations and better farming practices. Agricultural occupations included the dairy maid (the largest category of independent female agricultural workers), housemaid, poultry maid, market gardeners, florists and nursery gardeners, itinerant agricultural labourers—haymakers, reapers and binders, hop-pickers—, farmers of both sexes, husbandmen and women, bee-mistresses, cidermakers (*Ibid.*; 1859b: 154–6).

While the work remained physically demanding, the quality of production had improved along with less strenuous human effort. But in those days of the Corn Laws and Poor Laws, agricultural labourers had low wages, high rents, and ultimately heavy responsibilities as the inevitable large family came along. Living quarters were inadequate for agricultural laborers, who were poorly educated in farming practices. Issues of equal pay and employment equity for male and female workers existed. Women's work in the agricultural context, Martineau shows, was often more arduous than men's work, partly because the latter were mainly involved in operating machinery. In some areas, such as dairy work, men were replacing women by the late 1850s. She points to the lack of understanding by the urban population of the difficulties faced by farmers. Martineau's optimism lies in the observation that this "vocation is now becoming one of skilled labour; and . . . qualifications and . . . wages must both rise" (Martineau 1861: 149).

Old and New Occupations

Martineau studied traditional but rapidly changing occupations, such as the soldier and the sailor, as well as new or changing occupations, such as the statesman, the artist, the policeman, the steelgrinder, in which the factors of technology, bureaucracy, psychological factors, stress and anxiety, pressures to produce, new health and safety hazards and environmental challenges were increasing.

Her discussion of the occupation of the statesman anticipates much in Weber's 1919 lecture on "Politics as a Vocation" (Weber 1946: 77–128). Politics requires education for good thinking and oratory, for which the aristocracy may remain, in 1861, best qualified because of classical education and early training in "hard official life" (Martineau 1861: 149–58). Political effectiveness depends on a prudent, temperate life, knowledge and experience of politics, and a character which is focused and free of anxieties and concern for others' opinions. Ambition is to be avoided:

> . . . heart-breaking discouragement is scarcely possible for a statesman who is sincerely and devotedly the servant of his country, and the well-wisher of every interest in it. If he can work towards his end, he must obtain more or less success: and if he is precluded from doing it, he yields up the responsibility to others, and still contends, for the satisfaction of the struggle. A steady will and a calm temper are almost certain of success. . . .

> We give up the great soldier on the battle-field, and the noble sailor at sea, in the moment of victory . . . . It need not be so in the field of political administration. There a man need not do and die. *He may do and live: and this is his duty, no less than his privilege.* (*Ibid.*: 157, my emphasis)

Political life has traditionally been unhealthy, she reminds the reader, because of the life style and the potentially corrosive nature of politics. In her pedantic manner Martineau maintains that the politician will survive and thrive "when the mind is . . . full of noble aims, and the heart of rational hope, while the intellect is kept equably at work on the highest order of business . . . " (*Ibid.*). Her descriptions of the devastating pressures and anxieties of office are, for us, quite contemporary.

Martineau was interested in new occupations, or those of new importance, as she studied the changing division of labour. The steelgrinder is an example of the first, and the policeman and the nurse of the second. She was concerned with the potential for upgrading occupations, for making them more professional, more effective and safer.

Working Conditions

It is difficult to analyze separately Martineau's discussions of working conditions in the new economy because, in fact, this concern constitutes a major theme throughout her writings. Included in this category are the actual parameters of the work situation itself, issues of wages, training, hours, technology, health, safety, and environmental consequences. Both the organization of the division of labour and the subsequent working conditions were affected by these, as well as factors of bureaucracy, psychological elements, stress and anxiety, and pressures to produce. As Martineau (1838a) argues in her article on "Domestic Service," the hazards to good relations at work and to health are, in a very real sense, everyone's responsibility. Nonetheless, she identifies particular problems which must be addressed by employers: low wages, long hours, overwork, employees' need for leisure and freedom from employer control. Employees, in turn, must avoid intemperance, anxiety, unnecessary impediments to good work performance; in other words, they must enhance self-rationalization. Workers should be able to enjoy the sympathy, if not empathy, of the employer. "Who that does not live by manual labour understands the feelings of those who do? How many of the hundreds of thousands of employers reflect on the early life of the servants they hire, and make allowance for them accordingly?" (*Ibid.*: 424).

Solutions for these problems, suggested by Martineau, include: promotion of the "prospects of rising" which can be perceived by the employees; the definition of work as honourable; an attitude of "the blessedness of work"; the establishment of a court of appeal for workers; and provision of health care for servants, and care in old age. Certainly in the case of domestic service which was demographically a large group in the 1830s, but also within the other occupational classes, she maintained that more research was needed into the psychological and social aspects, the cultural variations, and the factors of social causation underlying the experiences of employee and employer.

Martineau uses the occupation of the baker to address issues of the material conditions of work in Victorian England, which, in the case of British factories and home industry alike were less than desirable in the 1850s: dust in the air from flour, coal, or metal shavings, loud noises from primitive machinery, unprotected machinery precipitating many accidents, crowded work spaces, extreme temperature changes, bad lighting, heavy weights, and excessive work. In comparing industries in terms of illness and absenteeism, for example, she finds:

> There are four trades that are more sickly [than bakers], and nineteen that are less so. . . . [F]rom 20 to 70 years of age, the bakers claim for 178 weeks of sickness . . . nearly three years and a half of such illness as renders them unable to work. The very most burdensome class is that of the potters, who are ill for 333 weeks of the same period; and the best are the clerks and schoolmasters, who claim for 48 weeks, or less than a year. But these figures do not show the full strength of the case. The clerks and schoolmasters are, in large proportion, living at nearly or quite the end of the term; whereas the potters were, for the most part, dead in a few years from the outset, and the bakers disappear, on the average, before the middle of the term. (Martineau 1861: 219)

The subtext of Martineau's analysis of "The Baker" is the theme of the efficacy of specialization, "the economy of division of employment" (*Ibid.*: 215). Commercial baking has become an occupation of increased importance for women, she observes, not because they are joining the profession but because of rising female employment in the workforce. Martineau makes the argument (reiterated decades later by Charlotte Perkins Gilman) against women having to reproduce in each home everyday the same cooking processes. In other words, the commercial production of foodstuffs was becoming a rational and necessary good. Unfortunately for bakers, "modern" bakeries, often underground with little light and air, were less than desirable workplaces in the 1850s.

> The men grow hoarse; they lose voice; they become short of breath; they spit blood, and die consumptive. . . . while the London builders were striking for ten hours' wages for nine hours' work, the bakers are agitating for twelve hours' work—which was a reduction very startling to the masters. . . . The

> average life of a journeyman baker ends at 42: some say at 40. (*Ibid.*: 219–20)

She looks to technology and faster methods of production as the hope for a reduction of hours and to healthier workplaces in the future.

Health, Safety and Environmental Issues

In her exploration of work and industry Martineau, like Marx, takes up matters which have to do with health and safety in the workplace, important elements in working conditions as we have just seen, and with the impact of economic production on the environment. As in other contexts, she reveals a deep interest in the natural world and in man's effects upon it. Her writings on health and occupation extend throughout her career as do those on food and diet, illness, health care and sanitation, and personal health practices (Martineau 1836c, II: 248–65; 1844b, 1845, 1849, 1859a, 1865).

In a series of articles in *Once A Week* on various occupations, Martineau focuses on work and health issues. The importance of a proper diet and desirable living and working conditions is fundamental to her discussions. And so she is very impressed with the agency of working girls in American textile mills who have created healthy, agreeable communities and living habits (Martineau 1844a). She is critical of the lifestyles of workers who dissipate themselves off the job and the dangers to which they expose themselves because of poor habits.

In analyzing conditions of health and safety for a range of workers from the statesman, the policeman, the steel grinder, and the artist, Martineau recognizes the almost inherent occupational hazards, particularly the psychological dimensions which are part of art, politics, policework, and manufacturing. In her view, the worker or employee must be proactive in dealing with them. For example, in the teaching professions the greatest threats to good health are personal anxieties about money and the privations of close friends and relatives, privacy, and personal freedom. The four types of teachers—schoolmistress, daily governess, family governess, specialized teacher—as defined by Martineau, experience somewhat different problems, but generally suffer from marginalization and lack of qualifications, which she maintains may be a significant cause of the disproportionate insanity and alcoholism among governesses, for example. As in the modern era, teachers of all sorts are among the poorest paid:

> What can be the state of nerves of a woman who, by laborious and precarious means, is earning a present subsistence, with no prospect whatever before her at the end of a few years, and no particular relish for the time which lies between? She cannot avoid hearing the dreadful stories that we all hear . . .

> of old governesses, starved, worn out, blind, paralytic, insane, after having maintained relatives, educated nephews and nieces, put themselves out of the way of marriage, resisted temptations of which no one but the desolate can comprehend the force, and fought a noble fight, without receiving crown or tribute. (Martineau 1861: 197)

Martineau also studied traditional but rapidly changing occupations, such as the soldier and the sailor. The benefits are many: travel, pensions, constant pay, balanced workload, lodging and daily needs met, security of income. Health and welfare problems dress, diet, daily routine were being attended to, but much room for improvement existed. Her important treatise on *England and Her Soldiers* of 1859 is an analysis and exposé of life and health in the military. Martineau had been corresponding with Florence Nightingale on the issues of health, housing, and medical care in the military and had launched a major publicity campaign in support of Nightingale and her request for government and public commitment for improvements. The problems ranged from lack of nurses, medical personnel, and equipment to weaknesses in the administration of sanitation and military hospitals. Clearly, she was making the case for modern military practices, for professionalization, particularly in terms of health, and all that that implied with regard to the training, preparation, and operation of military personnel at all stages. Some of the solutions were bureaucratic: greater coordination and exchange between the Military and Medical Departments, the establishment of Hygiene as a separate Department (more soldiers were killed by problems deriving from poor hygiene than from wounds in battle), thorough and practical military medical education, establishment of general hospitals abroad and at home, establishment of the Army Medical Department whose rules and regulations are related to its function rather than to military structures as a whole, and improved organization and provision of Supply, so that the tragedies of disorganization of the Crimea will not be repeated (Martineau 1859a: 270–82).

Sailors experienced a slightly different occupational context, many of the problems having been identified and tended to. Health and diet on ship had to be addressed, as well as means for allaying boredom on long voyages with entertainment, reading, and schools. The greatest health hazard for sailors was their own indulgence in excesses while on shore. It is ironic that she commented on the "health hazards" of philandering military personnel several years before the Contagious Diseases Acts of 1866 and 1869, which blamed women for venereal disease among the military and instituted laws to harass and punish them. Martineau participated in the campaign led by Josephine Butler against the Acts. Sailors, she observed in an earlier article, were generally and strongly attached to their profession (Martineau 1861: 253).

With regard to environmental issues, Martineau, like Marx, understood that humans must live off of, as well as with, nature. She took an almost romantic delight in describing humans' use of nature, as in her light essay on "The Life of a Salmon," which expounds on the life cycle of this species in a sympathetic and informative account (Martineau 1861: 326–35). Her articles on "Our Farm of Two Acres" (*Ibid.*: 269–313) elaborate on proper agricultural practices of terrain and tillage, dairy and meat production, and the poultry yard to enhance the returns on one's work and to knowledgeably work with the natural world.

These were very popular articles indeed, along with those which dealt with the impact of weather patterns and changes in nature on food production, such as 1859 articles "Flood and Its Lessons," "Drought and Its Lessons," and "The Weather and the Price of Food in 1860" (Martineau 1861). Noting the inequality of rainfall and water supplies generally throughout England, she recalls the rare occasions of flooding in years past. She points to the increase in tillage and pasture and the drainage of the fens, an issue existing even today, which have precipitated changes in water systems and a lack of control, such as in planned arterial drainage. The result was the flooding of land, particularly in valleys. Humans had damaged the natural water-courses, put up dams for steam power unthinkingly, and failed to set up systems of drainage. In the situation of drought, alternative measures were required to reserve water and to use irrigation systems to distribute water properly. In the face of seemingly uncontrollable natural events, information and strategies would have to be disseminated to ensure the necessary food supply without waste or further environmental damage, according to Martineau. Consideration must be taken as to what products would best be imported. Among other measures she sites the need for greater knowledge of meteorology and better practices of drainage and irrigation to compensate for "the irregularities of the seasons," doing so "by the devices of human forethought" (Martineau 1861: 379).

As a keen observer of nature, Martineau, throughout her writings, traces its impact on the economy as its major resource. This sensitivity to the links between humans, their diets and food supply, the economy, and the ultimate well-being of society, exhibited by many in Martineau's generation, contrasts with our current assumption that the new industrial economy ignored all considerations of the environment, conservation, and the general balance of nature. Precisely because, as has been discussed, industrialization emerged gradually, in uneven and often reticent patterns, humans' awareness of their dependence on nature and of the effects of the economy on nature predominated. The important role of agriculture in industrialization reinforced a continuing concern with the uses and limits of nature, and the ways in which these determine importation policies, trade relations, and labour supplies.

One of the industries closest to her heart is bobbin production, in large part because of the presence of a bobbin mill in Ambleside. Barrels, hoops, posts, rails, and bedsteads were also products of the industry. Here she paints a romantic picture of industry in a rural setting (Martineau 1861: 442):

> This is not much like visiting Birmingham or Manchester manufactories. For the muddy canal, we have a cataract of water "softer than rain-water," the proprietor assures us, and clear as starlight. The very sight of it, slipping over the weir, and drowning the stones below, makes one thirsty. Instead of the coiling smoke, we have the balancing gossamer above the stream . . . Instead of attic-windows opposite, we have the old rookery. The rooks are our spies and gossips here; and they and the babbling waters seem to be telling tales against each other, all the year round . . . We asked the proprietor whether he had ever to complain of want of water. "Very rarely, indeed," said he.

But she is quick to point to the inevitable clamor of industry:

> "And the noise; is it always like this?" . . . "O yes" . . . perhaps his men do not know what an infernal din they are living in, with those circular saws, and the whirring of a multitude of wheels and lathes. (*Ibid.*)

She observes the large stacks of timber and poles—beech, ash, mountain-ash, sycamore, "seal" (sallow), hazel, birch and alder. Remarking on the Ambleside "industrial" scene including the mill proprietor Mr. Horrax's ivy-covered and flowered home adjacent, she writes:

> There is an unspeakable charm in seeing the commonest manufacturing toil cheered and brightened by the presence of that antique and ever-young beauty, which is supposed to be mournfully displaced by the establishment of the arts of life." (*Ibid.*: 443)

She quickly added that Ambleside suffers rather little from workers' intemperance. The process of bobbin-making is then described in detail (*Ibid.*: 444–6).

This scenario captures Martineau's perspective on industrial work. One must savour the beauty of nature even while using it. In the same way, one must use and benefit from new mechanized production by disciplining oneself both at and away from the machine. One must regulate one's behaviour off the job just as machines control one's activity at work, part of the self-rationalization theme suggested earlier. Industrial accidents are generally, she claims, due to worker negligence. Problems of humans' encounters with machines were seen as generally human-derived: carelessness, daring, stupidity, workers' negligence or dissipation (as a worker's "getting in the way of the machine"). It is clear that worker responsibility increases with the machine age.

THE MEANING OF WORK AND THE WORK ETHIC

The importance of the meaning of work on the individual level can be seen throughout Martineau's studies; that is, she assumes that some level of meaning and satisfaction is the right of each person. Furthermore, the meaning of work is played out in the relations of work between employer and employee, among employees, and in work activities in general.

The work ethic is a critical element in the new economy, as Martineau sees it, in guaranteeing high quality in the products, employment security, and good wages for the workers, as in the electro-gilding and plating industry, for example (Martineau 1861: 406–7):

> There may be seen nearly four hundred men and boys employed, diligently and constantly, upon work of so high an order, that the wonder is how, in the imperfect state of our popular education, so many can be found to manage such processes. . . . Here must be no Monday laziness after Sunday's rest; no caprice as to going to work or staying away. Like time and tide—like brewing and dyeing—the work at Messrs. Elkington's cannot wait for men's humours . . . . "We find you six days' work, and you are to find six days' labour." And the wages given are such as to justify this compact being made stringent. They rise from twenty-five shillings to three pounds a week, according to the nature and quality of the work.

Here again the theme of self-rationalization in relation to work activity is a prominent one.

MACHINE TECHNOLOGY AND THE RISE OF MANUFACTURES

A significant period in Martineau's explorations of work, occupations and industry began in autumn of 1851 when she began investigating Birmingham manufactures. Not only had she retained her interest in the expanding British economy and its social consequences, but since the days of the Reform Bill and political and class movements deriving from recent economic development, she was fascinated with Birmingham's industrial development as well as its leadership (see Berg 1985; Joyce 1980).

Birmingham may have been the "second" industrial center after Manchester, according to Eric Hobsbawm, but by 1850 it had developed into a significant producer (see Timmins 1866). Although a variety of manufacturers were to be found there, the metal trades were perhaps the strongest. Consumer goods and household items (jewelry, guns and pistols, buttons, buckles, chains, seals, rings, charms, snuff boxes, for example) seem to have been particularly predominant in Birmingham's industrial scene (Hobsbawm 1968: 34, 186; Berg 1985: 287–314). Birmingham's success has been attributed to geography, its unincorporated political status which meant fewer controls, its religious toleration, and its lack of transportation in the early stages, which accounted for its industrial growth and for the "predominance of the manufacture of small articles" by skilled workers and artisans (Berg 1985). Birmingham's dynamism can be seen in its predominance as a center for inventions and patents. Greater flexibility in employment regulations meant that apprenticed, non-apprenticed, and women and children's labour were used. Martineau, as Maxine Berg (1985) much later, shows that the division of labour became more gendered as new industries and machinery were introduced.

Martineau's studies of Birmingham industries contained descriptive details of actual production processes, including the treatment of raw materials, the workforce and the manufacturing division of labour, technological aspects of production, labour-management relations, equity issues, and health and safety. She provided historical background on each industry as well. In a political economy framework, Martineau discusses the economics of production and consumption, the need to balance supply and demand, competition in the marketplace, and the importance of scientific knowledge for industrial development. The sociological dimensions of these accounts are furthered in her examination of the social structure of work, occupational training which sometimes reflected the guild system, arduous work conditions, the impact of machine technology on workers, the intricacies of production, class consumption and saving, and issues of health, wages, and child labour.

Martineau investigated nine industrial sites and an evening school for women on which she submitted as many articles to Dickens. The articles were highly successful in informing the public of current developments in production; numerous industrialists requested that she visit their establishments. She continued her research which subsequently expanded into Scotland and Ireland and included matters of agriculture, health, transformations in nature effected by new industries, and selected occupations. Many of the resulting articles appeared in *Once A Week* and *Chambers's Journal* during the 1850s.

Of particular interest to Martineau were the historical roots of production. Birmingham's industries had developed in conjunction with agriculture over several centuries; and by the nineteenth century Birmingham was a major industrial centre in England. Indeed, many of the industries Martineau studied—brass, coppersmithing, glass, jewelry, buttons, guns, to name a few—had been established early in the eighteenth century. She understood the influence of not only geography, population, and agriculture, but also of the Nonconformists in building industrial enterprises of a variety of size. Economic historians have acknowledged the influence of the Huguenots in the seventeenth and eighteenth centuries to have been a significant factor in the emergence of industrialization in England, and particularly in establishing a community of toleration in Birmingham (see Court 1938; Berg 1985).

Martineau traces the early world history of specific industries which she investigated. In the case of needles, for example, she relates that Lebanon (Eden) was perhaps the first site of sewing, that Egyptians used needles of wood, American Indians, needles of porcupine quills and threads of deer sinew, and Greenlanders and South Sea Islanders needles of fish bone (Martineau 1861: 475). She points out that modern needles were first made by Elias Krause, a German who went to England (Whitechapel) in 1565, although the original steel needle is attributed to the Spanish (*Ibid.*: 476). In a brief history of arms, quite literally the first weapon of warfare, she crosses the globe and the centuries to show the prevalence of the bow and arrow and the sling and stone, and the sword "the cutting and thrusting instruments of battle . . . the most terrible kind . . . ," all replaced by the invention of gunpowder. Tracing the history of the musket, from 1520, to cannons, guns, pistols and revolvers, she comments not only on the crudeness of many such weapons but also on the current British policy of furnishing weapons around the world, often to fight British soldiers. She also considers weapons not used for manslaughter, such as the walking stick used to shoot birds, the whip gun which houses a gun in the handle, and the plantation gun used for the detection of poachers, which fires a blue rocket or warning ball. In other examples, she traces products such as window covers, whether made of glaze, shutters or parchment existing in various forms in England and various kinds of glass and its manufacture. Copper, apparently the most prevalent metal in the world, was used with tin to make brass by the ancient Greeks and Egyptians, and by Romans who imported the tin from England. Still used in varying degrees in many products, nineteenth-century England was importing copper from Australia and South America. The production and constant improvement of products were seen as part of the history of humans providing themselves with necessary and desired products.

The social organization of industry is a significant dimension of Martineau's investigations. She demonstrates her awareness of how mechanization has changed and enlarged that organization, moving from a medieval guild and artisan structure, as in the production of gold chain, to an increasingly specialized division of labour with incremental changes in the size and composition of the labour force in terms of gender, age and class (Martineau 1861: 451). While the factory system emerges in modernity in new centralized form, the artisan shop and family workroom not only remain but in some cases thrive. The example is given of artisan shops in the jewelry industry for instance, still thriving and producing high quality products (*Ibid*.: 455–6), the workshops typically attached to the home.

Nevertheless, the new industrial setting, according to Martineau, meant that pay for one's work is better, factories are "light and airy" places of enthusiastic workers (*Ibid*.: 470), workers enjoy pecuniary independence, and many employers invest genuine interest and resources in the workers. In the tradition of political economy she points out that the costs of improvements in the factory, such as additional water to run a fan which removes dust from the factory room in needles production, were often shared by employer and workers alike (*Ibid*.: 482). The fact that workers had to share with employers the costs of measures to improve safety and comfort at work has been verified by contemporary historians (see Court 1938; Berg 1985). Martineau agreed that continual improvement of the production system is necessary to remain in business; workers as well as employers must be forward-thinking, adaptable to change, and willing to sacrifice in the short-term for long-term gain. The relations between employer and employee must be cooperative, as must those among employees. Where this breaks down, as in John Hutton's London coach-manufactory where workers' jealousy and subsequent violence disabled a skilled co-worker, several workers lost their employment and the products were thereafter imported (Martineau 1861: 554).

Discussions of electro-gilding and plating in Birmingham give considerable details of the process from the designs to the molds, to embossing, castings, hand-decorating, soldering, smoothing and finally cleaning in potash. The products are burnished, finished and sent to the troughs for silver, where magnets and wires are used, or gild. Smoothing and polishing follows (*Ibid*.: 407–13).

In describing the weaving industry Martineau takes the reader through the processing and dying of the wool, which is teased, fanned, carded, combed, and spun before spinning and reeling, washing and drying with centrifugal force, and warping to prepare for weaving (*Ibid*.: 401). Preparation of silk for the making of cloth involves many steps: the raw gummy silk is thrown (twisted or twined), boiled, wrung, boiled again, bleached with sulphur, separated, dyed in an elaborate setup, wrung out, pressed and dried in a hot chamber. Thus are some six and a half tons of silk prepared for weaving each week (*Ibid*.: 415–20). The actual process of weaving involves making the looms, filling the spools, drawing and "reading in" the pattern, tying of cords or strapping, and weaving (*Ibid*.: 423–6).

The tracing of nail and screw manufacture is reminiscent of Adam Smith's discussions. The sheets of iron are cut into strips according to the length and width of the nails which are then produced as the sheets are fed into machines. One worker, called a "minder," tends four machines, assist-

ed by a boy for each machine, whom he must pay weekly (*Ibid*.: 432–3). The making of screws, curiously enough, involves some boys, but mostly women who run the machines which produce the screws, finish the threads, snip and "nick", making the slits on the heads, and worming, which makes the threads (*Ibid*.: 430–6). The screws must then be baked, dried, bolted, counted, and packed. Likewise, the manufacture of buttons is described in detail as she observes women working the machines which punch, drill, stamp, polish and finish buttons by the hundreds of grosses each day.

Martineau's personal knowledge and experiences as a seamstress, prior to becoming a writer, contribute to her enthusiasm about the production of covered buttons, stamped buttons, acorn buttons, and various kinds of pearl buttons. She traces the process of producing the latter, from the work of the divers who retrieve the shells from the ocean's floor to the ultimate product of pearl buttons and handles for knives and paper-cutters. At the time Birmingham, employing thousands of workers, supplied nearly all the world's pearl buttons. Buttons were finished off in kitchen industry as housewives sewed forty to sixty gross daily to stiff paper. Similarly her seamstressing experience is reflected in her investigation of needle manufacturing, a truly Smithian narrative. As she relates the production of 5,000 needles per hour and 10,000 heads per hour, each step from the cutting of wires to final packaging is carefully described and analyzed. The reader is reminded that Redditch remains the leading producer of needles precisely because people there do not shun new machinery and new ideas, as elsewhere.

The production processes of other industries—weaving, gun-making, glassmaking, copper products, wallcoverings, and watches—are described in extraordinary detail. Throughout, the advantages of mechanization, the division of labour, the efficient, non-wasteful use of resources, and the new availability of affordable consumer goods are reiterated. Martineau remained convinced that the technological revolution manifest in modern factory production would yield largely positive outcomes for society. She was particularly impressed with the quantitative increase in machine production over hand production, allowing workers to spend time in finishing products, as in the production of shawls:

> A capital machine now intervenes, with its labour-saving power; this time, of French invention. Formerly, it took two girls a whole day to cut off the refuse threads from the back of a shawl. But this machine, superintended by a man, does it in a minute and a half. (*Ibid*.: 504)

Ironically, the women in the shawl shop are still doing much handwork: darning over faults in the fabric, putting silk fringes on shawls, knotting, twisting or picking out knots and blemishes from the fringes, brushing, folding, and packing them. Exemplifying the almost universal trend in the gendered division of labour, the machines for cutting and steaming were operated by men, and the tedious and detailed hand-finishing was done by women.

GENDER AND CLASS RELATIONS

Martineau's studies of occupations began in the context of her studies of American society in which she gave particular attention to the employment and underemployment of women. For privileged (middle-class) women, she observed, "the sole business of woman" was wife and mother, neither of which they did especially well, in her view, for lack of knowledge and training. The absence of occupation for these women in America was the most significant factor in their economic and emotional dependence and almost infantilization. The women who worked, those unmarried and of modest or meager economic circumstances, were restricted by and large to seven occupations: domestic service, teaching, needlework, keeping boarders, mill work, typesetting, and bookbinding (Martineau 1837, III: 131–51).

We have then, in *Society in America*, the beginnings of Martineau's extensive research on women's work including her empirical evidence that "occupation" was equally important for women as for men, particularly in the new industrial economy. In 1834 Martineau (1837) observed the women working in the bookbinding trade as folders and stitchers who were self-supporting, but working in deplorable conditions. It is well known, of course, that Martineau was extremely impressed with the consequences of independent paid employment for women, in the case of the Lowell mill girls, for instance (Martineau 1844a; 1859b: 166). She sees the employment of women in industry as offering new opportunities both for financial rewards and self-development, on the one hand, and for exploitation and vulnerability of workers, especially women workers, on the other.

Edith Abbott (1906) showed that Martineau underestimates perhaps the significant participation of women in various employments in the United States even in the 1830s. However, Abbott emphasizes that women's participation in manufacturing and industrial work (at home and in organized factories) is significant in certain industries: the textiles, shoemaking, and bookbinding. Abbott points out that Martineau was not, in *Society in America*, surveying women's employment specifically, but rather developing a critique of a culture which rather systematically discouraged or prevented women from realizing economic independence, development of occupational skills, and therefore their self-realization in general. In Martineau's chapter on women's occupations, she reminds us of the hardships for all:

> One consequence, mournful and injurious, of the 'chivalrous' taste and temper of a country with regard to its women is that it is difficult, where it is not impossible, for women to earn their bread. Where it is a boast that women do not labour, the encouragement and rewards of labour are not provided. It is so in America. In some parts, there are now so many women dependent on their own exertions for a maintenance, that the evil will give way before the force of circumstances. In the meantime, the lot of poor women is sad. (Martineau 1837, III: 147)

Martineau's theme focused on the need to recognize that many women work, that others need to find work, and still others should work to avoid the "forlorness of female idleness and the folly of pride in the gentility of idleness" (Martineau 1865: 409). Factors behind this view had to do with the reality of the increasingly low sex ratio (more females than males) in the United Kingdom as a result of male emigration, the growing proportion of female workers, especially of female independent breadwinners, and the necessity for women to make their own way financially. Women needed occupational opportunities because the changing times in Britain meant that women were increasingly self-supporting, often with several dependents.

As Martineau investigated different occupations and industrial settings, she analyzed and affirmed the significance she had already discerned of the gender dimensions of the division of labour, of employee relations, and of industrial organization. She identified discrimination, ghettoization, patriarchal practices, and the increasingly gendered division of labour which worked to exclude women from full participation in the workplace and therefore from an acceptable income (Martineau 1859b). Any work that women customarily do at home is poorly paid when done in the workforce, she found. Women's work, such as sewing, nursing, cooking, both is and is not professional, and therefore is likely to be considered little more than ordinary. Additionally, women's work is often invisible, as in the cases of agricultural labour, household labour, work in their husbands' businesses and artisan shops. Their work is difficult and burdensome. Lower paid women, such as the maids of all-work, are likely to carry heavy workloads and therefore risk life and health.

In certain industries women were excluded all together. The exclusion of women from watchmaking by the men of Coventry, for instance, meant that British watches could not compete in cost to Swiss watches made by women in cottage industry (Martineau 1861: 491). Gender exclusion was breaking down in the ribbon industry, but in pottery factories men used subtle tactics to keep women uncomfortable and unwanted, such as not providing them with handrests while painting dishes and pots. Electro-gilding and plating is an industry well suited to women who are excluded for want of training. While she recognized that men remained the owners, managers, and supervisors of modern industrial organization and women furnished cheap labour in most of the non-machinized areas of production, she rejoiced that women had employment at all. Even working in rather unhealthy circumstances, as in the lacquering rooms in the brass works ("one wonders that they can be healthy, sitting in such a heat, and in such a smell"), the women earn good wages and have their own incomes (*Ibid*.: 570).

We have seen that Martineau's important articles on "Female Industry," "Domestic Service," "Modern Domestic Service," and contributions to *The Guide to Service* made significant contributions toward the understanding of women's employment in the nineteenth century. In her survey of Birmingham industries she describes the work of women which is, at the time, becoming increasingly prevalent and important. For example, in the manufacture of screws and nails, of which there are eight establishments in Birmingham, women are preferred in a ratio of ten to one to boys because "their attention is more steady, and they are more careful of their own flesh and blood" (*Ibid*.: 434). They are paid by piecework, operating the "worming" machines for the screws ("and can easily earn ten shillings per week"). But while Martineau delights in women's employment, she wonders if women can balance work and home for which they alone are responsible.

> As I turned away from the hundreds of women thus respectably earning their bread, I could but hope that they would look to it that there was no screw loose in their household ways, that the machinery of their daily life might work as truly and effectually as that dead mechanism which is revolving under their care, for so many hours of every day. (*Ibid*.: 437)

Martineau is committed to the idea that women must be able to fit into the new economy, as seen in her condemnation of women's so-called reluctance to learn about business. Perhaps she is really sharing the contradiction of women's desire or need for paid work and their responsibilities at home. In the manufacture of decorative home furnishings, for example, she observes that, although we might expect women to be more suitable by head and hand for fine finishing work, they comprise only a fourth of those workers. Why?

> The reason is, that women do not learn the business and stick to it, as men do . . . Girls . . . never . . . look upon it as the one settled business of their lives. They marry, or they think of marrying . . . it commonly happens that a home and a baby call them from the manufactory as soon as they have become thoroughly trained to their work. (*Ibid*.: 386)

In the making of gold chains women and girls again predominate, "bright and diligent," as she describes them. Martineau recognizes the strain of such work on the eyes:

> . . . very blinding work, but we are assured that it becomes so easy, by practice, that the girls could almost do it with their eyes shut. In such a case we should certainly shut ours; for they ache with the mere sight of such poking and picking, and ranging of the white rings . . . (*Ibid.*: 452–3)

Such a response is, rather uncharacteristically, both unsympathetic and naive, and critical and sarcastic.

Martineau considers the future prospects of women in industry to be bright as she observes that men have had to give place to women in several industries, as in the ribbon industry. And women will persevere as the guild traditions decline and they are given other opportunities to prove their talents. "The women will obtain whatever liberty of occupation is reasonable, because whatever is reasonable becomes practicable, sooner or later" (*Ibid.*: 492). Inroads are being made by wives of mechanics who learn the trade, and who, if not allowed to practice it, instruct their daughters in it. It is ironic that Martineau is, in some instances, quite sanguine about technology and industrialization as sources of women's economic improvement and freedom, even while indicating in many studies the ways in which women's work is generally considered unskilled, less valuable, and somehow secondary in production processes. As work is mechanized, men take over, and women are often left unemployed and deprived of income from the cottage industries which had been rather abundant (Berg 1985: 129–58). It must be remembered as well that occupational rights and opportunities did not exist for married women in most fields, so that to be a teacher, industrial worker, household servant or other worker and to be economically independent, one had to give up the idea of marriage.

Martineau's many discussions of women and work coincide with those of such astute contemporary economic historians as Maxine Berg, and the earlier Ivy Pinchbeck and Alice Clark who continued Martineau's work on women and industrialization (Clark 1919; Pinchbeck 1930). There can be no doubt that Harriet Martineau was among the first social analysts to call attention, as she did in many instances, to gender differences in the labour market and the workplace, about which we need to know much more.

Domestic Service

In the study of nineteenth-century occupations, domestic service could be considered important work by virtue of numbers alone. In the United Kingdom there were over a million domestic servants by 1831; 75 per 1,000 of the female population and 18 per 1,000 of the male population

(Martineau 1838a: 409). Underlying Martineau's studies of domestic service is the observation that

> . . . the peculiarity in the life of domestic service is subjection to the will of another . . . . The wages are given in return for the obedience of service quite as much as for the industry itself. (*Ibid*.: 411)

Martineau interprets service occupations, such as domestic service for example, as existing on a continuum between slavery and contract labour. She finds that in many respects, domestic service "combines some of the worst features of each: the requisition of obedience and subjection to caprice of the first, and the uncertainty of maintenance of the last" (*Ibid*.: 413). Domestic service can be used, she claims, as a paradigm for societal relations, "important in itself . . . and symptomatic of some things out of itself" (*Ibid*.: 408).

For Martineau domestic service is a critical site of class relations. Domestic service is an "exponent of the general relation between employers and employed . . . perhaps the mildest exemplification . . . of the opposition of interests and tempers between the two classes concerned" (*Ibid*.: 410). Martineau points out that relations between employer and employee are defined to a great extent by the historical and social contexts in which they exist. She contrasts the attachment in such relationships in Scotland, for example, where clan membership often means the two parties are related ("their service has a mixture of worship in it"), with Ireland, where the treatment and housing of servants is "wretched" and relationships are "treacherous," and, further, with America, where the same servants may find themselves in "a new state of things . . . they begin better . . . and rise in respectability in proportion as they gain an insight into their new position" (*Ibid*.: 416). Poisoning these relationships, particularly in the British context, are the factors of: (1) asceticism, often imposed upon servants by employers such that little of life's enjoyments are available; (2) the spirit of commercialism, which is "eminently selfish" and threatens mutual trust; and (3) the reserve and unsociableness of the British national character, which prevent offenses from being explained and anger from being dissipated (*Ibid*.: 419). The "evil of arbitrary rank . . . poisons all our social relations; and domestic service among the rest" (*Ibid*.: 414). In contrast, the American domestic enters into an agreement with the employer on "certain kinds and quantities of work for a certain amount of domestic provision and pecuniary recompense" (*Ibid*.: 428). Obedience is not part of the contract, servants are independent and voice their complaints where such exist. In brief, relations in the domestic realm reflect the historical reality of social interdependence in each particular society, but the causes of these differences "will sooner or later peremptorily demand research, contemplation and the forethought which it would be wise to exercise early" (*Ibid.*: 409).

Martineau's titles in Knight's 1838–39 *The Guide to Service* series included: *The Maid of All-Work*; *The Housemaid*; and *The Lady's Maid*. The series was intended to inform young people about their occupational options and to provide useful information leading, according to Martineau's intention, to improvement in skills and in "spirit and temper" in various departments of trade and service. Included in these didactic primers for domestic workers is Martineau's own sociological analysis of these occupations and the relations between employer and employee:

> If the publications . . . are grounded on such right principles, and conducted in . . . a just spirit . . . to ameliorate the relation between master and servant, they will be among the most permanently useful books of the time. (Martineau 1838a.: 410)

Her books in the *Guide to Service* series focus on various household occupations and emphasize issues of health and safety, as well as work responsibilities and obligations, which must be addressed by employer and employee alike. Attention must be given in the household to sensible dress, good diets, adequate sleep, fresh air and exercise, leisure time, and respect among household members. Opportunities in the new division of labour abounded in the many specialized roles connected with the household provided the necessary training or education was obtained. Martineau saw this development as only positive and encouraged women and men to avail themselves of these opportunities.

She contextualizes domestic work within the changing class structure and various household situations and develops a typology of domestic workers: maid of all-work, housemaid, lady's maid, dressmaker, charwoman, housekeeper, cook, nursemaid, gatekeeper, inn servant (excluding governesses and other teachers). Robert K. Webb (1955: 38–59) suggested that the *Guide to Service* writings fall within a middle-class genre designed as much to control as to inform the working classes in the evolving industrial society. That Martineau, by virtue of such writings, participated in that endeavour only reminds us that she was not immune from class interests and motivations. The guides were, in the end, training manuals, preparation for the duties of a household employee.

Nevertheless, her analysis of domestic relations concerned "the limits of obedience to the employer's will," particularly the all too frequent abuse of power exercised by the "woman of the house," as much as with improvement of the quality of work by the servant. The employer's exercise of power and control, or rather attempts to do so, extended into all aspects of the servants' lives. Women in particular, suffered from oversupervision in all affairs from dress to choice of friends with whom to socialize. As she emphasizes, "next to governesses, the largest class of female patients in lunatic asylums is Maids of All-Work" (Martineau 1838a: 423). Women who themselves are "suffering under arbitrary power" are ill prepared for their own use of power over female domestic servants. Nevertheless, Martineau remained optimistic that these relations could improve with proper education on all sides. "Cooperation is natural and practicable . . . obedience is spurious if it springs from anything but respect or love" (*Ibid.*: 413).

The "maid of all-work" is the classic case of a worker who suffers from an overabundance of tasks and resultant fatigue, and therefore loss of comfort, health, self-respect, adequate compensation, emotional deprivation, and lack of resources in time of illness. Martineau was correct in suggesting that labour associated with drudgery, overwork, and unhappiness is also poorly paid in wages and prestige—"the multifarious character of maid's work . . . oppresses her faculties more than the mere toil wearies her limbs" (Martineau 1861: 158–66). This solitary occupation, suggested by the title "maid of all-work" is found most frequently in families of lower rank. A penetrating psychological portrait of a typical maid-servant provides the clearest picture of the life of such a worker, her utter despair and loneliness and persistent alienation in her relationship with her employers (Martineau 1838a: 425–7). Martineau remains convinced that the difficulties of these relationships are a function of society in transition from an "empire of physical to that of moral force." Education and a constructive understanding of the nature and purposes of work on both sides will provide the route to improvement in these relations. Indigenous to all this is the problem of women's relation to work. Women are divided into two classes: "those who must work and those who need not or cannot." Until women's relation to work is equal to that of men, corruption and exploitation will typify domestic relations. The self-education of the employing class and the engendering of mutual respect are required for the domestic scene to change sociologically (Martineau 1838a: 432; 1838d).

Twenty-five years later, in an article on "Modern Domestic Service" of 1862, she reiterated many of her earlier concerns, as they had remained part of the domestic landscape. Domestic service was a continuing tradition in Britain. Maids of all-work constituted over 400,000 workers in the English census of 1860, by far the largest single category of domestic workers. Poor work conditions, health problems, little training, poor wages, sleep deprivation, and often destitution in old age remained serious challenges to the well-being of women in this occupation. The maid of all-work is a generalist; she has to do everything "somehow" and cannot be expected to excel in anything (Martineau 1859b: 158–9). Inevitably, the maid of all-work, who works hardest and longest hours of all household servants, continues to be paid the lowest wages. Women domestic servants, and especially maids of all-work, along with governesses, remained in 1862 over-represented among victims of insanity, ill health, and premature death.

In her 1859 analysis of "Female Industry" Martineau examines the entire phenomenon of women's work in Britain. Using Census data and nine reports and books on women's work in England and the United States, she explores women's participation in the major economic sectors: agriculture, mining, fishing, domestic service, service occupations, commerce, clothing, sewing and textiles, home manufacturing, governess, nursing, the arts. She reveals the growth in the number of women employed in these sectors: three million of six million adult Englishwomen are working for subsistence in 1859; two of the three million are self-supporting. With regard to domestic service, she develops a typology based on title, responsibilities, and pay and shows the inequities even within a largely female industry. She calls, therefore, for the removal of old obstructions with the aim in both national and private life to be "to provide for the free development and full use of the powers of every member of the community, . . . [including particularly] the independent industry of our countrywomen" (Martineau 1859b: 173). In both the *Guide to Service* series and in her analytical articles on work, Martineau is both educating employers and employees about the norms and practices of their relationships and asserting a sociological analysis of the historical and social factors operative in the work, especially domestic work, context.

Teaching

Martineau's typology of teachers includes the following: schoolmistresses, private (family) governesses, daily governesses, and special teachers of music, drawing, dance and other arts. In her analysis of each category in terms of responsibilities, prestige, control over one's work, and personal satisfaction, one sees the historical roots of contemporary prejudices (Martineau 1861: 188–202). Schoolmistresses enjoy greater control over their work and greater personal satisfaction, no particular health liabilities, but considerable prejudice, in fact social stigma and some shunning. She reports (Martineau 1861: 188) that families are reluctant to reveal that their wives or daughters work in education, and that the local book club of a London suburb prohibited anyone engaged in education as a subscriber! Enduring problems posed by students or parents are compensated by the independence which the schoolmistress enjoys.

The daily governess, a fairly large category of 60,000 in 1861, also enjoys the relief of living independently of employers. Although technically not overworked, she is fatigued if she takes her job seriously because she typically works in two or three families six days a week, twelve hours a day

(*Ibid*.: 190). She generally has some relatives to support and with whom, typically, she lives. New institutions, such as the Ladies Reading Room on Langham Place, were beginning to emerge to combat isolation and intellectual torpor for these teachers. The family governess, portrayed in Brontë and in Martineau's 1838 novel, is the best-known and perhaps most troubling of teachers. Martineau does not approve of the love-lorn governess in these portrayals whose privacy has been invaded and whose employers are seen as ogres. She believes this vocation, the most frequent choice in teaching employment, consequently suffers from too many bad governesses. Martineau, who considered becoming a governess but could not due to her hearing problem, condemns those who are "adventuresses" hoping to catch a husband, fawning liars and ignorant pretenders seeking bread and board, or victims of poor health looking for shelter (*Ibid*.: 193). She questions the assumptions that "to know a thing is to be able to teach it, and that intercourse with children is a thing which everybody is capable of" (*Ibid*.: 194). Doctors report a disproportionate occurrence of insanity and alcoholism among governesses. The causes seem to revert to lack of ability and preparation, and the strains of being with the children and of dealing with anxious parents. Financial strains and the absence of security in old age further contribute to the stresses of the governess (*Ibid*.: 197–8).

A major obstacle here is the absence of combinations (unions) for governesses until Sir George Stephens made it an issue. Although new financial institutions, including pensions, and counseling for governesses had been initiated, more needed to be done. Marriage itself is generally precluded. Qualifications and the public valuation of the profession required improvement. Nonetheless, Martineau regarded the occupation of governess, while requiring a good strong character and disposition and diligent, dedicated work, as an interesting and rewarding, if not remunerative, profession.

Needlework and Sewing

The third major occupation for women of the period was needlework and dressmaking. Martineau herself worked as a seamstress for a year following her father's death and prior to embarking on a writing career. This is the most oppressed class, according to Martineau, "the grief and shame of society from the day when Hood published the 'Song of the Shirt'" (Martineau 1861: 226). Because sewing is a universal feminine activity, professional seamstresses not only have to compete with the entire sex but also are consequently the worst paid. A major obstacle is the lack of training in the labouring classes. "In short, sewing both is and is not, a professional occupation" (*Ibid*.: 227).

The solution for the dismal prospects of seamstresses is technology—the sewing machine which will make the work endurable, the quality of the work better, production greater and cheaper, and the physical and moral strains of these poor women reduced. Reporting the 1851 Census data on seamstresses, Martineau reveals the increasingly specialized division of labour with more women in the paid workforce and the need, therefore, for more sewing to be "put out" to professional specialists. They are classified as dressmakers and milliners, the largest category (*Ibid.*: 202, 448), shirtmakers and plain sewers, glovers and hosiers, hat and bonnetmakers, shoebinders and sewers, and staymakers, plus a miscellaneous category (*Ibid.*: 232). Overwork and exploitation by privileged women remains one of the greatest problems for the dressmakers of such ladies. She describes (Martineau 1838a: 410) the scene in a large country house where ladies of high rank indulge themselves and place high demands on the dressmakers:

> They [the dressmakers] are for the most part young, and many have not done growing. It is near midnight of the second night of working when they should have been sleeping, and they are to sit through the whole of this night and the next day: that is, three days and two nights of incessant sewing; an occupation which cannot be safely pursued for more than a few hours at a time. These girls are fed high—roast beef, porter, port wine: the rooms are kept light and hot: every stimulus is applied. Three at once drop off their chairs fainting; they are plied with strong green tea, and they resume their work. As often as they are sinking, more strong green tea is given them;—their eyes are dim, their skin burns, their hands tremble, their voices are hysterical,—but the ball dresses are finished; and when they come to be paid for, more or fewer of them turn out bad debts. These are facts.

Given conditions among dressmakers at the time, Martineau recommends against entering the occupation. The same could be said about the handsewers (embroiderers) in Ireland. Again, she predicts that the sewing machine will bring an end to exploitation; "it can embroider beautifully already," although handwork will always be needed to some extent. It should not be long before the health of needlewomen is restored to the level of other occupations.

Nursing

Nursing is both a traditional and an emerging occupation in the time of Martineau and Nightingale. Caring for the sick was a long traditional activity but now the need, particularly in the context of the Crimean War, had increased significantly for knowledgeable nurses, "there is an immediate and urgent demand for many thousands . . . of trained nurses" (Martineau 1865: 412). The 1851 Census showed 40,000 nursemaids in Great Britain, mostly tending sick children, and about 25,000 attending sick adults. The proposal to fix the number of nurses at one to twenty-five patients seemed an impossible goal at that time. Martineau expresses surprise and regret that this particularly suitable woman's occupation is scanty in numbers and so poorly performed.

Nursing as a profession in Britain was officially born in 1860 with the opening of Florence Nightingale's School of Nursing at St. Thomas Hospital, London. Martineau shares with Nightingale, following the latter's encouragement, a commitment to campaign for sanitary reform and improved health care in both the military and civilian populations. Martineau's *England and Her Soldiers* (1859a), which utilized data provided her by Nightingale on the causes of mortality in the army during the Crimean War, made the case for better hygiene and the use of trained nurses among the military, who suffered far higher death rates from preventable diseases, unsanitary practices, and poor diet than from wounds. Thus she joins Nightingale's campaign to get public recognition of the need and importance of nursing as a profession and the need for better administration and organization in the hospitals. Good education and training would significantly improve the standards of treatment of the ill in a variety of care institutions as well as in the military. Martineau (1865: 411–12) considers nursing to be perhaps the greatest opportunity for women who need or want to work, within, of course, the framework of the qualifications needed to do quality nursing:

> Who would imagine that all the time there is a vocation for women almost entirely neglected in this country;—an occupation combining the advantages which Adam Smith represents as alternatives—of social repute and pecuniary profit;—an employment undisturbed by any jealousy of men, congenial with all the best instincts of women, universally honoured, and better paid than any other woman's work, except . . . that of queens and of actresses! . . . The occupation is Nursing.

In several articles in the 1860s Martineau campaigns for women to join the nursing profession by indicating the types and locations available for nursing, including, following training, work in country parishes among the poor, the village hospital, poor kitchens, workhouse infirmaries, family and home nursing, nursing in the colonies, monthly (maternal) nursing, military nursing. In terms of the content of nursing, her 1860 comparative review of Nightingale's [1860] *Notes on Nursing: What It Is and What It Is Not* and her own experiential *Life in the Sick-Room* (Martineau 1844b) provides a critical examination of what constitutes good nursing from the point of view of the nurse, on the one hand, and of the patient, on the other. Of particular concern is to bridge "this impassable gulf between the experience of the sick and the well" (Martineau 1860a: 409). The two books complement each another especially in their treatment of the sociology of the patient-caregiver relationship.

WORK AND FAMILY LIFE

Martineau's studies frequently explore the impact of the changes in industry and work on the social lives of workers and workers' families, on gender as it defines women's work and industrial positions, and on the lives of children. Perhaps the major underlying assumption about work realities for Martineau is the fact that paid work is a necessity for women as well as for men, and in many instances for children. She believes the conditions under which economic needs are met reveal much about the social order and the dynamics and politics of gender and families.

In the economy of her era, work units are either families or gendered units in a traditional division of labour. In the weaving industry, for example, men weave while women spin, wind and piece the fabrics. But typically, especially outside of urban areas, the entire family related itself to a particular industry, so that children moved into these work places as they matured and established their life's work. Martineau warns assiduously against such "family specialization" as it heightened the vulnerability of the family unit as well as individual family members, should the industry or factory close, cut back or excessively mechanize. Repeatedly, therefore, she stresses the importance of occupational and industrial diversification within families. From her early political economy tales she lectured the working classes about the importance of developing such strategies, of budgeting, of becoming literate, of seeking further training, and of saving for the inevitable hard times. She decried the absence of pensions and recognized that old age, particularly for women workers, is financially difficult.

Far from condemning the factory as a negative environment, Martineau saw it as a site of freedom and improvement. In analysing the Kendal weaving industry, for example, she claims that "the morals and manners of the mill-workers are superior to the weavers who do their work at home, . . . which is sadly small and unwholesome" (Martineau 1861: 397), although communities and regions vary somewhat on this count. The sociability of the factory contributes to good mental and physical health through conversation in noisy circumstances, which after all exercises the lungs! Workers form sports clubs which encourage wholesomeness of entertainment. Although irreligious herself Martineau notes the positive influence of the clergy and the church for the labouring classes. She commends the Kendal weavers who have resisted union representatives from the south, established themselves as a quasi-guild, and made an agreement with their employers on a moderate wage-rate with a compensation fund for the slack seasons (*Ibid.*: 396–7).

A nourishing leisure life is found among progressive working-class communities and work establishments. The importance of literacy and libraries for the working classes is a favourite theme of Martineau who directs a great deal of her writing to such audiences. She notes that the presence of libraries and reading rooms for workers, as in the Birmingham glass works, for example (Martineau 1861: 529), reduces the temptations of the public-house and increases worker improvement as well as the quality and length of family time:

> There the workman may enter at any hour during the day, and find a good fire, a table covered with newspapers and other periodicals, and some comrades reading the news. There is a good and increasing library; and the men may take the books home. . . .

In studying the industrial scene she surveys the issue of literacy and is encouraged to report in many cases, as in the Victoria Works needle factory in Redditch, the most progressive of the needle-producing communities, that worker literacy is increasing. The owner of Victoria Works hires no child under ten in his employment. Of the workforce in this case, "thirty-eight can read and write; fourteen read, but do not write; and only three can do neither" (*Ibid*.: 480).

In addition to feeding the mind, it is important, she reminds us, that workers and their families benefit from the availability of new consumer comforts, one of the significant outcomes of industrialization:

> We must hope that the improvement will proceed, and that, while dismissing from under their hands, to the houses of the great, the articles of luxury and beauty which Birmingham supplies, the men of Birmingham will aspire to have their own humble homes furnished with every needful comfort, and brightened by that intellectual enlightenment, and that peace of mind about their families and their future, without which neither luxuries nor comforts can yield any true and lasting pleasure. (*Ibid*.: 415)

Martineau analyzes the ways in which consumer goods are gendered, as in the case of watches. Sizable pocket watches are made to suit the preferences of Scottish males, while women's watches are "scarcely bigger than one's thumbnail. As little ladies' time is not supposed to be very valuable, it is not insisted that these should go well" (Martineau 1861: 494). The cultural meanings of goods and their social functions in various societies are fascinating to Martineau. For example, the universality of the shawl, with its differing class and economic gradations in various cultures, signals its importance as a product of exchange and expression whether manufactured or handmade, whether inexpensive or of the most exquisite and costly craft. Likewise, some items have become more available, less costly and therefore of practical rather than prestige value, as with carriages for instance (*Ibid*.: 559).

THE BENEFITS OF TECHNOLOGY AND GLOBALIZATION

Martineau is well aware that the national economic processes and changing structures which she is describing reverberate on the level of international trade and globalization. In contextualizing economic institutions in their larger contexts, she expresses her optimism about technology. In her description of the production of Birmingham jewelry we see Martineau's loyalty to Birmingham industry even in the face of others' prejudices against it. She notes the careful use of all materials to avoid waste, and declares her sense of injustice about the "middle men" who live off the labour of others, filling their pockets and driving prices up (*Ibid.*: 450). Although machines now do the work of cutting stones for jewelry, many steps and people are involved in the processes of jewelry and chain production. She explores the guild tradition, its transformation within modern industry, and the blessings which mechanization has brought to the workers:

> In 1830, the making of gold chains occupied a dozen or twenty people in Birmingham. Now the establishment we are entering, alone, employs probably eight times that number. Formerly, a small master undertook the business in a little back shop; drew out his wire with his own hands; cut the devices himself; soldered the pieces himself; in short, worked under the disadvantages of great waste of time, of effort, and of gold. Into the same shop more and more machinery has been since introduced as it was gradually devised by clever heads. This machinery is made on the spot, and the whole is set to work by steam. Few things in the arts can be more striking than the contrast between the murky chambers where the forging and grinding . . . are going on, and the upper chambers, light and quiet, where the delicate fingers of women and girls are arranging and fastening the cobweb links of the most delicate chain-work. (*Ibid.*: 451)

Martineau understands the significance of the expansion of world trade which affords both opportunities and threats to the British economy. While Britain must be aware of its own interests, world trade was becoming a reality which she generally endorsed. The detailed account of gold chain-making indicates her appreciation of a division of labour continually expanding as required for one product (*Ibid.*: 455):

> All this hard work; . . . all these scores of men, and women, and children, busy from year's end to year's end; all those diggers far away in California; all those lapidaries in Germany; all those engineers in their studies; all those ironmasters in their markets; all those miners in the bowels of the earth—all are enlisted in making gold chains; and some of us have no more knowledge and no more thought than to call the product "Brummagem shams!" [The

> latter is a pejorative term for Birmingham meaning "showy but inferior and worthless"—SHD]

Always the optimist on technological change, Martineau greets the progress in communication products and looks forward to a greatly improved future. In the technology of writing, for example, she imagines developments far beyond the primitive cedar pencil or the new ever-pointed pencil of her day, greeted first with enthusiasm and then skepticism as to whether it would be serviceable (*Ibid.*: 457):

> We are so saucy as to look beyond our improved pencils; beyond pen and ink; beyond our present need of a cumbrous apparatus to carry about with us . . . perhaps Electric Telegraph has spoiled us; enabling us to imagine some process by which thoughts may record themselves; some brief and complete method of making "mems," without the complicated process of writing down hundreds of letters, and scores of syllables, to preserve one single idea. All of this, however, is as romantic now as ever-pointed pencils seemed to be at first; and instead of dreaming of what is not yet achieved, let us look at the reality before our eyes.

Martineau imagines a technology not unlike the computer which she would likely have embraced—a technology enhancing communication and easing contact between people over large distances. A prolific author, she might have expanded even further her prodigious body of writing! Finally, it must be reiterated that Martineau observed and clearly understood the transformations in work, and in the product as well, created by technological change. Concerned that a balance be maintained between supply and demand and that cheap goods should refer to "widely available" and not "inferior," she strongly endorsed new technologies and recommended that everyone accept and adjust to the new realities.

CONCLUSION

Industrial production and trade flourished in Britain in the middle of the nineteenth century because of British manufacturing monopolies in many cases and because of established imperial relationships with nonindustrial nations, which served as sources of materials and markets for products (Hobsbawm 1968: 134–53; Church 1975). Undoubtedly Martineau, like her fellow countrymen, suffered from great enthusiasm and inflated optimism about Britain's industrial dominance in the present and future, although she was quite aware, perhaps more so than her contemporaries, of the potential threats to British industry by foreign, particularly American, competition.

It is clear that Martineau's accounts of her investigations and their findings, as well as numerous writings on economic issues throughout her life, reveal not only a carefulness in her research, but an understanding of the processes of industrialization which concurs with the best historical and theoretical discussions on the subject today. Her work is based, as well, on considerable personal (familial) and empirical experience of these matters. She insists that economy and production must be understood not only in technical but also in moral and sociological terms, and that this understanding must be seen against societal transitions in the economy, in class and class relations, in technology, and in trade and commerce. She emphasized the role of artisans and skilled labourers in the expansion of industrialization, the relation of family and work in home production, the ways in which technology shapes social relations, networks, and community, the influential roles of small workshops and middle-sized businesses and industries in building Britain's industrial economy, the significance of agriculture in the new economy, the rise of commerce and the impact of international (rather than simply local) markets, and the importance of both the advantages and the limits which nineteenth-century British industry enjoyed. Martineau's observations both contribute to and affirm the importance of small manufactures as they evolved into centrally organized factory systems, and of the existence of various forms of proto-industrialization which laid the foundations for the rise of organized labour, capital, entrepreneurship, and technological innovations.

By relating Martineau's empirical investigations of industries and occupations of all kinds to her philosophical presuppositions about work, it becomes possible to identify the philosophical themes embedded in her empirical analyses. We have seen empirical examples of her concerns regarding work and the self, work and society, and work and the state. She believed that products, and therefore the standard of living, would be improved through specialization, improvements in production processes and better distribution. "The economy of division of employments is sure to prevail so there is little use in opposing it" (Martineau 1861: 215).

CHAPTER EIGHT

The Florence Nightingale–Harriet Martineau Collaboration

Lynn McDonald

THE ENORMOUSLY PRODUCTIVE AND INTERESTING COLLABORATION between Florence Nightingale and Harriet Martineau began on Nightingale's return in 1856 from the Crimean War when she sought support for the recommendations from her first royal commission on the sanitary condition of the army. By that time, both were famous women and each knew of the other. Martineau was Nightingale's senior by eighteen years and was a well-established author and journalist; Nightingale, of course, was the heroine of the Crimean War. This essay documents their mutual interest in—and collaboration on—a variety of social issues.

Martineau and Nightingale exchanged numerous letters and the epistolary record of their collaboration warrants extensive coverage in the projected *Collected Works of Florence Nightingale*, now under the editorship of the present author (the first three volumes are scheduled for publication 2001). The letters are long and full, including personal concerns, the reporting and analysis of intellectual problems and strategizing on the related activism required to set them straight. Today, most of the correspondence reposes in the British Library (Additional Manuscripts 45788, hereafter cited as "AM"); other sources include the University of Birmingham and the National Library of Scotland. Only a few of these letters are in Vicinus and Nergaard (1990) and in Martineau (1990). All the correspondence between these two remarkable women will be included in the electronic version of Nightingale's *Collected Works*, and a considerable portion will also be published in print form.

Martineau was acquainted with the Nightingale family, and recalled, in her *Autobiography*:

> During the whole time of my illness [in 1843], comforts and pleasures were lavishly supplied to me. . . . Among other memorials of that time which are still preserved and prized in my home are drawings sent me by the Miss Nightingales, and an envelope-case, (in daily use) from the hands of the immortal Florence. I was one of the sick to whom she first ministered; and it happened through my friendship with some of her family. (Martineau 1877b, I: 464)

This early background (see also Martineau 1990: 167) set the stage for what became a significant alliance on several matters of mutual interest.

Nightingale knew and admired Martineau's work. It is not clear, however, if she knew her most sociological books, namely *Society in America* (1837) and *How to Observe Morals and Manners* (1838b). Nightingale liked her novels and her fictionalized accounts (notably the woman drunk) in the *Illustrations of Political Economy* (1832–4). She read Martineau's *Eastern Life, Present and Past* (1848) before she took her own trip to Egypt in 1849–50. Her grandmother gave her a copy of Martineau's *Traditions of Palestine* (1830) in 1832. It is not obvious what book Nightingale had in mind (about half of Martineau's life's work had by then been published) when she allowed to Martineau:

> . . . your book, though it must be some eighteen years since I read it, stays by my memory, as everything you write does. And I believe I could repeat it pretty nearly all, as I could nearly all your *Deerbrook* and much of your *Political Economy* tales. (Letter, 8 February 1860, AM 45788 f61)

Nightingale had read her *Life in the Sick-Room* (1844b) while she was ill and liked "some" of it "exceedingly," but did not agree on much of the material (Letter, to Beatrice Clough, 21 March 1844, Balliol College Archives). A letter to Julia Ward Howe recounts that "the Queen is going to add a *babby* and Miss Martineau a *book* to the already too numerous swarm" (Letter, to Julia Ward Howe, 26 December 1845, reproduced in Richards (1934): 330–31). A subsequent letter to Ward Howe, 28 July 1848, described Martineau's *Eastern Life* as one of the most discussed books. She recounted that John Murray would not publish it "because, he said, he never published anything against Christianity—dunce!" (reproduced in Richards 1934: 342). Late in life, Nightingale's diary records her reading (probably re-reading) *Retrospect of Western Travel* (1838c). She read Martineau's posthumously published *Autobiography* (1877) promptly on its appearance in print.

During the Crimean War (1853–1856), Martineau made flattering references to Nightingale's work in her *Daily News* articles (or "leaders")—see especially 2 June and 18 December 1855, as well as 22 January 1856, and she wrote to Nightingale on 8 December 1858:

> In whatever I did, in the war-time & after it, in relation to yourself, my object was to have you entirely *let alone*. . . . What I could do I did to keep the crowd off you, & leave you air & space & liberty. The thing was impossible, of course, but it was right to try. (Martineau 1990: 166)

She was an obvious person for Nightingale to turn to for help in her media campaign, and the progressive *Daily News* was an obvious outlet. The collaboration was a practical one, of two prominent women with causes to promote, who shared an empiricist epistemology and many points of broader culture, but who differed substantially on religion, women's rights and the role of government in society. Martineau's chief causes were women's equality and the abolition of slavery. She worked also on the reform of government, foreign and imperial policy (especially India and Ireland), health care, scientific agriculture and the environment, and food security. Nightingale's chief concerns were health care (broadly conceived and including midwifery), social reform, administrative reform in government, India, theology and religion (including comparative religion). They early came to terms with their differences on the status of women's issues. Martineau attempted to interest Nightingale in the care of the mentally ill and her particular alternative therapy interest in magnetic fields, in both cases without success.

Throughout their collaboration, Nightingale most often took the initiative. It was Nightingale who clearly sought Martineau's help, with one important exception (when Martineau suggested extending Nightingale's military medical reforms to the Northern army in the American Civil War and Nightingale followed up with alacrity).

Martineau was a Unitarian, devout in her youth but later became an outspoken agnostic and atheist. Nightingale was a deeply-religious person—albeit with an extremely unconventional theology—who maintained the intensity of her faith throughout her life. Both were rationalists, however, and this allowed them to work together. Nightingale's God ran the universe by law, without recourse to miracles, and sought active human participation. Thus, despite significant differences in the philosophical details of their respective theologies, they maintained a constructive working relationship. Politically, their respective views were complex and not always congruent. For example, Nightingale's politics were often to the left of Martineau's. But, adding to this complexity, Martineau's thinking changed over time—she later moderated the *laissez-faire* economics so dramatically exhibited in her early *Illustrations of Political Economy*, and where the rights of women, slaves, and free-thinkers were concerned, Martineau's positions were often radical.

Methodologically, Nightingale and Martineau complemented each other. Martineau published on theory and methodology and was an astute sociological observer, as amply demonstrated in *Society in America* and elsewhere. For quantitative arguments, Martineau relied primarily on secondary data collected by the Census and other government enterprises. Nightingale, on the other hand, conducted surveys and collated questionnaire data for the purposes of applied social action. Nightingale's methodological mentor was Adolphe Quetelet (cf. Halbwachs 1934)—whose views were compatible in many respects with Martineau's. Martineau provided Nightingale with a numerate and effective ally who responded positively to Nightingale's effective marshalling of powerful and persuasive quantitative data during the fight against the Contagious Diseases Acts.

The two shared a pragmatic, naturalistic approach to sociological explanation, integrating factors of the biophysical environment with the social and economic. The recent ecological critique that the founders of sociology emphasized the social to the exclusion of the *biophysical* applies to neither Martineau nor Nightingale. Martineau frequently wrote on environmental subjects in her journalism, articles which reveal her to have been as interested in agricultural drainage as Nightingale was in sewers. Martineau's leaders for the *Daily News* covered numerous aspects of scientific agriculture, rural life, food and nutrition, irrigation and water quality. There is even early treatment of the threat of species extinction and cruelty to animals, again subjects for which Nightingale's private correspondence shows concern. Nightingale also wrote extensively on issues of irrigation and deforestation in India.

The Nightingale-Martineau collaboration covered four major subject areas:

1. The reform of army medical/nursing services, initially in Britain, then extended to the United States and elsewhere;
2. Health care, health promotion/preventive medicine and midwifery;
3. The fight against the Contagious Diseases Acts; and
4. The reform of Britain's administration of India.

Sketches of their work together in each of these areas follow below.

REFORM OF ARMY MEDICAL/NURSING SERVICES

Nightingale requested Martineau's help to win support for the recommendations of the Royal Commission on the Sanitary Condition of the Army in the East (for discussion, see McDonald 1994: 206–11). Martineau speedily offered not only to write leaders for the *Daily News* but produced a popular book, *England and Her Soldiers* (1859a), copies of which Nightingale purchased and distributed. Nightingale also turned to Martineau in her lobbying efforts to get a progressive appointed as the next Secretary for War, to ensure that the Commission's recommendations would be implemented.

In asking for Martineau's help, Nightingale showed herself as sometimes impatient and fussy. Whereas Martineau's writing style was smooth and easy, Nightingale's was brusque and sharp. At one point, Nightingale evidently did not consider her friend's newspaper articles sufficiently tough and sent a more pointed one, presumably as an example of what she wanted, but it was never published. The excerpts below show too that Nightingale could wield a witty and sarcastic pen:

> The Royal Commission (on the Sanitary State of the Army) while exposing defects in present sanitary arrangements and their results to soldiers, appears to have carefully considered the means of remedy. Two plans come out in the evidence: one to place the whole sanitary administration under an officer quite unconnected with Army Medical Department, the other to use the department and its officers for preserving health as well as curing disease. There are strong arguments for both methods. . . .
>
> The Royal Commission appears to have considered that the machinery might be improved and rendered efficient by two measures: (1) educating every medical officer in the specialties of hygiene; (2) creating a council to be attached to the Army Medical Department of three members, one for hygiene, one for hospitals, one for statistics . . . . In considering our progress in army reform we ask what has become of this council? Are the deliberate recommendations of a royal commission of "experts" to be adopted and future armies saved or has the whole plan so carefully considered and so intelligently framed been shelved by the genius of dulness and stupidity in the War Office to which Great Britain from time immemorial has committed the destinies of her soldiers, in peace and in war?
>
> Why all this delay? Has not the time arrived when the nation should call for a Royal Commission of Inquiry into the manner in which the interests of the army are neglected through the ignorance of a set of obscure paid officials who in all probability would never have been able to earn their salt in any other walk of life?
>
> The House of Commons last session decreed barrack reform by an unanimous vote sanctioning by the national voice one recommendation of the royal commission. Our columns show from time to time the progress which is made. Let them also tell the War Office that unless other equally necessary reforms are carried out it is quite possible that better men may be found to attend to the health and efficiency of the army. (Included with Letter, 23 January 1859, AM 45788, ff23–27)

In one instance, Martineau proposed action and Nightingale responded by providing information on army medical/nursing services to the United States during the Civil War. Martineau thereby pursued her great cause of the abolition of slavery by drawing, in part, on Nightingale's special expertise. Nightingale, of course, wanted her material to be used by everybody (and it should be noted that she was decorated by *both* sides in the Franco-Prussian War). Martineau, however, was relieved that they lacked a communication channel to the Southern forces in America and thus nothing of help was sent to the confederacy. Further, Martineau thought the slave-owning Southerners were too debased to have put Nightingale's data to good use (see the correspondence for September and October 1861, AM 45788, ff125–62).

Martineau of course was more identified with the Northern cause than Nightingale, having taken a strong antislavery position early, when few other opinion leaders did. In the course of the Civil War, Martineau was forced to defend her support of the North in the face of its atrocities, or alleged excesses. Excerpts from the following letter show similar views with Nightingale, indeed with many women theorists, on the need for time for institutional change. Martineau's defense of the North is reminiscent of the liberal defenses of the French Revolution by Catharine Macaulay (1790), Mary Wollstonecraft (1794), and Germaine de Staël (1796–8):

> I wonder at friends of America being disappointed now, though they have plenty of reason to be vexed. After thirty years of political delinquency, thirty years of cowardly and base subservience to the pro-slavery faction ruling the country, how could the North be expected to start up complete in virtue when the hour of regeneration arrived? There is a long and dreary purgation to be gone through, a long retribution to be borne, before republicanism *begins* to run its course in that country. I am not surprised at anything now because I have been disgusted at the leaders of society there for one quarter of a century. I wish you knew how furious some of the best of them are with me now! My course is to get justice for them *here* [in Britain], as far as I can, and to put their case, with all their faults, plainly before them *there*. (Letter, Martineau to Mr. Lucas, 23 Jan 1862, M.S. Eng. Lett. D. 397, f208, Bodleian Library Archives)

The letter also slammed the *Times* for its hostile coverage of the Northern side, another sore point Martineau shared with Nightingale, who railed constantly over the London newspaper's conservatism, complacency, and cowardice.

HEALTH CARE

The correspondence exchanged between the two women each recounts progress on and problems with their causes of the day, together with descriptions of personal circumstances, bereavements and their own illnesses. Martineau warmly supported Nightingale's work to make nursing a viable profession for women, to improve the skills of midwives and midwifery practice, and to train all women to be, in effect, nurses for themselves and their families. Nightingale's landmark *Notes on Nursing* was distributed in January 1860—and thus Martineau must have been among the first to read it for in a letter dated 19 January 1860 she called it a "work of genius." Martineau wanted to help in its diffusion. "It is so real and so intense that it will, I doubt not, create an order of nurses before it has finished its work" (AM 45788, f59). Martineau (1860a) promptly published an enthusiastic thirty-page review in the *Quarterly Review*. She also published a shorter "Reverie after Reading Miss Nightingale's 'Notes on Nursing'" in the June issue of *Fraser's Magazine* (Martineau 1860b). Further, Martineau proposed placing anonymous reviews in the *Edinburgh Review* and the *Daily News*, but Nightingale warned that the identity of the author of *any* review would "leak out." "If a review article does not fall dead—and depend upon it this will not—people always ask, whose is it? And people always find out. Ultimately *everybody* will known that *you* have written it" (AM 45788, f62).

Nightingale confided in her friend at various stages on the development of the training school for nurses at St. Thomas's and the establishment, and later closure, of a training institution for midwifery. Martineau (1865) took up a long-standing Nightingale complaint about women not wanting to train for the profession—despite opportunities and well-paying jobs going begging—in an article on "Nurses Wanted" published in *Cornhill Magazine*.

Neither woman accepted the dominant chemical model of medicine, either in principle or in their own practice (Martineau experienced a cure through hypnotism while Nightingale took water cures at Malvern spa). Martineau pronounced herself "much further in approbation of homeopathic treatment" than Nightingale. She had watched it for twenty-three years, "and I am as sure as I can be of anything future that it will supersede any other principle and method yet known" (Letter, 19 January 1860, AM 45788, f60). Both saw environmental facts as important in the etiology of disease (Nightingale especially considered better *housing* as essential for better health). Both considered good nutrition as key. Martineau wrote on food policy at a general, systemic level and gave practical advice for improved nutrition for the poor. Nightingale emphasized diet in all her writing on patient care and was instrumental in changing catering practices, including the institution of formal training for military cooks, in the army.

Martineau made at least one effort to engage Nightingale's interest in the therapeutic use of magnetism. A letter otherwise on Nightingale's recent publication of *Notes on Nursing* raised the issue delicately:

> If you will not for a moment think it needful to reply, I will add a thing or two: I see no reference in any of your books to an important precautionary method which it is possible may not have come under your study—that of

> putting heads north and south (the patient's head to the north). The reason cannot be stated with scientific precision but it is supposed to belong to the relation between the human electric current and the current of terrestrial magnetism. However that may be, the fact seems to be indisputable that in cases of extreme exhaustion or irritability, the position of the patient makes the difference between sleep and sleeplessness—and therefore at times between life and death.

Martineau's letter also provided a reference to a treatise on the subject and warned that "the distress when the patient lies east and west is often very great, in puerperal cases, in nervous fevers and insanity, and in great feebleness of any kind" (Letter, 19 January 1860, AM 45788, f60).

Martineau was less involved in Nightingale's considerable, and moderately successful, efforts to institute professional nursing in workhouse infirmaries, a major step in the establishment of a public health care system. Still, she was, as ever, a trusted confidante as the following two excerpts show. Nightingale had used publicity over the death of a man in a workhouse to urge consideration of a better *system*:

> I have also had to see Mr Villiers and by Mr Villiers' desire, Mr Farnall [his deputy], to confer about introducing trained nursing into London workhouse infirmaries. They are much more frightened at the death from the Holborn Union than they "let on." I was so much obliged to that poor man for dying. The man was lost for want of cleanliness. (Mr. Villiers says he shall never hear the last of it in the House of Commons.) It was difficult to me to recognize the earnest Corn Law repealer in a man who, as far as I saw, felt merely as if he were rehearsing a speech for an angry debate in the House. (Letter, 12 February 1865, AM 45788, f281)

The second excerpt shows reform tactics, notably the need not to let proposed changes appear too substantial so as not to put off the conservatives:

> With regard to our workhouse nursery, I will just say that, if London Boards of Guardians were to get a scent that the Poor Law Board was colloquing with Miss Nightingale to nurse their workhouses, it would upset the whole scheme. For, though the Poor Law Board has the power of forcing nurses upon the Guardians, the Guardians have a very unpleasant power of dismissing any officers of their own, who give information they don't like. Indeed, part of the scheme I shall have to work myself with the Guardians if at all, whose backs are always set up by the Poor Law Board. (Letter, 22 February 1865, AM 45788, f293)

CONTAGIOUS DISEASES ACTS

In their collaboration on the Contagious Diseases Acts, Nightingale first raised the issue with her friend in 1861 (Letter, 24 September 1861, AM

45788, f128). They agreed entirely, Nightingale's feminism here being as keen as Martineau's. Neither accepted the dominant view, sanctioned by the entire establishment of state, church, and the medical profession, that men had greater sexual needs than women and were less able to restrain their sexuality when unable to express it in legitimate marriage (as was frequently the case for men in the army and navy). Both rejected the view that the compulsory inspection/treatment of women prostitutes reduced syphilis, insisting instead on changed social conditions to reduce recourse to prostitutes. Nightingale cited data showing no reduction in rates of venereal disease where compulsory inspection and treatment was practiced: "There is absolutely no evidence that there is less syphilis among populations under police restrictions and certificates of health than among populations under none. It is pure assertion" (Nightingale 1862: 1).

At Nightingale's request, Martineau placed four leaders in the *Daily News* during September 1863. The articles clearly use Nightingale's statistical material and arguments, but they are cautious in tone. They were republished as a booklet (Martineau 1870), again unattributed, in the repeal campaign in 1870.

On 14 March 1864, Nightingale sent Martineau a report on syphilis in the Army in India, with her considered remarks on the medical aspects of the matter:

> The present movement should be discussed under the head of public morality, public policy, public utility. Proof of all three—overwhelming proof—ought to be produced. Medical *opinion* is absolutely worthless except as to the treatment. As to prevention, that is another thing. About that, they have given us no evidence at all. My evidence is (but all Paris police papers are kept so secret that I cannot produce any) that the Paris police, the only people who know anything about it, state that there the disease among the prostitutes is very small, among the men is very much *increasing*; that, in thousands of cases among *men* examined and traced at great expense, *not one* was traced to a diseased woman. The act of vice between a man and a prostitute, even not diseased, seems to produce the disease, but not invariably . . .
>
> The *Times* letters are not worthy of notice. They are merely medical opinion. If, after careful *statistical* inquiry, there were proof to show benefit, there would still be left the question of policy and morality. As regards soldiers, until we have provided men with rational means of work and recreation for their spare time what can we expect but dissipation and disease?
>
> I am afraid there is too much reason to fear what the government may do. . . . We are not idle—I sent all your former *Daily News* articles (cut out and pasted) to Lord de Grey [War Minister]. (Letter, 14 March 1864, AM 45788, ff253–6)

Note Nightingale's condemnation of *medical* opinion. She was convinced that medical treatment was counterproductive for understanding public health issues. Sanitarians had to be statistically trained to see trends and then ascertain where to intervene; medical doctors were trained to treat individual cases after the disease occurred, not to prevent.

In April, 1864, Nightingale learned of the preparation of a bill for Parliament. She was then carrying out an enquiry "by which I hope at least to procure a clause punishing all procurers and solicitors and also to call the attention of the House of Commons to the fact that justices won't convict even on the existing law against 'bawdy houses'" (Letter, 28 April 1864, AM 45788, f163). Late in May, she advised Martineau of the content of the second draft of the bill. At this point she still thought that the legislation would not go through: "I don't believe any House of Commons will pass this bill. Any honest girl might be locked up all night by mistake by it" (Letter, 31 May 1864, AM 45788, f269).

Martineau published two more leaders in the *Daily News* arguing for positive measures to prevent "vice" rather than the punitive measures for control of the act. Her leader of 10 May 1864 ended with the statement:

> At the moment the lesson conveyed by the discussion in the House is that we have much to do yet in affording our soldiers a fair chance for their health and their morals before we betake ourselves to any perilous and questionable direct interposition between them and snares which can be best dealt with indirectly—by superseding evil by good.

Martineau argued in a similar leader, on 3 June, 1864, for the merits of gymnasia, reading rooms, workshops, cricket clubs, etc. In pointed discussion of the Contagious Diseases Act, she contended on 2 July 1864:

> After such facts as these, delivered to us by the highest authority, who will argue on behalf of the questionable methods proposed from time to time for dealing with vice and disease in the Army? We have created the evil by subjecting our soldiers to unnatural restraints and to temptations which are therefore irresistible, and there are some among us who propose to meet the mischief by arrangements which, however legalized, must ever be morally illicit. The other method . . . consists in allowing the laws of Nature to operate on the mind and body of the soldier as on those of other men, permitting his faculties to be exercised and his moral nature cheered by the same incitements and achievements which keep men temperate and healthy in other callings. Henceforth there will be no sort of excuse for proposing to resort to artificial and debasing expedients before the fullest trial has been made of the sound and natural methods which are indicated by the very constitution of the human being and the world in which he lives.

The bill was introduced in June 1864 and passed in July with scarcely any debate. Nightingale remained active behind the scenes for the next years while Martineau came to play a more public role. Martineau's anonymous letters from "An Englishwoman," published 28–31 December 1869 (and reprinted in Martineau 1985: 239–67) launched the repeal movement that was ultimately successful. Martineau's language here was much bolder than her earlier writing on the topic. On 29 December 1869, she wrote:

> Up to the date of the passage of these bills every woman in the country had the same rights as men over her own person, and the law extended its protection over all alike, of both sexes, and altogether without regard to any question of character, manners and calling. Prostitutes were as other women, and as men, in their claims upon the law. Now it is so no longer. Any woman of whom a policeman swears that he has reason to believe that she is a prostitute is helpless in the hands of the administrators of the new law.

She reported on 30 December 1869, on evasion of the laws abroad, where they had been in operation longer than in England:

> A provision of prostitutes has been made in places and under conditions which the law does not reach—as where the servants of refreshment houses are always on hire, under the disguise of dear drink, payment for amusements &c.; and the landlord's house is a brothel, unsuspected or impenetrable. . . . there are instances on record of medical officers and the police being actually in the pay of the prostitutes, these wretched women being held at the mercy of the extortioners by threats of being informed against.

The last letter in the series, 31 December 1869, is especially strong and succinct, stating the women's "solemn protest" against the acts and the way they were passed:

> . . . Because, so far as women are concerned, they remove every guarantee of personal security which the law has established and held sacred, and put their reputation, their freedom and their persons absolutely in the power of the police.
>
> . . . Because it is unjust to punish the sex who are the victims of a vice, and leave unpunished the sex who are the main cause, both of the vice and its dreaded consequences; and we consider that liability to arrest, forced surgical examination and, where this is resisted, imprisonment with hard labour, to which these Acts subject women, are punishments of the most degrading kind.
>
> . . . Because these measures are cruel to the women who come under their action—violating the feelings of those whose sense of shame is not wholly lost, and further brutalizing even the most abandoned.

> . . . Because the disease which these acts seek to remove has never been removed by any such legislation. The advocates of the system have utterly failed to show, by statistics or otherwise, that these regulations have in any case, after several years' trial, and when applied to one sex only, diminished disease, reclaimed the fallen, or improved the general morality of the country.
>
> . . . Because the conditions of this disease, in the first instance, are moral, not physical. . . . We hold that we are bound, before rushing into the experiment of legalising a revolting vice, to try to deal with the causes of the evil, and we dare to believe that with wiser teaching and more capable legislation those causes would not be beyond control.

This final letter to the *Daily News* was signed and included a specific appeal to join the struggle for repeal. The names of Nightingale and Martineau led the list of signatories, with Josephine Butler, who thereupon took over the leadership, third. Nightingale declined to become a vice-president of the new organization but she did send a supportive message to the founding conference of the international repeal society, 1877 in Geneva. Nightingale's message was acknowledged by Josephine Butler on 1 July 1877 (Letter, B25, Woodward Biomedical Library).

In contrast, Martineau both joined and took a public role in the new society. As a journalist, she was greatly sensitive to press treatment of the campaign: indifference largely, ridicule and hostility otherwise for their cause, active support for the acts. She protested the unfairness of the press when the *Pall Mall Gazette* published a long article, by Elizabeth Garrett, in favour of the acts, but refused to publish a joint letter by Martineau and Butler on the other side. Her last agitation for repeal was a letter to a friend in 1871, copied to a Member of Parliament (Letter, to Isabella Spring Brown, 16 July 1871, f30, National Library of Scotland).

INDIA

Elisabeth Sanders Arbuckle's (1994: 317–30) updated list of Martineau's unsigned leaders shows that Martineau began publishing on India in the *Daily News* as early as 1853, before the collaboration with Nightingale, indeed before Nightingale apparently had taken any interest on the subject. She took up the subject in earnest only in 1857, with the infamous "mutiny," or the "First War of Independence" as it would be called later by Indian nationalists. It must be noted that Martineau's two books on India are largely favourable to British rule: the descriptive *British Rule in India* (1857), and the more prescriptive *Suggestions Towards the Future Government of India* (1858). Martineau, from 1857 until 1861, published nine to ten leaders each year on India. Her focus was primarily economic: finance, taxes, tariffs, manufacturing and currency reform, with some leaders on education and women. When the report of the Royal Commission on the Sanitary Reform on the Army in India (instigated by Nightingale) came out in 1863, she gave it considerable attention (sixteen leaders in 1862, seventeen in 1863, ten in 1864, eight in 1865 and two (out of only fifteen articles total) in 1866. Martineau (1863) also published an article in *Macmillan's Magazine* to publicize the royal commission report, "Death or Life in India," a reversal of the title Nightingale often used.

Martineau and Nightingale complemented each other in their interests in India, the former supporting sanitary reform measures while highlighting economic factors, the latter stressing the basics of disease and famine, fully understanding that remedy could only be achieved by social and political change (see, for example, Nightingale 1863, 1874). A leader in the *Daily News* regarding the royal commission report gave both enthusiastic endorsement and a useful overview of this long and complex work:

> At last we have the long-promised sanitary report about military life in India, which if wisely and boldly used will save more lives than the most fatal of Indian wars has ever extinguished and preclude more sickness than will remain to be treated. The commission appointed in May 1859, chiefly through the influence of Lord Herbert and Miss Nightingale, was charged to make inquiries under eight heads. It was to ascertain the amount of mortality and sickness in the European and native forces in India, and the main causes of both, to point out what military stations are unhealthy and why, to recommend wholesome sites for new stations and indicate whether good positions can be found within easy reach of those unhealthy ones which, for military reasons, cannot be given up, to afford guidance as to the best construction of barracks, huts, hospitals and tents, to inquire into the regulations and practice for preserving the health of the troops, and enforcing care by an effective medical and sanitary police, to ascertain what is the present organization of the Army Medical and Sanitary service, to point out how a system of medical statistics may be established throughout India, and how the facts may be brought into comparison with those of the diseases and mortality of the rest of the population, native and European and, finally, to recommend such a procedure as may best preclude the causes of death and sickness. . . . No other book exists which affords such a disclosure of the character and details of life in India . . . .
>
> Such a state of things warrants and demands courageous treatment, and a liberal disposition in Parliament and people to do what can be done in the way of remedy now, and prevention for the future. The recommendations of the commission seem to be adequate to the occasion. We shall bring them forward another day. (*Daily News* 16 July 1863: 2)

Martineau joined Nightingale in considering money lenders as a curse to India. Both gradually moved to an appreciation of traditional culture in the administration of India. Both initially supported reform from the top, through a royal commission and the implementation of its recommendations by the Government of India (see, for example, Martineau's glowing endorsement of the royal commission in her *Daily News* leader 16 July 1863: 2). In later life (and after Martineau's death), Nightingale gave considerable encouragement and practical assistance to the Indian nationalist movement.

CONCLUSION

The Nightingale-Martineau collaboration was productive, but was conducted at a distance rather than face-to-face. Agendas were moved, points won, lives saved and improved. At the personal level it produced a mutually supportive correspondence, but nothing more. Martineau did try once, when visiting London, to call on Nightingale, who put her off. Martineau accepted the situation with good grace and nonetheless continued to give Nightingale her active support. In a similar light, Nightingale never met J.S. Mill, but in that case she invited him for a meeting while he preferred to keep things on paper. Perhaps Martineau's fame made Nightingale hold back (or possibly Nightingale was simply callous).

Nightingale declined joint authorship of the popular work Martineau prepared in 1859 concerning the first royal commission report. *England and Her Soldiers* in fact appeared with Martineau's name as the sole author (quite rightly so as she had done all the writing—but Nightingale had provided the data, up to supplying printer's plates for the statistical graphs, and vetted the text for errors). In a revealing letter to Arthur Hugh Clough, a friend, research assistant and relative by marriage, Nightingale observed with reference to Martineau:

> It would be *impossible* to use *our joint names*. If the *Times* puts in that John Stuart Mill is a disciple of Comte, I shall be put in as an apostle of H. Martineau. (Letter, to A.H. Clough, 10 January 1859, Balliol College Archives)

Nonetheless, Nightingale and Martineau collaborated productively through the mail on issues ranging from medical and nursing services in the military, health care, and prostitution and venereal diseases on the one hand, to reform of the British administration in India on the other. Martineau (1910) wrote Nightingale's obituary—while both women were still living—to be published on the occasion of Nightingale's death. Of Nightingale, Martineau observed (1910: 202):

> Many of the wisest of men and women have said that talk about the powers and position of women is nearly useless, because all human beings take rank, in the long run, according to their capability. But it is true, and will remain

> true, that what women are able to do they will do, with or without leave obtained from men. Florence Nightingale encountered opposition—from her own sex as much as the other; and she achieved, as the most natural thing in the world, and without the smallest sacrifice of her womanly quality, what would beforehand have been declared a deed for a future age.

So too for Martineau. Together, and individually, the work of both women contributed enormously to the shape and substance of the modern world.

CHAPTER NINE

Harriet Martineau and the Positivism of Auguste Comte

Susan Hoecker-Drysdale

> We find ourselves suddenly living and moving in the midst of the universe,—as a part of it, and not as its aim and object. We find ourselves living, not under capricious and arbitrary conditions, unconnected with the constitution and movements of the whole, but under the great, general, invariable laws, which operate on us as a part of the whole. . . . If it be desired to extinguish presumption, to draw away from low aims, to fill life with worthy occupations and elevating pleasures, and to raise human hope and effort to the highest attainable point, it seems to me that the best resource is the pursuit of Positive Philosophy, with its train of noble truths and irresistible inducements.
>
> —— H. Martineau, from her preface to *The Positive Philosophy of Auguste Comte* (1853)

TRADITIONALLY, HARRIET MARTINEAU'S PLACE IN SOCIOLOGY WAS ROOTed in her work of translation and condensation of Auguste Comte's (1830–42) *Cours de Philosophie Positive*, which for the past one hundred and fifty years has been considered the founding document of the discipline. In that context, little inquiry was made by sociologists about Martineau's own intellectual position on Comtean positivism, beyond a minimal exploration of the relation between the two thinkers at the time of the translation. Although Martineau's motivation to do the project was based on her stated view that Comte's work was needed among the English-speaking public, her decision to do the project had as much to do with her own understanding and interest in positivism, her views on science, and her perception of the need for a science of society. In this regard, Shelagh Hunter (1995: 102) offers an analysis of Martineau's intellectual lifecourse, referred to as her "progress of worship," suggesting that her earlier Natural Theology became Natural Science and that a spiritual basis for her social concerns was continuous and consistent as she moved increasingly toward science. We can see in this "progress of worship" the link between knowing and understanding and action and altruism in Martineau's work and life, and the continual and necessary relation for her between reason and imagination. Indeed, the connection between knowledge and human improvement, to be mediated by scientific truth, is apparent in the quote above as Martineau prepares the reader for *The Positive Philosophy of Auguste Comte*. However, Martineau was far from being a "disciple" of Comte or a strong supporter of Comtean positivism. What exactly was her intellectual perspective on positivism, on science, on the Comtean system, and on sociology as an emerging discipline?

This essay attempts to trace the project in some detail with the aim of specifying and elucidating the meaning of positivism for Martineau and her position on science and sociology. To accomplish that, we will: (1) examine and situate Martineau's project to translate and condense the six volumes of Comte's *Cours de Philosophie Positive*, 1830–42, (2) present some understanding of Martineau's own assessment of Comtean positivism; and (3) sketch Martineau's epistemology or—more accurately—her philosophy of science.

It is helpful to distinguish between French positivism and English positivism, or more accurately between Comtean positivism and English positivism. W.H. Simon (1963: 4), in his excellent historical account, has shown that positivism for Comte was

> more than a method; it was a system of affirmations, a conception of the world and of man. . . . What is fundamental is the assumption that the phenomena of human thought and of social life are continuous with the phenomena of the inorganic and organic world of nature and therefore susceptible of investigation by analogous methods which will yield comparably reliable results.

This widely shared assumption (Mill 1865: 8–9) was articulated within the Comtean system by the interlinking of the Law of Three Stages and the Classification (Hierarchy) of the Sciences. The human mind had evolved culturally from a theological stage of anthropomorphic gods, to a stage of metaphysical abstractions, and finally to the scientific or positive stage where truth was derived through particular scientific methods and disciplines. The disciplines themselves had emerged, according to Comte, in a particular logical and historical sequence from mathematics, to astronomy, physics, chemistry, biology, and finally sociology, in an order of decreasing generality and increasing complexity and interdependence. The point for Comte was that, in the development of the final scientific (positive) stage, sociology would take its place at the head of the positive sciences in providing the "system" required to understand humanity in order to serve it, in part by reorganizing it and instilling humane values. Pickering (2000: 26) reminds us that the definition of the "positive," for Comte, was "the real, the useful, the certain, the precise, the relative, and the constructive," a reaction in part against the perceived "negative" or critical orientation of the Enlightenment.

Johan Heilbron (1995: 234) observes that the *Cours* was intended by Comte, not as a "discourse on the positive method," but as a contribution toward the establishment of social science as positive science, which would then, and only then, make possible a theory of science. Positive philosophy as a theory of science, in turn, would help to balance the increasing division of scientific labor, serve didactically as a new epistemology for reforming education, contribute to more interdisciplinary perspectives and general points of view, and provide a basis or guidelines for social reform (*Ibid*.: 235). One can see, for example, that Comte's thinking about sociology, its concepts, methods, and progressive direction reflects what he saw as its close relationship with biology (*Ibid*.: 246–9). The relations between the disciplines, in terms of their objects of study, therefore could be determined—the more complex, the more dependent, and the lower the degree of generality. This epistemological model was more original, more comprehensive, more systematic, and more empirically directed than any previous or contemporary expositions by others (*Ibid*.: 237–8). Comte does, of course, outline not only the structure of sociology (social statics and social dynamics, the study of order and change or progress, respectively), but also its methods—observation, comparison, experimentation, historical method, and statistics. He insists on the relativity of facts and therefore of knowledge, and maintains that "absolute reality can never . . . be perfectly unveiled" (Comte, quoted in Pickering 2000: 31). Original or not, he had provided a systematic epistemology for a new science of society.

Given the historical and intellectual roots of many of these ideas in French post-Revolution and anti-Enlightenment organicism, Comte concluded that serving Humanity, the focus and goal of all knowledge, meant nothing short of the reorganization of society, a reconstruction which must proceed ultimately from a "subjective synthesis," that is, an inner moral and mental transformation situated in the Religion of Humanity. In the end, as Simon (1963: 4–6) argues, Comte did not advocate the "abstemious empiricism" generally associated with, particularly twentieth century, positivism. Heilbron (1995: 259) asserts that "it was only in a trivial sense that Comte belonged to the genealogy of logical positivism."

Comte was a systems thinker, who assumed that ideas and beliefs were fundamental to social change and to a notably conservative societal reorganization. Comte always appreciated the importance of theory in science, as a step toward scientific or "positive" truth, and the central role of ideas in history. This meant that the new society was to be knowledge-based with, according to Simon (1963: 4–12), the scientists of society in power and organized around a secular religion. Mary Pickering (2000: 29) maintains that, on the contrary, Comte asserted a separation of powers, to balance the societal system, with the industrialists in charge of practical, material affairs and the positive philosophers as custodians of morality, ideas and feelings (as a counterbalance to the potential greed and egoism of industry). She reminds us that:

> Comte wanted positive philosophers to be men who had a general knowledge of all the sciences, especially sociology . . . [who] understand the impact of the natural environment and human nature on society and the application of positive method to social phenomena. (*Ibid.*)

And, that Comte was interested in encouraging intellectual well-roundedness and altruism in the positive philosophers (*Ibid.*).

Later, as his ideas about the Religion of Humanity developed, Comte saw himself as head, as the High Priest, with disciples and a rank and file of women, workers, artists, intellectuals, and industrialists. Comte's ultimate society was meant to be communal in spirit, anti-materialist, affectively-oriented, and hierarchically structured. Moreover, his methodological interests shifted from the "objective method" to the "subjective method," from scientific truth and rationality to subjective truth emanating from the irrational—from sentiment, feeling, spirituality.

Two points made by Simon (1963: 11–12) are particularly salient in discussing the essence and historical development of Comtean positivism: (1) positivism lent itself to different interpretations and emphases, so that one might be drawn to the intellectual or the emotional, to the analytic or synthetic, or to the hierarchical or the communal aspects; and (2) the fact of the existence of disciples, discipleship, and an organized religion created rather extraordinary and complicated circumstances. Difficulties arise, not only in the historical understanding of positivism as a philosophy and new epistemology but also, in the reality of the cultist character of French positivism, with its complicated relationships between the followers and the temperamental leader who demanded loyalty and monetary support and could not tolerate criticism. Indeed the fate of Comtean positivism might have been quite different had it not taken an affective, charismatic turn. As Simon (1963) observes, Comte's relationship with interested intellectuals, particularly those who were British or American, was perhaps more fruitful and less turbulent than with those who considered themselves his true disciples, although he managed to alienate numerous intellectuals with his complaints that they were not sustaining him financially.

French positivism then can be seen to emphasize the hierarchical and logical interconnections of the sciences, the quest for permanent laws of the relations among things (T.R. Wright 1986: 19) discovered by scientific method which enables prediction and therefore action, the hegemony of sociology and its established subject matter to lead social progress, affect or subjectivity as the driving force in society, and ultimately a sociocracy which would be organic and anti-individualist. The goals of French positivism were toward synthesis and utility (T.R. Wright 1986: 18–22).

What of English positivism? Simon makes the distinction between Comte's "disciples," who subscribed to the subjective, religious goals of the Religion of Humanity and who were committed to convincing others of Comte's philosophy (e.g., Congreve, Harrison), and his "apostles" or teachers, who were interested in exploring Comtean positivism and utilizing it within the context of science without subscribing to the religious system connected with it (Simon 1963: 10–11). Many of the latter, including Martineau and J.S. Mill, eventually rejected both Comte and his version of positivism. English positivists indubitably were drawn to selected aspects of Comtean positivism. George Lewes did much to popularize Comtean positivism in England; George Eliot encouraged Lewes, as well as W.M.W. Call in his aborted effort to translate Comte (Haight 1940). Comte significantly influenced Mill's ideas in his *System of Logic* (1843) and his *Utilitarianism* (1863). There were in fact "disciples" in the persons of Richard Congreve, Edward S. Beesly, John Henry Bridges, Frederic Harrison, and numerous other British professionals. As T.R. Wright's excellent account of the impact of Comtean positivism in Britain demonstrates, these individuals, for a time at least, were extremely active in spreading Comte's doctrines and in helping to establish the Religion of Humanity as the Positivist Church.

For Mill, Lewes and others, the positivist principles would provide a systems approach for social science, the methodology for the empirical investigation of the social world, and the foundation for social reorganization, for the "humanization" of society. But Mill, like Harriet Martineau, rejected Comte's views of women, his narrow ideas on liberty, and his reactionary politics. Mill was, however, in the mid-1850s drawn to the Religion of Humanity (T.R. Wright 1986: 44). In fact, he was more interested in the possibility of a humanist religion than in the reorganization of society.

Comte's interest in social science was at general levels, the study of the whole. His great law of human evolution, the Law of Three Stages, became his repeated universal and permanent law. He was less interested in specialization among or within the social sciences and in empirical research (Heilbron 1995: 266); although he gives us rather definitive elaborations on the methods of sociology. The British positivists were more straightforwardly inductivist in that they believed in the tentativeness of facts and the generalized nature of knowledge. Laws of nature *per se* might be discovered by science but general permanent laws for social life did not exist. And, while they were sympathetic to Comte's secularism, many British thinkers did not wish to reject religion altogether nor to dismiss the idea of an Ultimate or First Cause or power. For Harriet Martineau, any First Cause which might exist was simply beyond the realm of science. She made her agnosticism public in her book with Henry G. Atkinson, *Letters on the Laws of Man's Nature and Development* (Atkinson and Martineau 1851).

Philip Abrams (1968) reminded us that the context for the origins of British sociology lay within three bodies of thought: political economy, ameliorism, and social evolution. Political economy had already provided a conception of society as rooted in individual self-interest which, if pursued in a wise and knowledgeable manner, did indeed serve society. One had, however, to understand the laws or principles upon which society functioned and that meant being informed of those laws and the "facts" of social reality. This might not be sufficient, however, because humans are fallible and do not measure up to the societal task. Problems had to be corrected. Philanthropy and ameliorism became the routes by which the English could gather the facts of social problems and establish effective courses of action to alleviate them. The closest the British came to a conception of the "social system" was in the doctrine of social evolution, sometimes called "evolutionary positivism" and most literally developed by Herbert Spencer, but not, in the end, part of the mainstream of the sociological *Weltanschauung* shared among English thinkers of Martineau's day.

British intellectuals had already accepted that society was moving into a new age with a new spirit and new problems. The generation of Carlyle and James Mill recognized that a new order would have to resolve the panoply of ideas and conflicting ideologies. But, as James Murphy (1968: iii-vii) points out, by the 1850s or so, some of the clashes had already been decided: secularism, new sciences, liberal and democratic movements, and a new class structure. It was no longer a question of constructing or reconstructing society but of using science, knowledge and technology to move ahead.

The attraction to Comtean positivism for British intellectuals in these circumstances was specifically to its system of knowledge, the methodology and unity of the sciences, and the preeminence of rational, logical truth, whether based in experience, in the study of the past or in the present/future. Positivism carried many meanings for different people. Seen by many in France and England as "an educational movement, moralistic, utopian, diffuse" and of course religious, many of those who looked to Comte's ideas on science and society reacted critically and negatively (Abrams 1968: 53–54). This is not to say that Comte had only French disciples. Beside such devotees as Littrè and Lafitte in France, England saw Richard Congreve, W.M.W. Call, E.S. Beesley, R.H. Bridges, and particularly Frederic Harrison become influential Comtean disciples who continued, in varying degrees, their devotion after Comte's death. With some exception, Harrison for example, his "moralistic" followers remained cultist and isolated; his critics, vociferous and distant.

However, it was the apparently systematic, unified structure of Comte's thought as well as his methodology for the study of society which appealed to British intellectuals, who as Enlightenment nominalists and Utilitarians for the most part, were far more liberal, even progressive, yet rather tentative and even ambivalent, on matters of science, religion and social reconstruction (Cf., Houghton 1957). In the 1840s, following the publication of the complete *Cours*, British intellectuals were drawn to Comte's secularism and scientific approach to knowledge and progress. Nonetheless, Comte's views of women (which fluctuated over his lifetime), his proposal for a quasi-religion and an affective community, and his demands for greater monetary support from his English "apostles," eventually cooled relations with many intellectuals.

Significant roles were played by Sir David Brewster, George Lewes, and John Stuart Mill in introducing their generation to Comte's ideas. Beyond that intellectual circle, however, Comte's views were known in the English world largely by reputation rather than directly (Murphy 1968: 96)—until the Martineau translation. Martineau is in many respects representative of the search for a scientific paradigm and a societal program, and therefore of the intellectual attraction to Comte's system, the subsequent assessment of it, and the ultimate reaction against Comte and his work. Our discussion will focus on Martineau's interest in and evaluation of Comte, as a means to understanding her philosophy of science.

MARTINEAU'S PROJECT TO TRANSLATE COMTE'S OPUS ON POSITIVISM

Why did Harriet Martineau take on the formidable task of condensing and translating six volumes of quite cumbersome writing by Comte into two volumes (reducing Comte's 4700 pages to 1000) of readable, useful text? What drew her to Comte? Addressing the first question, she gives, in the Preface, four major reasons for taking up the task. First, Comte deserved recognition and credit for his work, which was, in her words, "one of the chief honours of the century." Second, the original text's difficult style ("rich and diffuse"), full of meaning but overloaded with words, did not do it justice. Third, her "strongest inducement was her deep conviction of our need of the book in my own country, in a form which renders it accessible to the largest number of intelligent readers." Fourth, it addresses the uncertainties of the age. "The supreme dread of every one who cares for the good of nation or race is that men should be adrift for want of an anchorage for their convictions . . . a large proportion of our people are now so adrift. The work of M. Comte is unquestionably the greatest single effort that has been to obviate this kind of danger" (Martineau 1853b: 5).

It should be remembered, in fact, that Martineau, as other British intellectuals, was drawn to Comte's work *because* of her already established convictions: that knowledge is relative to its time and context; that knowledge has evolved through various historical stages; that science provides the new and vital means to understand a changed and very modern world; that human truths are tentative and rest on interpretation. These ideas are apparent in her earliest essays in the *Monthly Repository* and certainly in her 1848 book on the Middle East, *Eastern Life: Present and Past* in which she analyzes religions and history in that part of the world.

Martineau saw the social sciences, particularly political economy and sociology, as potentially providing a new foundation for "intellectual and moral convictions" which could be shared by all classes (Hoecker-Drysdale 1992). At the heart of the matter is her concern to make the public aware of the "great, general, invariable laws" operating in society, to inform them about the laws of progress and their realization (Martineau 1853b). But science itself had to become more systematic and unified:

> While our science is split up into arbitrary divisions; while abstract and concrete science are confounded together . . . while the researches of the scientific world are presented as mere accretions to a heterogeneous mass of facts, there can be no hope of a scientific progress which shall satisfy and benefit those large classes of students whose business it is, not to explore, but to receive. (*Ibid.*: 5)

In 1830, before she wrote the tales of political economy, Martineau was introduced to the work of Claude-Henri, Comte de Saint-Simon, by the French socialist Gustav D'Eichtal, who was visiting her friend William Fox in London at the time. She became enthusiastic about French positivism (Hoecker-Drysdale 1992: 28, 47). Particularly important to her were Saint-Simon's ideas on the progressive evolution of society, the goal of positivist and systematic knowledge, and the proposal of a new discipline to study society. Other projects, travel, and nearly five years of invalidism intervened, however, before Martineau returned to French positivism specifically. After publishing her controversial book with Atkinson in 1851 in which she declared her agnosticism (Hoecker-Drysdale 1995), she returned to her earlier curiosity about Comte:

> After hearing Comte's name for many years and having a vague notion of the relation of his philosophy to the intellectual and social needs of the time, I

> obtained something like a clear preparatory view, at second-hand, from a friend, at whose house in Yorkshire I was staying . . . in 1850. What I learned then and there impelled me to study the great book for myself; and in the spring of 1851 . . . I got the book and set to work. I had meantime looked at Lewes's chapter on Comte in Mr. Knight's Weekly Volume and at Littrè's epitome; and I could thus, in a manner, see the end from the beginning of the complete and extended work . . . I conceived the scheme of translating the *Philosophie Positive*. (Martineau 1877, II: 57)

Within two days of receiving the book, she "began to dream of translating it" and on the third night, she "sat up late,—not dreaming, but planning it" (*Ibid.*). A close friend soon suggested that she give an abstract of Comte's philosophy in one or at most two volumes. The suggestion of a kind of condensation, rather than literal translation, fit well with her aim of bringing Comte to the British general readership as well as scholars and intellectuals.

Martineau, like many of her contemporaries, was searching for an affirmation, and perhaps a completion, of her ideas (Murphy 1968: 87), which may explain her emotional response to the work of translation itself, "many a passage did I write with tears falling into my lap" (Martineau 1877b, II: 72). That enthusiasm continued for many years, even as she distanced herself from Comte and his later philosophy. In 1855 she wrote:

> If I were now to live and work for twenty years, I could never enjoy anything more. The vast range of knowledge, through which one is carried so easily, is a prodigious treat, and yet more, the clear enunciation, and incessant application of principles. (*Ibid.*: 71)

For George Lewes, John Stuart Mill, and Harriet Martineau, the goal was to propagate Comte's ideas on positivist science, to make them accessible to members of society including, especially for Martineau, to the middle and working classes, so that this knowledge could be employed through various means to further social progress. As Martineau (1853b: 5) put it, "the growth of a scientific taste among the working classes of this country is one of the most striking of the signs of the times." Lewes and Mill were engaged in lengthy correspondence with Comte and were at least apostles, if not disciples, of Comte for several years (Lewes longer than Mill). They were much more ardent followers and believers in Comte's philosophy than Martineau. Mill and Comte found much common ground regarding the need for a new moral order:

> They shared the view that, to complete the revolution, new beliefs, new institutions, and a new morality had to be put in place, thereby ending the anarchical, transitional period and ushering in a new organic type of society. They

> also agreed that regeneration and reconstruction—filling the void of disbelief and lack of authoritative values—would have to take place in the realm of ideas, philosophy, and morality . . . (Hamburger 1995: 72–75)

This emphasis led Mill to "sympathize with some of the main features of what later emerged as Comte's religion of humanity" (*Ibid.*). Mill (1865: 1866), of course, subsequently became a well-known critic of Comtean positivism. Although he continued to share with Comte the idea of the need for a secular religion in society, Mill refused to publish in Comte's "anti-Christian" journal because he did not wish to go public regarding his atheism, to which Comte replied that Mill lacked courage and conviction (Hamburger 1995: 75). Hamburger maintains that the most prominent disagreement between Mill and Comte had to do with the status of women (*Ibid.*: 74). People like Mill and Martineau were of course attracted to different aspects of Comte's thought—he, to the moral and religious aspects; she, to the scientific and practical dimensions.

There had been considerable controversy over who should do the translation. George Eliot, consort of George Lewes, objected to Martineau on the grounds that her translation would be popular rather than specialized in nature. Eliot recommended Wathen Mark Wilks Call, a young Oxford protegé of Richard Congreve, who had already completed three volumes of an abridged translation. John Chapman agreed and suggested to Martineau that she give up the idea. However, she refused "to relinquish the task" (Haight 1940: 209–10), particularly because she recognized that Call's translation would not be "in popular form" and thereby unaccessible to the general reader. Chapman would have preferred Call, after the scandal of the Martineau-Atkinson volume which he had just published, but another event changed the situation and probably Chapman's mind as well.

A final element which impelled Martineau to embark on the project was *funding*! On August 1, 1851, a wealthy admirer of Comte, Edward Lombe, contributed £500 Sterling through John Chapman to Martineau for "support of a great literary work" (Comte's *Positive Philosophy*), which Lombe himself had originally wished to translate (Haight 1940: 55). The money was considerably more than necessary for publication expenses; Chapman wanted to use some of the money for other projects as well. But Lombe intended the funds specifically for Martineau's translation/condensation of Comte. She placed the money, so designated, in a trust to be used to pay for disseminating the final product. Although Chapman suggested she take £150 and use the rest for publication purposes (he was the publisher!), she decided to take £200 for her work, pay Chapman's expenses only, and provide Comte with the remaining amount. The three parties later shared the small profits from the book's sales (Martineau 1877b, II: 66–7).

Writing to Holyoake on October 6, 1851, she commented:

> It was only yesterday that I ascertained that Mr Mill is not translating the work, nor intending to do so. (I hear) elsewhere that he will by & by publish a book on Sociology, according much with Comte's views . . . . Another gentleman *was* doing it,—*not in popular form*—& he, seeing that he cannot compete with our advantages, offers,—in the most good-humoured way,—to merge his scheme in ours, & to give me the use of his MS,—on the sole condition that he shall claim, whenever he thinks proper, his share of the honour of introducing Comte to the English! If I find his M.S. of any substantial use (of which I have no doubt) I shall send him some small portion of the money . . . . Meanwhile, Mr. Lombe writes freely of the affair; and we think we ought to make the project known, to save others from entering upon useless labour.
>
> We believe there will be two 8vo [octavo] vols. I don't see how any justice can be done to the work in less. We will make it as cheap as we possibly can; and I am giving my very best pains to the task. (Martineau to Holyoake, British Library, AM 42726, f3)

Martineau tells us in her *Autobiography* how she went about the task of translation and condensation, which took from June 1, 1852, followed by interruptions until December, until October 10, 1853, essentially one year and four months with a few months break. She enjoyed exploring:

> The vast range of knowledge, . . . the clear enunciation, and incessant application of principles . . . . I became "strengthened, stablished, settled" on many a great point; I learned much that I should never otherwise have known, and revived a great deal of early knowledge . . . : and the subdued enthusiasm of my author, his philosophical sensibility, and honest earnestness, and evident enjoyment of his own wise range of views and deep human sympathy, kept the mind of his pupil in a perpetual and delightful glow. (Martineau 1877b, II: 71–72)

Her method of working included translation and condensation of Comte's pages during the day, and, usually in the evening, study of the subjects covered in the volumes. It should be recalled that Martineau had a classical education and so was well acquainted with the nineteenth-century understanding of the sciences, as well as humanities and arts. In the process she revived her previous knowledge and gained new knowledge. "Thus, my work was not mere translation: it involved quite a different kind of intellectual exercise; and, much as I enjoy translating . . . it is pleasanter still to combine with this the work of condensation" (*Ibid.*: 72). This version of Comte was "a very free translation," as she later said in the Preface, "more a condensation than an abridgement: but it is an abridgement too" (Martineau 1853b: 8). She worked at it four to five days a week and tried to average twenty-five to thirty pages each day. Professor John Nichol of Glasgow reviewed, at Martineau's request, the first three books on mathematics, astronomy, and physics, in which he found no errors, added only a few notes and observations, and recommended some further condensation in the section on physics (Martineau 1877b, II: 72).

Martineau's motivation lay particularly in her concern to avoid misinterpretations of Comte and to quell some of the public ignorance about his work. She relates numerous instances in her writings and letters of encounters with individuals who claimed to know the content of someone's book and ideas, but who in fact had never read or even seen the book concerned. Claims that Comte stated that theology was finished or that we can know nothing but phenomena, omitting "and their laws," meant that partial- or mis-interpretations were causing serious problems in the acceptance or even fair hearing of Comte's ideas. That his ideas were about not only the rise of the scientific paradigm for knowing, but also about the collapse of old orthodoxies may help to explain the low sales of the translation in the decades immediately following publication. Martineau wished to bring Comte's ideas to the general English reader but she refused to analyze or in any way criticize Comte's ideas in her Preface to the translation.

In April, 1853, preceding the November publication of the two volumes, Martineau wrote to George Holyoake:

> . . . We hope it will come out at the beginning of next season. Two thick volumes. Price not determined till we see precisely the size, but as cheap as we can make it.—Entre nous, I have made arrangements for Comte (who is, as you know, very poor) having a chief share of the profits: & profits there will be, as I apply Mr. Lombe's money mainly to the expenses of publication. I say "*entre nous*" because I am very desirous that M. Comte should not know of my intention till there is some money to send. If you see reason to think that the book will be aided in any quarter by your mentioning the fact to any discreet person, you can do so. Only, it must not get round to M. Comte." (British Library ADD MS 42726, Folios 9–10)

Competition from George Lewes, who two months before Martineau's translation had published *Comte's Philosophy of the Sciences*, a summary previously serialized in the *Leader*, had little effect, particularly in the opinion of Comte. He was so impressed with Martineau's work and dedication that he replaced his original with her version in his *Bibliotheque positiviste du proletaire au dixneuvieme siecle* and wrote to her of his deep appreciation for the quality of the result:

> Je n'hésite pas à vous announcer que vous avez rendu votre nom inséparable du mien, en exécutant le seul travail qui subsistera parmi tous ceux qu'a déjà suscités mon livre fondamental. (Comte 1902–5, I: 143)

More will be said about the relationship and correspondence of Comte and Martineau, below.

Exactly twenty years after Martineau's death in 1876, Frederic Harrison, the Comtean positivist, wrote an introduction to a new edition of Martineau's translation of the *Positive Philosophy*, in which he also restored the last ten pages of Comte's text which Martineau's condensation had originally omitted. Harrison (1895), a barrister, historian, writer, literary critic, and positivist, gave Martineau full credit for the quality of her translation, the praise received from Comte and readers generally, the fact that her condensation had, in turn, been translated into French, and her generosity in sharing the profits from the book with Comte. But he harshly criticized her for the omission of the last ten pages of Volume Six and restored them to the new edition. Recognizing that Comte's later works were not before Martineau at the time of her translation, he argued that they are crucial because they anticipate Comte's later writings like the *Positive Polity*, in which Comte elaborates on his Religion of Humanity, the reorganization of society, and his synthesis of the sciences. Here Comte made the case for positive *philosophy* over scientific rationality alone and displayed his hope that sociology would be the basis of a new spiritual power for humanity which science itself could not provide (Pickering 1993: 539–604).

Martineau considered Comte's discussion—in these last pages—of philosophy and his quest for a new foundation for society to lack both credibility for the reader and relevance for the discipline of sociology. References in the last pages to "final reconstruction of human society," "the new philosophical synthesis," "the philosophy of the Social Polity," and "the reorganization of Morals" on a positive basis were, to Martineau, inappropriate and premature, as well as disconcerting. She had notified the reader in the Preface, after all, that his discussion of future works had been omitted:

> It will be observed that M. Comte's later works are not referred to in any part of this book. It appears to me that they, like our English criticisms on the present Work, had better be treated of separately. Here his analytical genius has full scope; and what there is of synthesis is, in regard to social science, merely what is necessary to render his analysis possible and available. (Martineau 1853b: 9)

She may have seen, in addition, the several comments by Comte in those pages regarding his weak financial standing,—"the humble and precarious form of material existence to which I am reduced . . . after a life of toil" and "my means of support may be snatched from me by blind prejudices and passions" (*Positive Philosophy*, 1896: 418–19)—as gratuitous and the possible basis for a misrepresentation of her motives for doing the translation. Her stated reason was that she wished to give Comte's analytic, rather than synthetic, genius full scope, that is, to strengthen the acceptance of Comte's sociological system as analytically useful. Becoming already suspicious of hints of the Religion of Humanity and of Comte's plans for social reorganization, she questioned the prudence and perhaps the specificity of this mix of sociology as a science and a moral philosophy, and therefore elected to omit the final pages which seemed unnecessary and irrelevant to the present work. Martineau was impelled to do the translation, after all, by Comte's analyses of the evolution of knowledge (and religion), the unity of the sciences through the positive method, and the protocol for a new science of society, sociology, which would provide the unifying "spirit of the whole" for all sciences (Pickering 1993: 681). She felt so strongly about the need for this work that she wished to focus on it alone, not other writings of Comte, in order to strengthen its reception.

"The English positivists received the work with rejoicing" (Webb 1960: 304). Positive reactions and reviews came from Lewes, Spencer, Holyoake, and even Harrison. Harrison himself predicted that "Miss Martineau's version . . . will long remain . . . as Comte himself said, the popular form of his great fundamental treatise" (Harrision 1896: xix). But he cautioned, as did Comte, that hers is a free condensation ("Miss Martineau's remarkable paraphrase"), and was so intended, and that Comte's original must be consulted by any serious student of philosophy (Harrison 1907: 335–43).

MARTINEAU'S ASSESSMENT OF COMTE AND WITHDRAWAL

When Martineau published *Cours de Positive Philosophie* in 1853, she had only recently published the infamous volume, *Letters on the Laws of Man's Nature and Development* with Henry George Atkinson, an enigmatic event to say the least, which scandalized the British public for its blatant anti-clerical, anti-church, secular, pro-scientific views (see Hoecker-Drysdale 1996). She was treated roughly by reviewers, friends, and family for this sin, and by her brother, theologian James Martineau, for a second time when he published a long-delayed review of her translation of the *Cours* in the *National Review*. It has been suggested that there was an element of revenge, therefore, in Martineau's deed of the Comte translation as she took "a delight in smiting her enemies who had patronized her for the *Letters*" (Murphy 1968: 88; also Hill 1989: xliii–xlviii). In her preface to the *Positive Philosophy*, Martineau (1853b: 11) wrote:

> My hope is that this work may achieve, besides the purposes entertained by its author, the one more he did not intend, of conveying a sufficient rebuke to those who in theological selfishness, or metaphysical pride, speak evil of a

> philosophy which is too lofty and too simple, too humble and too generous for the habit of their mind.

As translator and editor she realized the work's limitations and its contributions:

> Whatever else may be thought of the work, it will not be denied that it ascertains with singular sagacity and soundness the foundations of human knowledge, and its true object and scope; and that it establishes the true filiation of the sciences within the boundaries of its own principle. (*Ibid.*: 5–6)

Martineau's relationship with Comte was marked by generosity and restraint. She shared the royalties with Comte, meager though they were. Sales yielded net proceeds of only £48 by 1854. A final payment of £23 from publisher John Chapman to Comte was delivered in 1856 by Herbert Spencer, who had been attracted to Comte's work at that time and whose own critique of Comte is fascinating (Cf., T.R. Wright 1986: 164–8). Profits from sales had totaled £117 over two years, assuming a profit of ten percent of gross return, probably no more than 1500 copies were sold (Murphy 1968: 96). Harriet gently broke the news to Comte as early as April, 1854, that sales were slow:

> I earnestly hope that you are prepared for the true nature of the reception in this country of your book. If so, you will not be surprised that there has not been one thoroughly favourable public notice of it. There ought to have been one in the *Westminster Review* and the editor strongly desired it. But the very few qualified men to whom he could look for that service have been in one way or another pre-engaged, so that part of your due appreciation is deferred . . .
>
> As for all the other reviews,—you have taught us what to expect of *littérateurs* who fill their pages. Wherever they have tried to go beyond mere invective, they have shown the most astonishing ignorance . . . . It is not this order of men that understand or will ever receive your work. It is *the men who do not write* that are your true disciples. The book is read and it must be by such. Down in that lowly valley where human life goes on under the feet of the proud, the seed is sown & will flourish. You and I shall never see the gathering of the harvest, except in the eye of faith; but I am sure that is all that we desire. (Martineau to Comte, quoted in Murphy 1968: 93)

Martineau's words probably mislead Comte in portraying on her part an exaggerated sense of enthusiasm and commitment to his ideas. She was interested primarily in the enlightenment of the working classes and most certainly stimulated Comte's hopes for a proletarian following (see Comte 1902–5, I: 143–6). Certainly the "eye of faith" did not refer to any religious interest or commitment on her part to Comte's religion, but perhaps to their common faith in the prospects for future society. She wrote to Holyoake in 1853, "I owe my expectations of the *eventual* influence of this book on the public mind are very high indeed" (British Library, ADD MS 42726, f10).

Martineau's dedication, objectivity and care in producing this foundational version of Comte compares with her restraint toward a public critique. In her preface, for example, she refused to reveal her criticisms, although she admitted that she had them. Her reaction to Comte's views on religion, women, domestic life, individualism and liberty was in effect more categorical but silent, in comparison with that of Mill who found much in common with Comte's critique of the Enlightenment, his quest for a new organic state, and his priority for a new secular religion—even if he rejected Comte's particular Religion of Humanity (see Hamburger 1995). She had realized even as she worked on the project that, whatever the harmony with her intellectual needs at the time, she could not accept Comte's vision of a highly centralized and controlled social system, a discourse of male authority, and a unitary public culture and opinion.

Recent research on Comte's views on women indicates that "his attitudes toward women were complex, contradictory, and variable" (Pickering 1996: 10). Pickering points to the fact that while Comte took a basically essentialist view and "valorized the differences" between the sexes in the first and last parts of his life, heavily misogynist attitudes prevailed in his middle period. At times, Comte emphasized the need for strong and improved relationships between the sexes, the importance of education for girls, and the crucial role of domesticity and nurturing. Although not in disagreement, Martineau would have had difficulty with his views in general. As Pickering notes, she probably would have found more common ground with his youthful appreciation of women, which had been influenced by Condorcet and Wollstonecraft. Comte tended to associate with strong women, and was very happy, it seems, to have a woman translate his *magnum opus*. That Harriet Martineau, throughout her lifetime, was fighting misogynist views and that feminism was a major issue for her created the expected difficulties in her assessment of Comte. Martineau was not prepared to compromise the goal of women's equality and freedom with a scientifically derived plan for society. At the very least, it can be said that their ideas of emancipation differed: for Martineau it meant economic, political, and social independence; for Comte, it meant freedom from financial want and material concerns, in a manner, freedom from the responsibilities of the public sphere.

Early British and American reviews of Martineau as translator and promoter of Comte's *Positive Philosophy* were significantly influenced by her agnosticism, her critique of the clergy dating from her American studies, her use of mesmerism, and her feminism, matters quite apart from Comte's work itself. Reviewers drew connections between Martineau and current movements on women's behalf (suffrage, dress, work, domestic equality, and so on) which were echoed in their reviews. Particularly in her American studies, she had challenged the authority and legitimacy of the clergy to define the moral norms of everyday life and had insulted them with charges of intolerance, selfishness and pride. It is not surprising that American sociology, founded as it was on religious and clerical underpinnings, relegated Martineau to the "dungeon of the discredited," all the while of course making good use of her translation! Harp (1995: 12) states that, though a few American intellectuals read Comte in the French, including David Croly and Lester F. Ward, "most stayed with Martineau's condensed English version."

MARTINEAU'S EPISTEMOLOGICAL FRAME AND PHILOSOPHY OF SCIENCE

Martineau's long-range attachment to the principles of Comtean positivism was selective. Most significant for her were the following tenets: (1) that empirical facts and their laws are the basis of all knowledge; (2) that there is a methodological coherence to the sciences, of which social science and sociology will be the latest representatives; (3) that the organization of knowledge and, therefore, of the human mind is unfolding logically and unfolding historically in accordance with the Law of Three Stages (Pickering 1993: 570); (4) that science is important for practical social needs, as well as for theoretical/intellectual purposes; (5) that theory and empiricism are interlocked; neither is useful or meaningful without the other; (6) that the possibility of an objective understanding of the world exists if previous theology and metaphysics are surpassed; and (7) that societal progress must be scientifically based. But most, if not all, of these tenets were elements of Martineau's philosophy prior to her study of Comte. Significantly, Comte had provided a detailed and systematic exposition of scientific knowledge—although not the first however, (see Yeo 1993)—which attracted and even thrilled Martineau, Mill, Spencer, and many others. That Martineau and Comte's shared convictions on science may explain why, for all her differences with Comte and her rather brisk withdrawal from any connections after 1854, when asked in 1873 for her opinion on the desirability to reissue the translation of the *Cours*, even though the first edition had not sold well, she strongly supported the idea.

However, both before and after Martineau's work of the translation in 1852–53, important differences existed between their epistemologies and scientific and social philosophies. She subscribed to the Necessarian version of Natural Law, which recognized both the influence of natural laws on human existence but, at the same time, the moral responsibility and agency of each individual. Influenced by utilitarianism, she believed that the whole point of knowledge, progress, and a rational moral existence is the improvement and well-being of members of society. In this regard, unlike Comte, she valued democracy and liberty in society, and completely rejected his views on women, workers, children, and his privileging of men and power elites, be they scientists, industrialists, or engineers. She believed, therefore, in convincing readers of all classes in society of the centrality of scientific knowledge for their lives and for social progress.

While she concurred with Comte's secularism, in the shedding of old theologies and metaphysical systems, Martineau was repulsed by his desire to establish a new quasi-religious morality and hierarchical social system, as she saw it. Martineau's original interest in positivism was to enable theoretical and empirical understanding of society and its structures and morals (values) in a critical sociological frame, and ultimately to make empirical findings and their interpretation available to the decision-makers and the public. This was far different from the authoritarian "management" (my term) approach of Comte. Martineau wanted to learn about social reality; Comte wanted, following his own philosophy, to reorganize it. It is not surprising then that she refused Comte's numerous appeals to translate his later works such as *Système de politique positive* and *Catéchisme positiviste*. And, Martineau apparently never recommended Comte's other writings to friends or readers (Murphy 1968: 103).

Martineau had been reading the work of Newton, Hartley, Priestley, Bacon, Kant, and Stewart since the 1820s and wrote about their ideas and her own view of science in the *Monthly Repository* during that decade. Her commitment developed early to Necessarianism, the principle of the inevitability of cause and effect in physical, natural, and social relations. She understood through associationism the basis of human development as rooted in the transmission of human sensations from the external world to the brain. She rejected the theory of innate ideas and the doctrine of free will. She was a positivist in insisting that the nonmaterial origins of phenomena are unknowable and perhaps unimportant and that knowledge of human nature can be found in material existence. We cannot say, however, that, as a materialist, she was a determinist, because individual human responsibility, choice and morality were, for her, inherent existential elements. She maintained that many aspects of the human mind and human faculties remained unexplored. She understood the linkage between science, enlightened knowledge and freedom and she was interested in the import of all three for the everyday lives of the members of society.

That she was a rationalist, an empiricist, a Baconian, and a social nominalist is clear. Her writings and letters in the 1820s demonstrate her early commitment to science, the moral sciences, and a science of society, and provide important background for understanding her later work in political economy and sociology. In the volume *Letters on the Laws of Man's Nature and Development* (Atkinson and Martineau 1851), published two years before her translation of Comte, we see her philosophy, somewhat muted in the shadow of Atkinson but nevertheless there, rather more developed but utterly consistent with her philosophy of science of the previous three decades (Postlethwaite 1984). The continued influence of Bacon was apparent. She and Atkinson wished to incite interest among the general public in the scientific study of human nature to aid their readers in understanding the lawful nature of the universe and the interconnections of the individual, the social, and the natural worlds. She had become increasingly secular and perhaps more strident about the issue of First Cause as unknowable. In a letter penned in 1856, Martineau (1877: 41) explained her philosophy:

> By Positive Philosophy, I mean not any particular scheme propounded by one author, but the philosophy of fact, as arising from the earliest true science, and rehabilitated by Bacon's exposition of its principles.

In this regard she and Comte were colleagues. Harp (1995: 12) noted that Comte "viewed much of his work as a development of Bacon's ideas, in particular," although others have argued that the influence of Descartes was equally strong. Martineau, reflecting Bacon's influence, subscribed to the necessity of empirical proof for scientific knowledge, while recognizing the vital role of theory in doing scientific and sociological work. She not only actually did a great deal of empirical research, such as her investigations of America, the Middle East, Ireland, and many British contexts, particularly with regard to work, industry, and education, but also developed a thorough methodology including protocols for the neophyte investigator in *How To Observe* (Hill 1989: xlviii–li). Comte's genre remained programmatic. Theory was always central to analysis and interpretation of empirical findings for Martineau, and she demonstrated that in her America studies particularly. Indeed, while translating Comte, she surely must have shed some tears as she mulled Comte's (1853: 27) words:

> If it is true that every theory must be based upon observed facts, it is equally true that facts cannot be observed without the guidance of some theory. Without such guidance, our facts would be desultory and fruitless; we could not retain them; for the most part we could not even perceive them.

Martineau had developed that very point in her treatise on *How To Observe Morals and Manners*, a book she outlined in 1834 and published in full in 1838. This work remains a momentous early exposition on the necessary interplay between fact and theory. Martineau, of course, went further to show how theory can be constructed, as, for example, in her typological analyses of suicide and of religion, and her macrosociological frame for the study of American society (Martineau 1837). The role of theory for her was not only to organize observations and facts, but also to facilitate interpretation and critique. She employs "immanent critique" to examine America's past and current social practices, particularly the relation of norms to behavior, principles to practices, values to concrete human relations, and the unobservable to the observable. In all her original sociological work, she did not hesitate to criticize the establishment, to analyze social conflicts and societal contradictions, and to expose the fates of the exploited and the marginalized.

Concerned with the imperatives of philosophical necessity, she nevertheless, as early as 1829, challenged those who subscribed to the uniformity of causation and necessary connections of cause and effect, preferring to focus on the *varying degrees* of certainty and predictability in the physical world and in human affairs. She thought it imperative to explore the variety of ways of knowing, to explore the nature of human nature as well as human organization. She carefully distinguished causation from correlation, fact from testimony, and law from cause:

> "Law" means in one sense *a decree of a Lawgiver*; & its province is *government*, Divine or human; its field is Society, & it admits the consideration of a *Cause*,—the supreme Will, spiritual or temporal—being the assumed Cause.
>
> In the other sense,—perfectly distinct from the first, "Law" means *the General Fact*, to which special facts may be referred, by which facts from a wide range of observation are classified,—that reference & classification constituting *Explanation* in its philosophical sense. In this sense the province of Law is *Science*, & its field is the whole range of natural phenomena. It has no cognizance of *Cause*.—This account of the two meanings of the term "Law" will be confirmed by any person trained to scientific reasoning. (Letter, to Henry Reeve, 7 August 1868, private collection)

Her concerns with the moral quality of life in society are reflected in her emphasis on the importance of sympathy, of agency and moral independence, of freedom from authority, and of the interconnections of motive and action, feelings and habits:

> The essentials of science and the essentials of human feelings, are substantially the same. The science does but enlarge our sense of the truth which is in us and around us, while widening the scope of our conscious action and rendering it more accurate. (Martineau 1858: 1120)

Positive sociology was, in her view and the view of many nineteenth century British positivists, to be scientifically grounded, but not uncritical. For

Martineau, this new science was to be value-free in precisely the Weberian sense as well as value-relevant in its concerns, addressing the complexities of values and behavior, but never presupposing the evidence, the findings or the conclusions.

The debate over the meaning and significance of positivism to British sociology is an interesting one, some taking the position that it was their concern with morality (Annan 1959: 14–15) and/or their interest in the regeneration of society (Farmer 1967), which drew the British to positivism. But it must be said that for Martineau, Mill, Spencer, Whewell, and others, the recognition of the importance of values and morals was not to be confused with a specific positivist moral and social program. Martineau, as the others, particularly rejected the imposition of any particular set of morals and values on society. Furthermore, as Hickox (1984: 13) has shown, the British sociologists in any case did not see themselves as a separate intelligentsia in society nor did they form an educated mandarin class, as in Germany, to facilitate becoming positivist leaders for the twentieth century.

In conclusion, perhaps Martineau's philosophy could be summarized thus: If science is to be relevant, to be historically grounded but critical in approach, if science is to be the spearhead of progress and social improvement, to serve all classes of society, it must be fearless to ask questions, to explore all problems and issues, and to serve, not the elites and structures of domination, but the common public good.

In an article in *The Spectator*, Martineau (1858: 1120) wrote:

> John Stuart Mill . . . has promised us a new work on "Sociology"; the first attempt towards placing "social science" upon something like a scientific basis. We do not disparage the attempt by any presumption that it must at once jump to completeness. No science is complete . . . . A science may be fragmentary, and still be a science; it all depends upon the method and ascertained principles.

EPILOGUE

Martineauian Sociology and Our Disciplinary Future

Michael R. Hill

I ARGUE ABOVE, IN CONCERT WITH MY COLLEAGUES, THAT WE MUST TAKE Harriet Martineau seriously, and that there are sound reasons for so doing. The history, sophistication, innovativeness, and continuing resonance of her work and ideas are dramatic, engaging, and impressive by all of the yardsticks used to assess the merit and importance of our sociological founders. We are asked, on occasion, "Yes, but what possible difference does Martineau make to sociology today?" Sheer impudence aside, it is a question to answer carefully, with probity, and our answers must be convincing rather than contrived. The gravity of the question comes home to us if we rephrase the query, to ask: "What possible difference does it make for sociology today if we had never heard of Durkheim, Weber, Marx, or Mead?" Presumably, many of us would reply that the absence of such major figures would make an enormous impact, that the shape and scope of sociology as a disciplinary enterprise would be quite else than it is without their contributions. Thus so with Martineau. Any sociologies (especially the received sociology of the standard textbooks) that lack the conscious acknowledgment, influence, and impetus of her work are necessarily strange and distorted versions of sociology. Likewise, the absence of Durkheim, Weber, Marx, or Mead would also create curiously strange and unrecognizable sociologies. Our discipline grows stronger from inclusion and dialogue, not from exclusion and silence.

When we take Martineau seriously, as intellectuals and scholars, we restore a bit of the balance to our discipline lost through decades of overloading our textbooks, theory courses, journals and monographs with "content" selected too often by institutionally-entrenched, virulently patriarchal gatekeepers. But the proverbial cat is now out of the bag. Martineau has been re-discovered, and the consequences of that event are evidenced in partial measure by the papers contributed to this book. We are now in position, collectively, to outline a serious reply to those who ask if knowing about Martineau "makes any difference." It is now possible to draw the contours of a Martineauian sociology. Doubtless future Martineau scholars may delineate these configurations in different ways—theoretical propositions, after all, are necessarily "working hypotheses" (Mead 1899) intended for subsequent modification and adjustment.

The practice and promulgation of Martineauian sociology holds considerable promise for the twenty-first century. It provides a personal, professional, and pedagogical alternative to the pervasive but bankrupt abstracted empiricism so prevalent during the last fifty years. The following core traits are representative of the values and sociological possibilities that Martineau personified and valued:

- Insistence on logically ordered and carefully reasoned expositions of social processes and situations.
- Fundamental quest for systemic understanding of social institutions as wholes, including their complexity and historical development, and the interconnections between institutionalized social structures.
- Respect for the direct empirical observation and in-depth qualitative investigation of social patterns, in contrast to today's near universal reliance on survey questionnaire data.
- Use of discourse as corroboration, never as primary empirical evidence.
- Appreciation for applied demographic, economic, environmental and epidemiological research, including careful, systematic reviews and analyses of government reports and census materials.
- Requirement for integrity, egalitarianism, and high moral standards in personal and professional conduct.
- Embrace rather than eschew sociological research into social questions in which one has deep personal interest and motivation.
- Sensitivity to ethnocentrism and its consequences.
- Recognition of the importance of conducting inclusive investigations across divisive social attributes, including gender, class, race, physical disability, and the like, together with active concern for oppressed peoples.
- Concern to understand everyday life and routine experiences.
- Sensitivity to the impact of metatheoretical assumptions on inferences and research design.

- Recognition of sociology as a socially purposeful activity, as encompassing far more than strictly academic, ivory tower enterprises.
- Dedication to a strong personal work ethic.
- Responsiveness to local as well as national social and political issues, together with a conception of sociology as a public service.
- Dissemination of sociological insights and findings to the lay public in comprehensible formats, including essays, editorials, didactic fiction, and newspaper columns.
- Sociological reflexivity, together with individual reflection on the self and its circumstances, capabilities, constraints, and opportunities.
- An abiding faith in the possibilities for human social improvement.
- Ever increasing capacity for personal growth and intellectual insight.
- Independence of thought, together with steadfast public commitment and private sacrifice when conscience dictates—and thereby necessitates—support for unpopular ideas and perspectives.

In our present era, where self-serving interpersonal impression management and raw professional aggrandizement are too often the norm at national sociological meetings and elsewhere within the discipline, Martineauian sociology provides a refreshing call for responsible disciplinary assessment, reflection, and action. In better understanding the early work of Harriet Martineau, we open the discipline of sociology to rational reform, greater applied relevance, and future renewal.

References

Abbott, Edith. 1906. "Harriet Martineau and the Employment of Women in 1836." *Journal of Political Economy* 14 (December): 614–626.

Abrams, Philip. 1968. *The Origins of British Sociology*. Chicago: University of Chicago Press.

Adam Matthew Publications. 1991. *Women, Emancipation and Literature: The Papers of Harriet Martineau, 1802–1876*. Marlborough, England: Adam Matthew Publications.

Annan, Noel. 1959. *The Curious Strength of Positivism in English Political Thought*. L.T. Hobhouse Memorial Trust Lecture, no. 28. London: Oxford University Press.

Arbuckle, Elisabeth Sanders. 1983. "Introduction." Pp. ix–xxiv in *Harriet Martineau's Letters to Fanny Wedgwood*, edited by Elisabeth Sanders Arbuckle. Stanford, CA: Stanford University Press.

———. 1994. "Appendix: Harriet Martineau's Contributions to the London *Daily News*." Pp. 317–430 in *Harriet Martineau in the Daily News: Selected Contributions, 1852–1866*, edited by Elisabeth Sanders Arbuckle. New York: Garland Publishing.

Atkinson, Henry George, and Harriet Martineau. 1851. *Letters on the Laws of Man's Nature and Development*. Boston: Mendum.

Beaumont, Gustave de. 1835. *Marie, or Slavery in the United States*. Translated by Barbara Chapman, with an introduction by Alvis L. Tinnin. Stanford, CA: Stanford University Press, 1958.

Beaumont, Gustave de, and Alexis de Tocqueville. 1833. *On the Penitentiary System in the United States and Its Application in France*. Translated by Francis Lieber, foreword by Herman R. Lantz, introduction by Thorsten Sellin. Carbondale: Southern Illinois University Press, 1964.

Berg, Maxine. 1980. *The Machinery Question and the Making of Political Economy, 1815–1848*. Cambridge: Cambridge University Press.

———. 1985. *The Age of Manufactures: Industry, Innovation and Work in Britain, 1700–1820*. Totowa, NJ: Barnes and Noble.

———. 1994. "Factories, Workshops and Industrial Organization." Pp. 123–50 in *The Economic History of Britain Since 1700*, vol. 1, edited by Roderick Floud and Donald McCloskey. Second edition. Cambridge (UK): Cambridge University Press.

Bonser, Helen A. 1929. "Illustrations of Political Economy: An Early Example of the Case Method." *Social Service Review* 3 (June): 243–51.

Broschart, Kay. 1991a. "Beatrice Webb." Pp. 425–31 in *Women in Sociology: A Bio-Bibliographical Sourcebook*, edited by Mary Jo Deegan. Westport, CT: Greenwood Press.

———. 1991b. "Ida B. Wells-Barnett." Pp. 432–9 in *Women in Sociology: A Bio-Bibliographical Sourcebook*. Westport, CT: Greenwood Press.

Bullock, Katherine Helen. 1992. "Harriet Martineau's Society in America: A Critical Reexamination." M.A. Thesis, Department of Political Studies, Queen's University, Kingston, Ontario (Canada).

Burns, Edward McNall. 1955. *Western Civilizations: Their History and Culture*. New York: Norton.

Carlyle, Jane Welsh. 1883. *Letters and Memorials of Jane Welsh Carlyle*, edited by James Anthony Froude. New York: Charles Scribner's Sons.

Cawelti, John G. 1963. "Conformity and Democracy in America: Some Reflections Occasioned by the Republication of Martineau's *Society in America*." *Ethics* 73 (April 1963): 208–13.

Chapman, Maria Weston. 1877. *Memorials of Harriet Martineau*. Boston: James R. Osgood and Company.

Church, Roy A. 1975. *The Great Victorian Boom, 1850–1873*. London: Macmillan.

Clark, Alice. 1919. *The Working Life of Women in the Seventeenth Century*. London: Routledge and Kegan Paul.

Collins, Patricia Hill. 1990. *Black Feminist Thought: Knowledge, Consciousness, and the Politics of Empowerment*. Boston: Unwin Hyman.

Collins, Randall, and Michael Makowsky. 1998. *The Discovery of Society*. New York: McGraw-Hill.

Commager, Henry Steele. 1947. *Theodore Parker: Yankee Crusader*. Boston: Beacon Press.

Comte, Auguste. 1830–42. *Cours de philosophie positive*. 6 vols. Paris: Bachelier.

———. 1853. *The Positive Philosophy of Auguste Comte*, translated and condensed by Harriet Martineau. Reprinted, New York: William Gowans, 1868; London: Kegan Paul, Trench, Troebner, 1893; New York: AMS Press, 1974.

———. 1902–5. *Lettres d'Auguste Comte à divers, 1798–1857.* 2 vols. Paris: Fonds typographique de l'exécution testamentaire d'Auguste Comte.

Costin, Lela. 1983. *Two Sisters for Social Justice: A Biography of Edith and Grace Abbott.* Urbana: University of Illinois.

Court, W.H.B. 1938. *The Rise of the Midland Industries, 1600–1838.* Oxford: Oxford University Press.

Courtney, Janet E. 1920. "Harriet Martineau." Pp. 198–239 in *Freethinkers of the Nineteenth Century.* London: Chapman and Hall.

David, Deirdre. 1987. *Intellectual Women and Victorian Patriarchy: Harriet Martineau, Elizabeth Barrett Browning, George Eliot.* New York: Cornell University Press.

Davidoff, Leonore and Catherine Hall. 1987. *Family Fortunes.* Chicago: University of Chicago Press.

Davis, Lennard J. 1995. *Enforcing Normalcy: Disability, Deafness, and the Body.* New York: Verso.

De Staël, Germanine. 1796–1798. *Des circonstances actuelles*, edited by Lucia Omacini. Geneva: Droz, 1979.

Deegan, Mary Jo. 1975. "Identity Change in Modern Society: A Case Study of Physical Disability." Ph.D. dissertation, Department of Sociology, University of Chicago.

———. 1978a. "Women in Sociology, 1890–1930." *Journal of the History of Sociology* 1 (Fall): 11–34.

———. 1978b. "Interaction, Drama, and Freedom: The Social Theories of Erving Goffman and Victor Turner." *Humanity and Society* 2 (February): 33–46.

———. 1981. "Early Women Sociologists and the American Sociological Society: The Patterns of Exclusion and Participation." *American Sociologist* 16 (February): 14–24.

———. 1983. "Sociology at Wellesley College, 1900–1919." *Journal of the History of Sociology* 5 (Spring): 91–110.

———. 1985. "Multiple Minority Groups: A Case Study of Physically Disabled Women." Pp. 37–55 in *Women and Disability*, co-edited by Mary Jo Deegan and Nancy Brooks. New Brunswick, NJ: Transaction Press.

———. 1987. *Physically Disabled Women and New Directions in Public Policy, 1977–1987.* (Public Administration Series, no. P-2307). Monticello, IL: Vance Bibliographies.

———. 1988a. *Jane Addams and the Men of the Chicago School, 1892–1918.* New Brunswick, NJ: Transaction Books.

———. 1988b. "Transcending a Patriarchal Past: Teaching the History of Early Women Sociologists." *Teaching Sociology* 16: 141–59.

———. 1988c. "W.E.B. Du Bois and The Women of Hull-House: 1895–1899." *American Sociologist* 19 (Winter): 301–11.

———., ed. 1991. *Women in Sociology: A Bio-Bibliographical Sourcebook*. New York: Greenwood.

———. 1994. "'The Marginal Man' as a Gendered Concept: A Feminist Analysis of Robert E. Park's Epistemology." Pp. 55–71 in *Robert E. Park and the "Melting Pot" Theory*, edited by Renzo Gubert and Luigi Tomasi. Trent, Italy: Reverdito Edition.

———. 1995. "The Second Sex and the Chicago School: Women's Accounts, Knowledge, and Work, 1945–1960." Pp. 322–64 in *A Second Chicago School? The Development of a Postwar American Sociology*, edited by Gary Alan Fine. Chicago: University of Chicago Press.

———. 1996. "'Dear Love, Dear Love': Feminist Pragmatism and the Chicago Female World of Love and Ritual." *Gender & Society* 10 (October): 590–607.

———. 1997a. "Disabilities, Women with Physical." Pp. 227–8 in *Women's Issues*, edited by Dawn P. Dawson and Margaret McFadden. Pasadena, CA: Salem Press.

———. 1997b. "Gilman's Sociological Journey from *Herland* to *Ourland*." Pp. 1–57 in *With Her In Ourland: Sequel to Herland*, by Charlotte Perkins Gilman, edited by Mary Jo Deegan and Michael R. Hill. Westport, CT: Greenwood.

———. 1998. "A Rose is Not a Rosa is Not a Roseann is Not a Rosemary: The Many Names of Mary Elizabeth Roberts Smith Coolidge." Pp. 163–95 in *Advances in Gender Research*, vol. 3, edited by Vasilikie Demos and Marcia Texler Segal. Stamford, CT: JAI Press.

———. 1999. "Jessie Taft" and "Dorothy Swaine Thomas." Pp. 254–5; 504–5 in *American National Biography*, vol. 21, edited by John A. Garraty and Mark C. Carnes. Published under the auspices of the American Council of Learned Societies. New York: Oxford University Press.

———. Forthcoming a. "Transcending 'The Marginal Man': Challenging the Patriarchal Legacy of Robert E. Park." In *Marginality*, edited by Rutledge Dennis. Sage Publications.

———., ed. Forthcoming b. *A Voice from Chicago: Fannie Barrier Williams and the African American Experience, 1893–1926*. DeKalb,: Northern Illinois University Press.

Deegan, Mary Jo, and Nancy A. Brooks, eds. 1985. *Women and Disability: The Double Handicap*. New Brunswick, NJ: Transaction.

Deegan, Mary Jo, and Michael R. Hill, eds. 1987. *Women and Symbolic Interaction*. Boston: Allen and Unwin.

———. 1991 "Doctoral Dissertations as Liminal Journeys of the Self: Betwixt and Between in Graduate Sociology Programs." *Teaching Sociology* 19 (3): 322–32.

Deegan, Mary Jo, and Michael R. Hill, eds. 1997. *With Her in Ourland: Sequel to Herland*, by Charlotte Perkins Gilman, with an introduction by Mary Jo Deegan. Westport, CT: Greenwood Press.

Deegan, Mary Jo, and Christopher W. Podeschi. Forthcoming. "The Ecofeminist Pragmatism of Charlotte Perkins Gilman." *Environmental Ethics*.

Deegan, Mary Jo and Linda J. Rynbrandt. 2000. "For God and Community: The Unitarian Female Ministers' Tradition and Chicago Sociology: 1892–1918." Pp. 1–25 in *Social Change for Women and Children*, edited by Vasilikie Demos and Marcia Texler Segal. (Advances in Gender Research series, vol. 4). Greenwich, CT: JAI Press.

Deegan, Mary Jo, and Ana-Maria Wahl. Forthcoming. "Arts and Crafts in Chicago and Britain: The Sociology of Ellen Gates Starr at Hull-House." In *Essays in the History of Sociology*, edited by Janusz Mucha, Wlodzimierz Winclawski, and Dirk Käsler. Toruń, Poland: Nicholas Copernicus University Press.

Denzin, Norman K. 1989. *Interpretive Biography*. Beverly Hills, CA: Sage.

Dewey, John. 1929. *The Quest for Certainty*. New York: G.P. Putnam's Sons.

———. 1934. *A Common Faith*. New Haven, CT: Yale University Press.

Drummond, James. 1902. *The Life and Letters of James Martineau*. New York: Dodd, Mead.

Du Bois, W.E.B. 1903. *The Souls of Black Folk*. Chicago: A.C. McClurg.

Durkheim, Émile. 1893. *The Division of Labor in Society*, translated by W.D. Halls, with an introduction by Lewis Coser. New York: The Free Press, 1984.

———. 1895. *The Rules of Sociological Method*, edited by George E.G. Catlin, translated by Sarah A. Solovay and John H. Mueller. New York: The Free Press, 1938.

———. 1897. *Suicide: A Study in Sociology*, edited by George Simpson, translated by John A. Spaulding and George Simpson. Glencoe, IL: Free Press, 1951.

———. 1972. *Émile Durkheim: Selected Writings*, edited and translated by Anthony Giddens. Cambridge: Cambridge University Press.

Farganis, James. 1996. *Readings in Social Theory: The Classic Tradition to Post-Modernism*. New York: McGraw-Hill.

Farmer, Mary E. 1967. "The Positivist Movement and the Development of English Sociology." *Sociological Review* 15 (March): 5–20.

Feagin, Joe R. Forthcoming. "Social Justice and Sociology: Agendas for the 21st Century." *American Sociological Review*.

Fish, Virginia Kemp. 1981. "Annie Marion MacLean: A Neglected Part of The Chicago School." *Journal of the History of Sociology* 3 (Spring): 43–62.

———. 1985. "Hull House: Pioneer in Urban Research During Its Creative Years." *History of Sociology* 6 (Fall): 33–54.

Fitzpatrick, Ellen. 1990. *Endless Crusade: Women Social Scientists and Progressive Reform*. New York: Oxford University Press.

Gane, Mike. 1988. *On Durkheim's The Rules of Sociological Method*. New York: Routledge.

Garfinkle, Harold. 1967. *Studies in Ethnomethodology*. Englewood Cliffs, NJ: Prentice-Hall.

Gillian, Thomas. 1985. *Harriet Martineau*. Boston: Twayne.

Gilman, Charlotte Perkins. 1898. *Women and Economics: A Study of the Economic Relation between Men and Women as a Factor in Social Evolution*, edited by Carl M. Degler. New York: Harper and Row, 1966.

———. 1904. *Human Work*. New York: McClure Phillips.

———. 1915. *The Dress of Women: An Introduction to the Symbolism and Sociology of Clothing*, edited with an introduction by Michael R. Hill and Mary Jo Deegan. Westport, CT: Greenwood Press, forthcoming.

Goffman, Erving. 1959. *The Presentation of Self in Everyday Life*. Garden City, NY: Doubleday, 1959.

———. 1963. *Stigma*. Englewood Cliffs, NJ: Prentice-Hall.

———. 1967. *Interaction Ritual: Essays on Face-to-Face Behavior*. New York: Harper and Row.

Gotsch-Thomson, Susan. 1990. "The Integration of Gender into the Teaching of Classical Social Theory." *Teaching Sociology* 18 (January): 69–73.

Haight, Gordon A. 1940. *George Eliot and John Chapman, with Chapman's Diaries*. Second edition. New Haven, CT: Yale University Press, 1969.

———. 1954–55. *The George Eliot Letters*. 7 vols. New Haven, CT: Yale University Press.

Halbwachs, Maurice. 1934. "Quetelet, Adolphe (1796–1874)." Pp. 23–5 in *Encylopaedia of the Social Sciences*, vol. 13, edited by E.R.A. Seligman. New York: Macmillan.

Hamburger, Joseph. 1995. Review of *The Correspondence of John Stuart Mill and Auguste Comte*, translated from the French and edited by Oscar A. Haec, with an introduction by Angle Cramer-Marietta. *Victorian Studies* 39 (Autumn): 72–75.

Harp, Gillis. 1995. *Positivist Republic: Auguste Comte and the Reconstruction of American Liberalism, 1865–1920*. University Park, PA: Pennsylvania State University Press.

Harrison, Frederic. 1895. "Introduction." Pp. v–xix in *The Positive Philosophy of Auguste Comte*, vol. 1, by Auguste Comte, translated and condensed by Harriet Martineau. London: G. Bell, 1913.

———. 1907. *The Philosophy of Common Sense*. New York: Macmillan.

Hassett, Constance W. 1996. "Siblings and Anti-slavery: The Literary and Political Relations of Harriet Martineau, James Martineau, and Maria Weston Chapman." *Signs* 21 (Winter): 374–409.

Hawkins, Richard. 1938. *Positivism in the United States (1853–1861)*. Cambridge: Harvard University Press.

Heilbron, Johan. 1995. *The Rise of Social Theory*, translated by Sheila Gogol. Minneapolis: University of Minnesota Press.

Hess, Elizabeth, Elizabeth Markson, and Peter Stein. 1988. *Introductory Sociology*. 3rd ed. New York: Macmillan.

Hewett, Phillip. 1978. *Unitarians in Canada*. Toronto (Canada): Fitzhenry and Whiteside.

Hickox, M.S. 1984. "The Problem of Early English Sociology." *Sociological Review* 32 (February): 1–17.

Hill, Michael R. 1984. "Epistemology, Axiology, and Ideology in Sociology." *Mid-American Review of Sociology* 9: 59–77.

———. 1987a. "Harriet Martineau's Novels and the Sociology of Class, Race, and Gender." Paper presented at the meetings of the Association for Humanist Sociology. Typescript. [Photocopy].

———. 1987b. "Novels, Thought Experiments, and Humanist Sociology in the Classroom." *Teaching Sociology* 15: 38–44.

———. 1988. "Research by Bureaucracy: Hattie Plum Williams and the National Commission on Law Observance and Enforcement, 1929–1931." *Mid-American Review of Sociology* 13 (Winter): 69–84.

———. 1989. "Empiricism and Reason in Harriet Martineau's Sociology." Pp. xv–lx in *How to Observe Morals and Manners*, by Harriet Martineau. Sesquicentennial edition. New Brunswick, NJ: Transaction.

———. 1991. "Harriet Martineau." Pp. 289–97 in *Women in Sociology: A Bio-Bibliographical Sourcebook*, edited by Mary Jo Deegan. New York: Greenwood.

———. 1993. *Archival Strategies and Techniques*. (Qualitative Research Methods Series, no. 31). Newbury Park, CA: Sage.

———. 1998. "Martineau in Current Introductory Textbooks: An Empirical Survey." *The Harriet Martineau Sociological Society Newsletter*, no. 4 (Spring): 4–5.

Hill, Michael R., and Mary Jo Deegan, eds. *The Dress of Women: A Critical Introduction to the Symbolism and Sociology Clothing*, by Charlotte Perkins Gilman, with in introduction by Michael R. Hill and Mary Jo Deegan. Westport, CT: Greenwood.

Hobsbawm, Eric. 1968. *Industry and Empire: From 1790 to the Present Day*. New York: Penguin Books.

Hoecker-Drysdale, Susan. 1992. *Harriet Martineau: First Woman Sociologist*. Oxford: Berg.

———. 1996. "The Enigma of Harriet Martineau's Letters on Science." *Women's Writing* 2 (Spring): 155–65.

———. 1998. "Harriet Martineau (1802–1876): Kritische Sozialforschung: Theorie und Praxis." Pp. 28–59 in *Frauen in der Soziologie: Neun*

Porträts, edited by Claudia Honegger and Theresa Wobbe. Munich: Beck-Verlag.

———. 2000. "Harriet Martineau." Pp. 53–80 in *The Blackwell Companion to Major Social Theorists*, edited by George Ritzer. Malden, MA: Blackwell.

Honegger, Claudia, and Theresa Wobbe. 1998. *Frauen in der Soziologie: Neun Porträts*. Munich: Beck-Verlag.

Houghton, Walter E. 1957. *The Victorian Frame of Mind, 1830–1870*. New Haven, CT: Yale University Press.

Hunter, Shelagh. 1995. *Harriet Martineau: The Poetics of Moralism*. Aldershot, England: Scolar Press.

Hutcheon, Pat Duffy. 1996. "Harriet Martineau and the Quiet Revolution." Pp. 70–96 in *Leaving the Cave: Evolutionary Naturalism in Social Scientific Thought*. Waterloo, ON, Canada: Wilfrid Laurier University Press.

———. 1998. "Renaissance Humanism and its Unitarian Offshoot." *Humanist in Canada* 125 (Summer): 22–7.

Jackson, A.W. 1901. *James Martineau*. Boston: Little, Brown.

Joyce, Patrick. 1980. *Work, Society and Politics: The Culture of the Factory in Later Victorian England*. New Brunswick, NJ: Rutgers University Press.

Knight, Charles. 1864. *Passages of a Working Life*. London: Bradbury & Evans.

Kurtz, Paul, ed. 1973. *Humanist Manifestos I and II*. Buffalo, NY: Prometheus Books.

Lamont, Corliss. 1949. *The Philosophy of Humanism*. New York: Philosophical Library, 1957.

Lehmann, Jennifer M. 1993. *Deconstructing Durkheim*. London: Routledge.

Lemert, Charles. 1993. *Social Theory: The Multicultural and Classic Readings*. Boulder, CO: Westview Press.

———. 1995. *Sociology After the Crisis*. Boulder, CO: Westview Press.

Lengermann, Patricia, and Jill Niebrugge-Brantley. 1996a. "Engendering Social Theory: Early Women Sociologists Theorize Domestic Service." Paper presented at the Midterm Conference, International Sociological Association, Research Committee on the History of Sociology, Amsterdam, The Netherlands. Typescript. [Photocopy].

———. 1996b. "Early Women Sociologists." Pp. 294–328 in *Classical Sociology*, by George Ritzer. New York: McGraw-Hill.

———. 1998. *The Women Founders: Sociology and Social Theory, 1830–1930*. New York: McGraw-Hill.

———. 2000a. "Classical Feminist Social Theory." Pp. 125–37 in *Handbook of Social Theory*, edited by George Ritzer and Barry Smart. London: Sage.

———. 2000b. "Early Women Sociologists." Pp. 291–6 in *Classical Sociology*, by George Ritzer. New York: McGraw-Hill.

Lewes, George. 1853. *Comte's Philosophy of the Sciences: Being an Exposition of the Principles of the "Cours de philosophie positive."* London: Henry G. Bohn.

Lipset, Seymour Martin. 1962. "Harriet Martineau's America." Pp. 4–42 in *Society in America*, by Harriet Martineau, abridged and edited by S.M. Lipset. (Social Science Classics Series). New Brunswick, NJ: Transaction, 1981.

Littrè, Émile. 1863. *Auguste Comte et la philosophie positive*. Paris (France): Hachette.

Logan, Deborah. 1999. "Fancy-work and Bluestockingism." *The Martineau Society Newsletter*, no. 11 (July): [12–17].

Lohrli, Anne. 1973. *Household Words: A Weekly Journal, 1850–1859, Conducted by Charles Dickens*. Toronto: University of Toronto Press.

Long, Judy. 1987. "Telling Women's Lives: The New Sociobiography." Paper presented at the annual meetings of the American Sociological Association. Typescript. [Photocopy].

Macaulay, Catharine. 1790. *Observations on the Reflections of the Rt Hon Edmund Burke on the Revolution in France*. London: Dilly.

Mannheim, Karl. 1940. *Man and Society in an Age of Reconstruction*, translated by Edward Shils. New York: Harcourt, Brace.

Martineau, Harriet. 1822a. "Essay on the Proper Use of the Prospective Faculty." Reprinted in *Miscellanies*, vol. 1, Boston: Hilliard, Gray, 1836: 224–30.

———. 1822b. "Essay on the Proper Use of the Retrospective Faculty." Reprinted in *Miscellanies*, vol. 1, Boston: Hilliard, Gray, 1836: 215–24.

———. 1822c. "Female Writers on Practical Divinity, No. I." *Monthly Repository* 17 (October): 593–96. [Signed, "Discipulus"].

———. 1822d. "Female Writers on Practical Divinity, No. II." *Monthly Repository* 17 (December) 746–50. [Signed, "Discipulus"].

———. 1823a. *Devotional Exercises, Consisting of Reflections and Prayers, For the Use of Young Persons*, by a Lady. London: Rowland Hunter.

———. 1823b. "On Female Education." *Monthly Repository* 18 (February): 77–81.

———. 1830. *Traditions of Palestine*. London: Longman, Rees, Orme, Brown, and Green.

———. 1831a. *Five Years of Youth; or, Sense and Sentiment*. London: Harvey and Darton.

———. 1831b. *The Essential Faith of the Universal Church: Deduced from the Sacred Records*. London: The Unitarian Association.

———. 1831c. *Providence as Manifested through Israel: An Essay . . . Issued by the British and Foreign Unitarian Association and addressed to the Jews*. London: The Unitarian Association.

———. 1831d. "On the Duty of Studying Political Economy." Pp. 272–88 in *Miscellanies*, vol. 1, by Harriet Martineau. Boston: Hilliard, Gray, 1836.

———. 1832a. *The Faith as Unfolded by Many Prophets*. London: The Unitarian Association.

———. 1832–1834. *Illustrations of Political Economy*. 25 nos. in 9 vols. London: Charles Fox.

———. 1834. "Letter to the Deaf." Pp. 248–65 in *Miscellanies*, vol. 1. Boston: Hilliard, Gray, 1836.

———. 1836a. "The Hanwell Lunatic Asylum." Pp. 230–48 in *Miscellanies*, vol. 1. Boston: Hilliard, Gray.

———. 1836c. *Miscellanies*. 2 vols. Boston: Hilliard, Gray. Reprinted, AMS Press, 1975.

———. 1836d. "On Moral Independence." Pp. 179–191 in *Miscellanies*, vol. 1, by H. Martineau. Boston: Hilliard, Gray.

———. 1836e. "Godwin's Thoughts on Man." Pp. 118–132 in *Miscellanies*, vol. 2, by H. Martineau. Boston: Hilliard, Gray.

———. 1837. *Society in America*. 2nd edition. 3 vols. London: Saunders and Otley, 1839.

———. 1838a. "Domestic Service." *London and Westminster Review* 29: 405–432.

———. 1838b. *How to Observe Morals and Manners*. Sesquicentennial edition, with a new introduction, appendices, and analytical index by Michael R. Hill. New Brunswick, NJ: Transaction, 1989.

———. 1838c. *Retrospect of Western Travel*. London: Saunders and Otley. Reprint edition. [n.p.]: Dover, n.d.

———. 1838d. *The Lady's Maid*. (*Guide to Service* series). London: Charles Knight.

———. 1839a. *Deerbrook*. 3 vols. London: Edward Moxon.

———. 1839b. *The Martyr Age of the United States*. New York: Benedict.

———. 1841. *The Hour and the Man*. 3 vols. London: Edward Moxon.

———. 1844a. "Letter." Pp. xvii–xxii in *Mind Amongst the Spindles: A Selection from the Lowell Offering: A Miscellany Wholly Composed by the Factory Girls of an American City*. London: Charles Knight.

———. 1844b. *Life in the Sick-Room*. Boston: Bowles and Crosby.

———. 1845. *Letters on Mesmerism*. London: Edward Moxon.

———. 1845–6. *Forest and Game Law Tales*. London: Edward Moxon.

———. 1848. *Eastern Life, Present and Past*. Philadelphia: Lea and Blanchard.

———. 1849. *Household Education*. Philadelphia: Lea and Blanchard.

———. 1853a. "The Deaf Playmate's Story." *Harper's New Monthly Magazine* 33 (February): 409–12. [This unsigned work by Martineau was wrongly attributed to Charles Dickens by *Harper's*. For attribution of authorship to Martineau, see Lohrli (1973: 360). This story also appeared, unsigned, in the unnumbered Christmas Issue of Charles Dickens' *Household Words* (Christmas 1852): 27–30].

———. 1853b. "Preface." Pp. 3–11 in *The Positive Philosophy of Auguste Comte*, by Auguste Comte, translated and condensed by Harriet Martineau.

Reprinted, New York: William Gowans, 1868; London: Kegan Paul, Trench, Troebner, 1893; New York: AMS Press, 1974.
———. 1854a. "Deaf Mutes." *Household Words* 9 (March 25): 134–38. [Unsigned, see Lohrli (1973: 361) for attribution of authorship to Martineau].
———. 1854b. "Idiots Again." *Household Words* 9 (April 15): 197–200. [Unsigned, see Lohrli (1973: 361) for attribution of authorship to Martineau].
———. 1854c. "Blindness." *Household Words* 9 (June 17): 421–25. [Unsigned, see Lohrli (1973: 361) for attribution of authorship to Martineau].
———. 1854d. "Results of the Census of 1851." *Westminster and Foreign Quarterly Review* 61 (April 1): 323–57.
———. 1855. *The Factory Controversy: A Warning Against Meddling Legislation*. Manchester, Engalnd: National Association of Factory Occupiers.
———. 1857a. *British Rule in India*. London: Smith, Elder.
———. 1857b. *Corporate Tradition and National Rights*. London: B. Routledge.
———. 1858. *Suggestions Towards the Future Government of India*. London: Smith, Elder.
———. 1858. "What is 'Social Science'?" *The Spectator* [31] (October 23): 1120.
———. 1859a. *England and Her Soldiers*. London: Smith, Elder.
———. 1859b. "Female Industry." *Edinburgh Review* 109 (April): 151–173.
———. 1859c. *Endowed Schools of Ireland*. London: Smith, Elder.
———. 1860a. "Miss Nightingale's *Notes on Nursing*." *Quarterly Review* 107 (April): 392–422.
———. 1860b. "Reverie after Reading Miss Nightingale's 'Notes on Nursing.'" *Fraser's Magazine* 111 (June): 753–57.
———. 1861. *Health, Husbandry, and Handicraft*. London: Bradbury and Evans.
———. 1862. "Modern Domestic Service." *Edinburgh Review* 115 (April): 409–39.
———. 1863. "Death or Life in India." *Macmillan's Magazine* 8 (August): 332–40.
———. 1864a. "Middle-Class Education in England: Boys." *Cornhill Magazine* 10 (October): 409–26.
———. 1864b. "Middle-Class Education in England: Girls." *Cornhill Magazine* 10 (November): 549–68.
———. 1864c. "Every two or three . . ." (London) *Daily News* (November 11): leader no. 2.
———. 1865. "Nurses Wanted." *Cornhill Magazine* 11 (April): 409–25.

———. 1868. "Salem Witchcraft." *Edinburgh Review* 128 (July): 1–47.

———. 1869. *Biographical Sketches*. New York: Leypoldt & Holt.

———. 1870. *The Contagious Diseases Acts, as Applied to Garrison Towns and Naval Stations*. Liverpool, England: Brakell, 1870.

———. 1877a. "An Autobiographic Memoir." Pp. 562–73 in *Memorials of Harriet Martineau*, by Maria Weston Chapman. Boston: James R. Osgood.

———. 1877b. *Harriet Martineau's Autobiography*, edited by Maria Weston Chapman. Together with M.W. Chapman's *Memorials of Harriet Martineau*. 3rd edition. 2 vols. Boston: James R. Osgood, 1878.

———. 1877c. "Letter." Pp. 40–50 in *An Epitome of the Positive Philosophy and Religion Explanatory of the Society of Humanity in the City of New York, Together with the Constitution and Regulations of that Society: To Which Is Added an Important Letter of Harriet Martineau in Regard to Her Religious Convictions*. Second edition. New York: The Society of Humanity.

———. 1910. "Earl Spencer and Miss Florence Nightingale." *Daily News* (August 15): 1–2. Reprinted in *Harriet Martineau on Women*, edited by Gayle Graham Yates, New Brunswick, NJ: Rutgers University Press, 1985: 192–202.

———. 1983. *Harriet Martineau's Letters to Fanny Wedgwood*. Edited by Elisabeth Sanders Arbuckle. Stanford, CA: Stanford University Press.

———. 1985. *Harriet Martineau on Women*, edited by Gayle Graham Yates. New Brunswick, NJ: Rutgers University Press.

———. 1990. *Harriet Martineau: Selected Letters*, edited by Valerie Sanders. New York: Clarendon Press, Oxford University Press.

———. 1994. *Harriet Martineau in the London Daily News: Selected Contributions, 1852–1866*. Edited by Elisabeth Sanders Arbuckle. New York: Garland.

———. 1995. *Harriet Martineau and America: Selected Letters from the Reinhard S. Speck Collection*, edited by R.A. Burchell. Berkeley, CA: Friends of the Bancroft Library.

Marx, Karl. 1844. *The Economic and Philosophic Manuscripts of 1844*. Moscow: Foreign Languages Publishing House, 1961.

Marx, Karl and Frederick Engels. 1846. *The German Ideology*. Moscow: Progress Publishers, 1976.

———. 1848. *The Manifesto of the Communist Party*. Pp. 469–500 in *The Marx-Engels Reader*, edited by Robert C. Tucker. Second edition. New York: Norton, 1978.

Mathias, Peter. 1969. *The First Industrial Nation*. London: Methuen.

McCulloch, J.R. 1825. *Principles of Political Economy: With a Sketch of the Rise and Progress of the Science*. London: Ward, Lock.

McDonald, Lynn. 1993. *The Early Origins of the Social Sciences*. Montréal: McGill-Queens University Press.

———. 1994. *The Women Founders of the Social Sciences.* Ottawa,Canada: Carleton University Press.

———. 1998. *Women Theorists on Society and Politics.* Waterloo, Canada: Wilfrid Laurier University Press.

———, ed. Forthcoming. *The Collected Works of Florence Nightingale.*

Mead, George H. 1899. "The Working Hypothesis in Social Reform." *American Journal of Sociology* 5 (March): 369–71.

———. 1934. *Mind, Self and Society*, edited and introduced by Charles W. Morris. Chicago: University of Chicago Press.

Mendelsohn, Jack. 1985. *Being Liberal in an Illiberal Age: Why I am a Unitarian Universalist.* Boston: Beacon Press.

Mill, John Stuart. 1865. *Auguste Comte and Positivism.* Ann Arbor: University of Michigan Press, 1968.

———. *Collected Works of John Stuart Mill.* 33 vols. Toronto: University of Toronto Press.

Mineka, Francis E. 1944. *The Dissidence of Dissent: The Monthly Repository, 1806–1838.* Chapel Hill: University of North Carolina Press.

Murphy, James. 1968. "Positivism in England: The Reception of Comte's Doctrines, 1840–1870." Ph.D. Dissertation, Columbia University.

Nevill, John Cranston. 1943. *Harriet Martineau.* London: F. Muller.

Nightingale, Florence. [1860]. *Notes on Nursing: What It Is, and What It Is Not.* New York: D. Appleton. Reprinted, New York: Dover, 1969.

———. [1862]. "Note on the Supposed Protection Afforded Against Venereal Disease by Recognizing Prostitution and Putting It Under Police Protection." Private and confidential, not published. [Copy available at the British Museum].

———. 1863. *How People May Live and Not Die in India.* London: Emily Faithful.

———. 1874. *Life or Death in India.* London: Spottiswoode.

Nisbet, Robert. 1988. "Tocqueville's Ideal Types." Pp. 171–91 in *Reconstructing Tocqueville's Democracy in America*, edited by Abraham S. Eisenstadt. New Brunswick, NJ: Rutgers University Press.

Oražem, Claudia. 1999. *Political Economy and Fiction in the Early Works of Harriet Martineau.* Frankfurt am Main: Peter Lang.

Park, Robert E. 1928. "Human Migration and the Marginal Man." *American Journal of Sociology* 33 (May): 881–98.

Park, Robert E. and Ernest W. Burgess. 1921. *Introduction to the Science of Sociology.* Chicago: University of Chicago Press.

Parke, David B. 1957. *The Epic of Unitarianism.* Boston: Beacon Press.

Payn, James. 1884. *Some Literary Recollections*, New York: Harper.

Peterson, Linda H. 1986. "Martineau's Autobiography: The Feminine Debate over Self-Interpretation." Pp. 120–55 in *Victorian Autobiography: The*

Tradition of Self-Interpretation, by L.H. Peterson. New Haven, CT: Yale University Press, 1986.
Pichanick, Valerie K. 1980. *Harriet Martineau: The Woman and Her Work, 1802–76*. Ann Arbor: University of Michigan Press.
Pickering, Mary. 1997. "A New Look At Auguste Comte." Pp. 11–44 in *Reclaiming the Sociological Classics: The State of Scholarship*, edited by Charles Camic. Malden, MA: Blackwell.
———. 1993. *Auguste Comte: An Intellectual Biography*, vol. 1. Cambridge: Cambridge University Press.
———. 2000. "Auguste Comte." Pp. 25–52 in *The Blackwell Companion to Major Social Theorists*, edited by George Ritzer. Malden, MA: Blackwell.
Pierson, George Wilson. 1938. *Tocqueville and Beaumont in America*. New York: Oxford University Press.
Pinchbeck, Ivy. 1930. *Women Workers of the Industrial Revolution*. London: Routledge and Kegan Paul.
Polanyi, Karl. 1944. *The Great Transformation: The Political and Economic Origins of Our Time*. Boston: Beacon Press.
Postlethwaite, Diana. 1984. *Making It Whole: A Victorian Circle and the Shape of Their World*. ColumbusH: Ohio State University Press.
Reinharz, Shulamit. 1989. "Teaching the History of Women in Sociology: Or Dorothy Swaine Thomas, Wasn't She the Woman Married to William I?" *The American Sociologist* 20 (Spring): 87–94.
———. 1992. *Feminist Methods in Social Research*. New York: Oxford University Press.
———., ed. 1993. *A Contextualized Chronology of Women's Sociological Work*. Waltham, MA: Brandeis University, Women's Studies Program.
Richards, Laura E., ed. 1934. "Letters of Florence Nightingale." *Yale Review* 24 (December): 326–47.
Riedesel, Paul L. 1981. "Who Was Harriet Martineau?" *Journal of the History of Sociology* 3 (Spring-Summer): 63–80.
Ritzer, George. 1996. *Classical Sociological Theory*. New York: McGraw-Hill.
Rivlin, Joseph B. 1947. *Harriet Martineau: A Bibliography of Her Separately Published Books*. New York: New York Public Library.
Rosenberg, Rosalind. 1982. *Beyond Separate Spheres: Intellectual Roots of Modern Feminism*. New Haven, CT: Yale University Press.
Rossi, Alice S. 1973. "The First Woman Sociologist: Harriet Martineau (1802–1876)." Pp. 118–24 in *The Feminist Papers: From Adams to de Beauvoir*, edited by Alice S. Rossi. New York: Bantam Books.
Rynbrandt, Linda J. 1999. *Caroline Bartlett Crane and Progressive Reform: Social Housekeeping as Sociology*. (Women and Sociological Theory, vol. 1). New York: Garland Publishing.

Saint-Simon, Henri. 1825. *De l'Organisation sociale*. In *Oeuvres choisies*. Brussels (Belgium): Lemonnier, 1859. Reprinted, Hildesheim, NY: Olms, 1973.

Sanders, Valerie. 1986. *Reason Over Passion: Harriet Martineau and the Victorian Novel*. New York: St. Martin's Press.

———., ed. 1990. *Selected Letters*, by Harriet Martineau. Oxford: Oxford University Press.

Scharff, Richard C. 1995. *Comte After Positivism*. Cambridge: Cambridge University Press.

Scott, Clinton Lee. 1964. *These Live Tomorrow: Twenty Unitarian Universalist Biographies*. Boston: Beacon Press.

Schutz, Alfred. 1971. *Collected Papers*. 3 vols. The Hague (The Netherlands): M. Mijhoff.

Simmel, Georg. 1950. "The Stranger." Pp. 402–8 in *The Sociology of George Simmel*, edited and introduced by Kurt H. Wolff. Toronto: Collier-MacMillan Canada.

Simon, W.H. 1963. *European Positivism in the Nineteenth Century: An Essay in Intellectual History*. Ithaca, NY: Cornell University Press.

Smith, Adam. 1759. *The Theory of Moral Sentiments*. Indianapolis, IN: The Liberty Fund, 1976.

———. 1776. *An Inquiry into the Nature and Causes of the Wealth of Nations*, edited by Edwin Cannan. London: Methuen 1950.

Smith, Dorothy E. 1987. *The Everyday World As Problematic: A Feminist Sociology*. Boston: Northeastern University Press.

Spender, Dale. 1982. "Harriet Martineau." Pp. 125–35 in *Women of Ideas and What Men Have Done to Them*, by Dale Spender. London: Routledge & Kegan Paul.

Sprague, Joey. 1997. "Holy Men and Big Guns: The Can[n]on in Social Theory." *Gender & Society* 11 (1): 88–107.

Stewart, Dugald. 1793. *Outlines of Moral Philosophy*. Edinburgh (UK): Creech.

———. 1854–60. *The Collected Works of Dugald Stewart*, edited by William Hamilton. 10 vols. Edinburgh: Constable.

Stinchcombe, Arthur L. 1982. "Should Sociologists Forget Their Mothers and Fathers?" *The American Sociologist* 17 (February): 2–11.

Stromberg, Roland N. 1963. *A History of Western Civilization*. Homewood, IL: Dorsey Press.

Sydie, R.A., and Bert Adams. Forthcoming. "Beatrice Webb and Charlotte Perkins Gilman: Feminist Debates and Contradictions." *Sociological Origins* 2 (1).

Terry, James L. 1983. "Bringing Women . . . In: A Modest Proposal." *Teaching Sociology* 10 (January): 251–61.

Thompson, Martha, and Mary Jo Deegan, eds. 1981. "Women Sociologists" (special issue). *Midwest Feminist Papers* 2: 1–103.

Timmins, Samuel (ed). 1866. *The Resources, Products, and Industrial History of Birmingham and the Midland Hardware District: A Series of Reports* . London: Robert Hardwicke.

Tocqueville, Alexis de. 1831. *Journey to America*. Translated by George Lawrence, edited by J.P. Mayer. Revised and augmented edition in collaboration with A.P. Kerr. Garden City, NY: Anchor, 1971.

———. 1835–40. *Democracy in America*. Translated by Henry Reeve. New edition, with a biographical notice by the translator and some additional notes. 2 vols. London: Longmans, Green, 1875.

———. 1967. *OEuvres complètes*, vol. 8, part 1: *Correspondance d'Alexis de Tocqueville et de Gustave de Beaumont*. Paris: Gallimard.

———. 1980. *Alexis de Tocqueville on Democracy, Revolution, and Society: Selected Writings*. Edited and with an introduction by John Stone and Stephen Mennell. (Heritage of Sociology). Chicago: University of Chicago Press.

Tristan, Flora. 1843. *The Workers' Union*, translated with an introduction by Beverly Livingston. Urbana: University of Illinois Press, 1983.

van Kleek, Mary. 1913. *Women in the Bookbinding Trade*. New York: Survey Associates.

Veblen, Thorstein. 1899. *The Theory of the Leisure Class: An Economic Study of Institutions*. New York: The Modern Library, 1934.

———. 1914. *The Instinct of Workmanship, and the State of the Industrial Arts*. New York: Macmillan. Reprinted, New York: Augustus M. Kelley, 1964.

Vicinus, Martha and Bea Nergaard, eds. 1990. *Ever Yours, Florence Nightingale: Selected Letters*. Cambridge: Harvard University Press.

Wallerstein, Immanuel. 1974. *The Modern World-System: Capitalist Agriculture and the Origins of the European World-Economy*. New York: Academic Press.

Webb, Robert K. 1955. *The British Working Class Reader 1790–1848: Literacy and Social Tension*. London: George Allen and Unwin.

———. 1959. "A Handlist of Contributions to the Daily News by Harriet Martineau, 1852–1866." Typescript. [Photocopy]. Updated in Arbuckle 1994.

———. 1960. *Harriet Martineau: A Radical Victorian*. New York: Columbia University Press.

Weber, Max. 1904–5. *The Protestant Ethic and the Spirit of Capitalism*, translated by Talcott Parsons. London: George Allen and Unwin, 1985.

———. 1946. *From Max Weber: Essays in Sociology*, translated, edited, and introduced by Hans Gerth and C. Wright Mills. New York: Oxford University Press.

Weiner, Gaby. 1983. "Introduction." Pp. i–xx in *Harriet Martineau's Autobiography*, vol. 1, by H. Martineau. London: Virago Press.

Wheatley, Vera. 1957. *The Life and Work of Harriet Martineau*. London: Jecker and Warburg.
Wilbur, Earl Morse. 1953. *Our Unitarian Heritage*. Boston: Beacon Press.
———. 1972. *A History of Unitarianism: Socinianism and its Antecedents*. Boston: Beacon Press.
Wilson, Edward O. 1998. *Consilience: The Unity of Knowledge*. New York: Alfred A. Knopf.
Winter, A. 1995. "Harriet Martineau and the Reform of the Invalid in Victorian England." *Historical Journal* 38 (3): 597–616.
Wollstonecraft, Mary. 1794. *An Historical and Moral View of the Origin and Progress of the French Revolution*. London: J. Johnson.
Wright, Conrad. 1954. *The Beginnings of Unitarianism in America*. Boston: Beacon Press, 1972.
———. 1982. *A Stream of Thought*. Boston: Unitarian Universalist Association.
Wright, T.R. 1986. *The Religion of Humanity: The Impact of Comtean Positivism on Victorian Britain*. Cambridge: Cambridge University Press.
Yates, Gayle G., ed. 1985. *Harriet Martineau on Women*, by Harriet Martineau, edited by G.G. Yates. New Brunswick, NJ: Rutgers University Press.
Yeo, Richard. 1993. *Defining Science: William Whewell, Natural Knowledge and Public Debate in Early Victorian Britain*. Cambridge: Cambridge University Press.
Zeitlin, Irving. 1971. *Liberty, Equality, and Revolution in Alexis de Tocqueville*. Boston: Little, Brown.

About the Contributors

MARY JO DEEGAN, IS PROFESSOR OF SOCIOLOGY AND WOMEN'S Studies at the University of Nebraska-Lincoln. She earned the Ph.D. in sociology at the University of Chicago and is the author of over one-hundred-twenty-five articles on sociology, American rituals, the history of women in sociology, and Chicago race relations. She has written/edited fourteen books, including her award-winning *Jane Addams and the Men of the Chicago School, 1892–1918* (1988). Other works include *The American Ritual Tapestry* (1998); *Women in Sociology* (1991); *American Ritual Dramas* (1989); *Women and Disability* (1985); and edited editions of *Play, School, and Society* by George H. Mead (1999); and *With Her in Ourland* by Charlotte Perkins Gilman (1997). She is the series editor of the *Women and Sociological Theory* series. Currently, she is editing the collected writings of Fannie Barrier Williams. Professor Deegan is an elected member of the first Council of the American Sociological Association's Section on the History of Sociology and is an active contributor to the Research Committee on the History of Sociology in the International Sociological Association.

Michael R. Hill, editor of *Sociological Origins*, earned doctorates in geography and sociology at the University of Nebraska-Lincoln and is now sometime Adjunct Professor of Sociology in the University of Nebraska and Iowa Western Community College. His projects have included an ASA/NSF grant that enables him to inventory the papers of the American Sociological Association at the Library of Congress. In addition to numerous articles, he is the author of *Walking, Crossing Streets, and Choosing Pedestrian Routes* (1984), *Archival Strategies and Techniques* (1993), editor of Harriet

Martineau's *How To Observe Morals and Manners* (1989), and co-editor of *Women and Symbolic Interaction* (1987) and Charlotte Perkins Gilman's *With Her in Ourland* (1997). He served ten years on the archives committee of the American Sociological Association and is Chair-elect of the ASA Section on the History of Sociology. Dr. Hill is a co-founder of the Harriet Martineau Sociological Society and is an active contributor to the Research Committee on the History of Sociology in the International Sociological Association.

Susan Hoecker-Drysdale earned her doctorate at Louisiana State University and is Professor of Sociology (Retired), Department of Sociology and Anthropology, Concordia University, Montréal, Québec. She was a Visiting Fellow, School of Advanced Study, University of London, 1997–98. Her publications include a biography, *Harriet Martineau: First Woman Sociologist* (1992); "Harriet Martineau" in *The Blackwell Companion to Major Social Theorists*, edited by George Ritzer (2000); "Harriet Martineau (1802–1876): Kritische Sozialforschung: Theorie und Praxis" in *Frauen in der Soziologie: Neun Porträts*, edited by Claudia Honegger and Theresa Wobbe (1998); "The Enigma of Harriet Martineau's Letters on Science" in the journal *Women's Writings: The Elizabethan to Victorian Period* (1995). Her current research and writing focuses on Harriet Martineau, selected women in classical sociology, and the history of feminist sociological theory. She is a founding member of The British Martineau Society and The Harriet Martineau Sociological Society, and a Lifetime Honourary Member of the Simone de Beauvoir Institute, Concordia University. Professor Hoecker-Drysdale is an elected member of the first Council of the American Sociological Association's Section on the History of Sociology and of the Executive Council of the Research Committee on the History of Sociology in the International Sociological Association.

Pat Duffy Hutcheon is a writer, sociologist and educator. Her Ph.D. in sociology is from the University of Queensland in Australia. Now retired, she taught in Education faculties at the University of Regina (where she became Head of the Educational Foundations Department) and at the University of British Columbia. She was also research advisor to the Health Promotion Branch of the Canadian Department of Health and Welfare and director of the Ottawa-based Vanier Institute of the Family. Her more than eighty publications include *A Sociology of Canadian Education* (1975) and three recent books: *Leaving the Cave: Evolutionary Naturalism in Social-Scientific Thought* (1996), *Building Character and Culture* (1999), and *The Road to Reason: Landmarks in the Evolution of Humanist Thought* (2001). She was named "Canadian Humanist of the Year 2000" by the

Canadian Humanist Association and is a recipient of the American Humanist Association's "Distinguished Humanist Award" for 2001.

Patricia Madoo Lengermann earned the Ph.D. at Cornell University and is Research Professor of Sociology at The George Washington University. She writes as a team with Jill Niebrugge. Together, their scholarship explores the history of sociology, sociological theory, feminist theory, gender and the relations among these four. Among other works, they are the authors of *The Women Founders: Sociology and Social Theory, 1830–1930* (1998) and "Classical Feminist Social Theory" in *Handbook of Social Theory* edited by George Ritzer and Barry Smart (2001). Pat and Jill were instrumental co-founders of the American Sociological Association's Section on the History of Sociology and are active contributors to the Research Committee on the History of Sociology in the International Sociological Association.

Helena Znaniecka Lopata was born in Poland and came to America during World War II. She obtained her Ph.D. in sociology from the University of Chicago and is Professor Emerita at Loyola University of Chicago. Her major research focuses on "the cosmopolitan community of scholars." Prior research and publications concerned American women, Polish Americans, widowhood, grief, and the history of Polish sociology. Among many notable projects, Professor Lopata edited, 1980–1983, the series on *Research in the Interweave of Social Roles* and is the author of *Occupation: Housewife* (1971); *Polish Americans: Status Competition in an Ethnic Community* (1976; 2nd revised edition 1994); *Circles and Settings: Role Changes of American Women* (1994); and *Current Widowhood: Myths & Realities* (1996). She is the elected Chair of the History of Sociology section of the American Sociological Association and Past President of the Society for the Study of Social Problems, Sociologists for Women in Society, and the Midwest Sociological Society. Professor Lopata is an active contributor to the Research Committee on the History of Sociology in the International Sociological Association.

Lynn McDonald earned the Ph.D at the University of London and is Professor of Sociology at the University of Guelph. In addition to an innovative theoretical analysis of *The Sociology of Law and Order* (1976), she has published extensively on women theorists, notably in *Women Founders of the Social Sciences* (1994) and an anthology, *Women Theorists on Society and Politics* (1998). McDonald is currently director of the *Collected Works of Florence Nightingale*, to be published in sixteen volumes beginning in 2001. She has also served as president of the National Action Committee on the Status of Women, Canada's largest women's organization, and was an elected member of the Canadian Parliament. Professor McDonald is an active contributor to the Research Committee on the History of Sociology in the International Sociological Association.

Jill Niebrugge earned her Ph.D. at the University of Kansas and is Visiting Professor of Women's Studies at Wells College and Professor Emerita at Northern Virginia Community College. She writes as a team with Pat Lengermann. Together, their scholarship explores the history of sociology, sociological theory, feminist theory, gender and the relations among these four. Among other works, they are the authors of *The Women Founders: Sociology and Social Theory, 1830–1930* (1998) and "Classical Feminist Social Theory" in *Handbook of Social Theory* edited by George Ritzer and Barry Smart (2001). Jill and Pat were instrumental co-founders of the American Sociological Association's Section on the History of Sociology and are active contributors to the Research Committee on the History of Sociology in the International Sociological Association.

Index